CW00394847

CLWYD ROCK

28 PEARTREE DRIVE
WINCHAM
CHESHIRE
CW9 6EZ
07818 077 492

Worlds End or Craig-y-Forwyn

CLWYD ROCK

Edited by
Gary Dickinson

CICERONE PRESS
Milnthorpe, Cumbria

© Gary Dickinson 1993
ISBN 1 85284 094 3
First edition: S.Cathcart, 1983
A Catalogue record for this book is available from the British Library.

ACKNOWLEDGEMENTS

The guidebook has not been written by any one person nor even any specific guidebook team, but rather a group people who know and love Clwyd. Each has contributed a script to a given area which was then passed around to other climbers to comment on and adjust as they saw fit. The names adjacent to a crag are the core writers for that section but they shouldn't be a) held totally responsible or b) given too much praise (it goes to their heads).

The writers who must take most of the credit and blame are: Dave Barker, Stuart Cathcart, Gary Dickinson, Jane Drinkwater, Gary Gibson, Greg Griffiths, John Moulding, Clair Osborne, Alec Williams and Simon Williams.

The authors of this guidebook would like to thank numerous people for their help in the compiling and checking of various stages of the manuscript, without which this guide would not have been possible. A special thank you goes to the following: Roger Bennion, Dave Boddy, British Mountaineering Council, Mal Cameron, Chester Mountaineering Club, *Climber and Hillwalker*, John Codling, Tony Crimes, Paul Day, Patrick Dickinson, Mike Frith, *High* magazine, Dave Johnson, Doug Kerr, Phil Lockett, Bev McConville, Rick Newcombe, *On The Edge*, Paul Stott, Walt Unsworth, Lee Webster, Les Williams, Rory Williams, Bill Wright and to all our families and friends who have had to suffer us over the past few years.

As editor, I would like to thank one and all for their hard work, patience and goodwill.

Gary Dickinson, 1993

Front cover: Sombre Music, Monks Buttress.
Climber: G.Gibson. Photo: H.Gibson

CONTENTS

U.I.A.A. INTERNATIONAL MOUNTAIN CODE

1. Observe restrictions and access agreements recognised by national mountaineering federations. Avoid any actions which might endanger access.

2. Do not disturb nesting birds or wildlife. Help protect flowers, respect sites of geological or other scientific interest.

3. Avoid actions which cause unnecessary erosion (such as taking short cuts on footpaths). Do not leave unnecessary waymarks.

4. Do not disturb livestock or damage crops or trees.

5. Do not leave any rubbish. Keep campsites clean. Avoid all risk of fire.

6. Where toilet facilities are not available, dispose of human waste in a sanitary manner (ie. bury it: away from water supplies, paths, or climbs, under rocks, soil, sand or deep crevasses).

7. Do not pollute fresh water supplies. Avoid unnecessary pollution to the snow pack.

8. Respect established climbing traditions in ethical matters such as the use of chalk, pitons, bolts etc. Avoid indiscriminate or excessive use of fixed equipment.

9. In mountain areas, use motorized transport sparingly and park considerately. Make use of public transport if practical.

10. On any excursion to remote or high mountains, observe the U.I.A.A. Kathmandu declaration and ethical code for expeditions.(It's a long walk to Craig Arthur!)

Advice to Readers

Readers are advised that whilst every effort is taken by the author to ensure the accuracy of this guidebook, changes can occur which may affect the contents. It is advisable to check locally on transport, accommodation, shops etc but even rights-of-way can be altered and, more especially overseas, paths can be eradicated by landslip, forest fires or changes of ownership.

The publisher would welcome notes of any such changes

INTRODUCTION

Clwyd, for one reason or another, is an area that has never seemed to have its rightful recognition as a major venue for the climbers in or around the North West of the British Isles. This is possibly due to its close proximity to Snowdonia and the wealth of routes to be climbed there, and with the North Wales limestone around Llandudno opening its doors to the sports climber, Clwyd gives the impression of being neglected by the mainstream of British climbers. Yet for those who do come here and sample the delights of the area, many are left with a deep feeling of affection towards Clwyd and its beautiful surrounds.

In climbing terms, Clwyd is relatively new to the onslaught of climbers. Because of this, there can be found a wealth of routes that would be lucky to see two ascents per year. What we hope to see is more climbers going to the less frequented crags and so ease the congestion that is starting to happen at some of the more popular places. There has been a lot of development in Clwyd since 1983. With climbing standards increasing, as the odd overlooked line being finally discovered, the area is at last gaining the respect of a lot of climbers who, several seasons ago, would have dismissed it off hand as they passed by on there way to "the Pass".

Most of the crags are situated in the Eglwyseg Valley, which runs from the north of Llangollen and ends in the popular Worlds End crag, with all the cliffs situated on its eastern slopes. The cliffs are composed of good quality limestone that is very quick to dry after rain, although they also tend to catch the breeze as well, which in the winter months can be very cold indeed. There is a good mixture of easy through to hard routes on most of the crags, so it makes life a pleasure when climbing with friends of mixed ability. The views from most of the crags in Clwyd are second to none anywhere in the U.K. Beautiful rolling vales scattered at random with tiny cottages and farms. Streams, woods and fields all fighting with each other to get the attention of the eye and just waiting for the climber to discover. (A lot more aesthetically pleasing than looking at the leader's backside!)

For provisions, the area is well served by the towns of Llangollen and Mold. Llangollen is a picturesque tourist trap that straddles the River Dee with an abundance of cafes and pubs, two quite good campsites, several petrol stations, public toilets, banks and general shopping facilities (although it does tend to get a bit crowded on weekends and bank holidays). Mold, on the other hand, is the capital town of Clwyd and has all the amenities you should require.

All map reference numbers are taken off Ordnance Survey maps, Landranger Series (1:50,000). Sheet numbers 116,117 and 126.

ACCESS AND CONSERVATION

Access and conservation cannot be divided, together they are an integral part of our ability to have a choice of crags. We should never forget that there are plants and animals that our recreation may endanger and people dedicated to conserving and preserving this flora and fauna. Therefore we must take every care to ensure that we do no harm to the environment. In the Clwyd area we are only climbing on a crag with the goodwill of the owner. Abuse of that goodwill can result in crags being lost to climbers for many years. Whatever your social viewpoint it is the owners' prerogative to keep their land to themselves. Any access granted has to be shared with others who also want to enjoy the area.

WILDLIFE

The main area to avoid is Pandy Quarry which should be avoided completely during February, March, April, May and June: it may seem to be rather a long time but there is no access agreement here. Other crags can also be affected and bans or restrictions appearing in the climbing press or elsewhere should also be adhered to. To claim we are ignorant of the facts is no excuse. Observing voluntary bans on certain crags is as important as it is essential, as is keeping to paths and avoiding unstable or delicate areas, especially scree slopes.

We are, as climbers, the people who will be noticed the most. While other recreationalists may be responsible for litter, fires or loose dogs, the very visible climbers will have been seen to be there for some time, while others have just passed through.

GEOLOGY

The major rock upon which we climb in Clwyd is limestone of the Carboniferous era. Limestone is formed in warm, clear, shallow seas and around 300 million years ago it covered a large area of Britain and was eventually to form the limestone crags of the Peak District, Yorkshire, Lancashire and Wales. However, unlike the Peak District and Yorkshire, the other rock that accompanies limestone, ie. gritstone, is all but absent in the area. Throughout the area the Carboniferous sediments dip eastward forming west facing escarpments such as in the Eglwyseg valley. The limestone, for those with geological knowledge, is a classic example of a carbonate ramp systems tract. Lying above the limestone but mostly buried is the local equivalent of the gritstone, the Cefn-y-Fedw sandstone. This outcrops to the east of Trevor Quarry forming the excellent bouldering area of Monument, and is very similar to the rock that is climbed upon in Northumberland. Above the Cefn-y-Fedw sandstone lies the coal measure which include the sandstones seen at Cefn Mawr quarry.

In general terms the region consists of two parts, a western portion of Ordovician and Silurian strata, and an eastern portion of the aforesaid Carboniferous sediments. To the south, in the Glyn Ceiriog valley, the rock consists of Ordovician and Silurian strata, forming the rock of Pandy Escarpment and Quarry. Pandy Escarpment consists of rock known as Pandy Ash, but is actually an agglomerate, a form of extrusive igneous rock. The rock at Pandy Quarry is also igneous but is instead intrusive.

HISTORY

Climbing first "began" in the area when H.J.Tinkler recorded some climbs in *Mountain Craft* in 1963. At that time he was an undergraduate at Liverpool University and realised the potential of the area while preparing his B.A. dissertation on slope development. He described about forty routes in the article, most of which were the result of a weekend visit by John Hesketh, including the classic Intensity which remained the hardest free climb in the valley for nearly a decade.

The majority of the routes described were on Craig Y Forwen, the photo accompanying the article being strangely absent of its foliage. Craig Arthur was at that time considered as being of interest only to the artificial climber, for whom it was said to hold "tremendous possibilities in airy situations". John Clements, Nick Hall and Martin Jones were amongst the first to start climbing at Craig Arthur. Unfortunately, with the death of Clements, the desertion of Jones to the Marines and departure of Hall from the area, little is really known of their explorations. With the arrival of Tom Hurley, Brian Riley and Dave Blythe the next stage of development began. This trio pegged the climbs of Nemesis, Scousers Slab and Chota Peg (now the Big Plop) before turning their talents to Snowdonia.

The Eglwyseg Cliffs were at that time, as elsewhere on limestone, regarded as practice grounds for aid climbing and many such ascents could be found at the majority of the cliffs in the area although a record of these was not kept.

Craig Arthur was still the centre stage for the next wave of development five years onwards. In 1969 Bob Dearman and Dave Riley began to investigate the crag. Tom Hurley joined the team and the result was the Girdle Traverse. Dearman then teamed up with Martin Pedlar to add the semi-free or free Swlabr, Badge and Scrapyard Thing (no prizes for guessing Dearman's musical taste at that time!). These routes were described in an article in *Rocksport* by Dearman in 1979. In the article he also appealed for information in the hope of being able to compile a complete guide to the area.

However, with all of Bob Dearman's good intentions the guide never reached publication, and he eventually handed the information over to Chester M.C., who, for a period were fired with the same intention. A few new routes were completed at their main haunt, Craig Y Forwen, during 1974 including

Close To The Edge but their guidebook ambitions soon dimmed, lacking anyone with sufficient motivation to see it through.

Such a person eventually materialised in the form of Stuart Cathcart, at that time a student at Chester College, who started his Clwyd career by climbing Digitron with Gerald Swindley in 1973. He first turned his attention to Maeshafn where the Burgess twins had previously climbed The Minstrel in 1972. During the next few years, Cathcart, aided and abetted by Swindley or Tom Curtis, systematically worked out the quarry, culminating in 1977 with the publication of his own guide to Maeshafn. At that time, the guide produced considerable interest, unfortunately taking the landowner by complete surprise. Alarmed by this sudden invasion the landowner promptly banned access to the crag, though the problem has since been ironed out. In 1976, unknown to most people, Ruthin School produced a guide *Ruthin Escarpment* (Pwllglas Rocks), which although not significant, Cathcart mentioning it in his guide as purely a bouldering area, did lead to a few routes of worth being established in the 1980s by Rory Williams and Alan Hill (known more for his contribution to Jersey climbing).

After Maeshafn, Stuart turned his attention to the rest of Clwyd limestone. In the Eglwyseg Valley many fine climbs were found along the length of the escarpment that were equal to or surpassed in quality those found at World's End. Such routes as Mental Transition, Solo in Soho, Jibber, Hyperdrive, and Any Which Way all climbed by Cathcart either solo, or with a variety of partners, are representative of the routes done in this era.

In contrast to the rapid development of the other cliffs at that time, Craig Arthur was slowly being brought to maturation. Following the ascent of Digitron in 1973, the cliff saw little activity during the next three years. However, from 1976 the pace quickened as Cathcart began to fill the gaps. Partnered by Gerald Swindley or Nick Slaney, he climbed the fine steep routes of Fall and Decline, Manikins of Horror and Swlabr Link plus the serious Deadly Trap, and in 1978 produced Survival of the Fastest, an impending crack and wall requiring the first bolt in the area for protection.

Meanwhile, the odd gems were still to be found at Craig Y Forwen where the fierce Shooting Star was climbed by Cathcart and Swindley in 1979. High above the ford, in full view of the parking space, two of the finest bits of wall on the crag remained unlead until the summer of 1981. In June, Cathcart, with Mal Cameron, climbed the prominent Taerg Wall, a superb pitch with the finest situation on the crag. The following month, as Cathcart's manuscript typing progressed along the upper tier, the urgency of climbing a "last great problem" became pressing, and three evenings of concentrated effort were required to produce Vertical Games, the crux move finally made to appreciative cheers from a youth group camping below.

In 1983 Cicerone Press published Cathcart's guidebook, which has had to serve the Clwyd area for so long. In the introduction to the guide Stuart wrote:

"I also feel sad in some ways that this guide book will undoubtedly promote considerable interest in the area and the atmosphere in which I made many of the first ascents will never really be savoured by other climbers."

It has been inevitable with the publication of the guidebook that Cathcart's prophecy would, to some extent, be fulfilled. Cathcart himself had left his final calling card in the summer of 1983, as the book was still at the printers, with Climb High up the centre of the Alison Walls. It was this route that gave an impression of the potential of the new climbing waiting to be done on the blanker and harder sections of cliff, a breakthrough possibly brought on by the development of Craig Pen Trwyn earlier in the year.

In place of Cathcart came several enthusiastic climbers ready to discover the potential of the area for themselves. Together, by the end of 1986, they had trebled the number of routes on Dinbren's Alison Walls.

In the December of the same year, John Codling added Dreadlocks and the classic Traction Trauma, climbs either side of Climb High, although Codlings initial interest in the area had begun over on Worlds End. Here he began to add a whole list of excellent routes to this popular cliff: Flashdance, Wasters Mall and Nurse Nurse to name but three.

Codling was not alone with these developments. His climbing partner, Steve Allen, added his own repertoire with two impressive routes lead on sight; both Line of Fire and Brigadier Gerard are in a completely different mould. Fred Crook also paid visits to Worlds End adding minor classics such as Titanium Man and Crystal.

But it was another local climber, at that time living in the valley, who was to have an even greater impact on the area. John Moulding had started his campaign in the September of 1983 with Eliminator, a free version of an old aid route on Craig Arthur, but was to play an important part in the development of the area with many important ascents over a number of years.

1984 was possibly Clwyd's most important year in terms of recent development as two competitive parties of active climbers began to attack the area in earnest. In the early part of the year the two Johns joined forces to provide a very assertive force and hence a number of outstanding climbs. The most impressive of these ascents lay on Craig Arthur where they attacked the wall above the traverse on Swalbr Link, Dance Of The Puppets being their reward. Then, with a variety of partners, they accounted for Survival Of The Fattest, Delaware Slide and the superb duo of Tres Hombres and Manic Mechanic, the latter requiring a couple of rest points later to be tidied up on an outside visit from Andy Pollit. At about the same time the ubiquitous Pat Littlejohn fought his way up an on-sight ascent of Friday The Thirteenth, another superb climb.

Other cliffs did not go unnoticed by this pair as a healthy air of expectancy hung over the cliffs. At Pinfold North Codling teamed up with Andy Grondowski to free climb The Bulger, thus giving the tremendous Atmospheres leaving only one point of aid low down. Moulding was no less industrious with a number of routes such as The Soft Machine and Demolition Man also laying siege to a desperate line at the left-hand end of Dinbren. In many ways Bolt From The Blue was a little ahead of its time and required a couple of rest points, yet clearly illustrated Moulding's desire to try and conquer even the most improbable lines (it was later to be free climbed by John Monks with yo-yos). Codling also managed the first free ascent of Mental Transition after another suitor had fallen from the last move clutching a broken flake, three days earlier.

That climber was Gary Gibson who had secretly, with a handful of friends, been adding many of his own routes. He had begun with such minor classics as Melody, Iceburn and In Search of Someone Silly, the latter appropriated after the cleaning exploits of John Moulding, but he later added much finer fair with Waltz in Black, Another Red Line and What's Going On. Towards the latter end of this short spell of development Gibson turned his attention to the fine wall to the left of Survival of the Fastest to come up with Punch and Judy, named in honour of his competitive partners!

Other climbers added the odd route here and there, some of which were no less important. The extremely talented Nick Dixon added perhaps the area's hardest route at that time with the thinly technical Dangermouse on Pinfold North and later accompanied it with a terse technical titbit in the form of Baron Greenbach. The Quick Tick Walls with its unlucky thirteen routes on Pinfold South were developed by a host of activists in the space of two weekends and Steve Boyden popped up to add the fine World's Edge to World's End.

Towards the middle of the year development began to fade and the area started to become quiet once more. The odd gem was created, most notable being Steve Allen's Technicolour Yawn and John Codling's Fire, but most of the activists began to allow the dust to settle and take stock of what had been left untouched.

1985 was altogether a much quieter year with only the odd route meriting mention. The previous years' activists returned for one important route each: Moulding with Killer Gorilla, Codling with Stress Test and Gibson with Through the Grapevine but the main protagonist of 1985 had to be Steve Boyden. In the latter part of May he added a quartet of excellent routes. Teaming up with Moulding he added the superb Rhiannon at Dinbren which required a point of aid and also created a bitter argument between Moulding and Codling, an issue that was eventually ironed out in 1987 when the pair teamed up for a free ascent. Boyden then turned his attention to the thin crack left of the ivy roof on the same crag. After a lot of effort, this yielded The Fog, a very impressive route. Not satisfied with this Boyden returned just a few days later to add a variation finish and a route even further ahead of its time for the area: Misty Vision.

For the next few years the trend was to continue with the same faces appearing to add important routes on a variety of crags. In terms of numbers the development had slowed to a trickle yet many of the routes were no less worthy than what had gone before and in many ways they were much harder.

In 1986 the pleasant Compact Wall was found and developed by Doug Kerr and friends to leave some good quality climbs in the lower extreme level. Ice, the compliment to Fire was produced at Dinbren by Codling and further to the left he also ascended a line left of El Loco, The Orgasmatron, with a point of aid. This move was free climbed in 1988 by Alan Doig to give the hardest move in the area but the whole route could not be completed, a completely free ascent being awaited with interest. Towards the end of the year Gibson, climbing with his brother Phil, turned his attentions to the main wall on Trefor Rocks which provided three new routes.

Interest through 1987 remained at the same constant level but this time it was Moulding who was to provide the most important routes. One day in May at Dinbren accounted for Baby Crusher and Bolt the Blue Sky and a return in August culminated in Walking with Barrence. Over at Pinfold South, the thin and bold Shoot to Thrill yielded to his onslaught. In between all this Gibson popped in one evening to grab I Punched Judy First, a short powerful problem and yet another reference to the healthy competition between the two.

In 1988 much attention was still centred on the Llangollen crags, namely Dinbren and Craig Arthur, but it didn't get away with all the action. Maeshafn received its hardest route with the ascent of Alex's Crack by Dave Johnson. Originally lead with a bolt runner, this blank wall between the two classics, The Minstrel and Mathematical Workout, was later soloed by Dave in accordance with a bolt ban being placed on the crag. At World's End, on the blank wall right of the original hard route Shooting Star, Mike Collins linked a series of desperate moves to give one of the hardest routes in the valley, Rudolf Hess.

Craig Arthur received four routes in 1988 the biggest and best being the plum line of Smoking Gun an inspired piece of climbing and route-finding from Moulding. He accompanied this with the technical Full Mental Jacket and the fine Steppin' Razor. Not to be outdone Codling gave the latter a companion route with Marie Antoinette, thus completing the development of this once-aided wall.

Moulding and Codling then switched their attentions to Dinbren, eventually coming up with a route each. The very technical Broken Dreams was Moulding's prize whilst Codling came up with Fat Boys, perhaps trying to tell the area's climbers something they didn't already know?

Whilst all this was going on Gibson was never far from the scene and inevitably added a whole string of new routes, some just space fillers and others far more important. In a single day he accounted for three fine routes: the fingery Fine Feathered Fink, the superb but desperate Cured and the innocuous Flowers are for the Dead. A little later he began to eye the walls to the right of Alison initially to come up with The Rivals. A flake, supported by glue, was used on this but came unstuck a year later. To sum up the irony of the name Moulding weighed in with a new ascent of this desperate line originally offering the new name of Savage Henry Cranks the Rad. Gibson's final important contribution lay just to the left and after three days of effort he came up with The Bandits, the hardest route on the cliff at the time of writing and again named tongue firmly planted in cheek.

In the last two years the pace of development has picked up again considerably thanks mainly due to the perseverance of one man. Gibson has laid siege to the area, coming up with over fifty new routes, mainly with the production of the forthcoming guidebook in mind. No crag was left untouched and some superb routes were climbed. In 1991, pride of place went to his activities on Craig Arthur where he had hitherto been relatively uninterested. The brilliant trio of One Continuous Panic, Heaven or Hell and These Foolish Things were added with his brother Phil and are probably destined for classic status given their fine climbing and well protected nature. Around the same time Gibson was also responsible for the impressive Black Poppies, the "sports" route Ten and the very technical Swelling Itching Brain a route named in direct reference to his own accident. Whilst this was the focal point of interest he also joined forces with Doug Kerr to create eight clip-ups on the hitherto neglected Monkshead Buttress which has since become a popular venue.

In 1992 Gibson continued his one man domination but this time spread his efforts more evenly across the area. Early on in the February, during a brief spell of good weather, The Planet was climbed but it was not until May and June when two months of perfect blue skies appeared that the real upsurge took place. Initially centring his efforts on Monks Buttress whilst doing guidebook work, the remaining gaps were duly plugged. Memorable Strains, Edgeley and the outstanding Screaming Lord Sutch were produced whilst Pierrepoint Pressure summed up his stranglehold on the cliff. Continuing on with the guidebook work his efforts then shifted over to Pinfold North only for him to realise the cliff's full potential; again impressive routes fell. The left-hand end of the cliff was liberally smattered with routes of which Whilst Rome Burns and U Got Me Bugged proved the best before the leaning walls of the bay area succumbed. Here the trio of Private Idaho, Planet Claire and Brainbox will probably prove to be classic test pieces in the years to come.

Interest slowly dwindled in July as the weather deteriorated although the odd gem was uncovered. At Craig Arthur the stunning Sunny Side Up Mix and Chilean Moon proved that there were still fine climbs to be found, but in August Gibson switched his attentions to the Devil's Gorge at Pantymwyn, a haven of dry rock in the prevailing showery weather. The first suitor to the overhanging wall was Simon Elcock who claimed the superb Coffee and Bananas but after a quick second ascent Gibson became enamoured by the place. Four fine climbs fell thick and fast namely The Ten Year Fog, An Ivory Smile, What's In A Word and Grand Canyon. It is without doubt that these latter two climbs along with Coffee and Bananas, will become very popular with the modern sports climber seeking solitude and steep, well protected limestone.

And what of the future for Clwyd at the beginning of 1993? Over the past ten years there have been some major changes in the ideals of new routing; bolts on certain cliffs have become accepted and some very impressive routes have emerged. The area still remains a relative backwater yet certainly deserves much more attention from the climber, a fact that this guidebook will, unfortunately, change. But that was said about the production of the last guidebook and still only a certain clientele came to sample Clwyd's superb climbing and atmosphere.

TECHNICAL INFORMATION

We have reverted to what has become the standard grading system in the U.K. which is an adjectival grade and a technical grade. The adjectival grade is a very brief description of the climb, which takes into consideration the protectability, the exposure, the landing, the situation of the route and the general seriousness of the climb. The system starts at easy and goes through to extremely severe with the extremely severe grades having a number after them, these extremes are numbered one to nine at the moment but, no doubt, will increase in the future. The adjectival grades that we have used in this guide are as follows:

MODERATE	HARD SEVERE
DIFFICULT	VERY SEVERE
VERY DIFFICULT	HARD VERY SEVERE
HARD,VERY DIFFICULT	E1, E2, E3, E4,
SEVERE	E5, E6, E7.

As you can see, the extremes can go on forever. The technical grades are a lot simpler, they are just a guide to physical difficulty of the route; a 4A should have nice big holds on a relatively easy angled piece of rock whereas a 7A would, for example, be undercut scratches on an overhanging mirror! (slight exaggeration). The grades we have used are as follows:

4A, 4B, 4C, 5A, 5B, 5C, 6A, 6B, 6C, 7A,

A typical route grading will look something like:

VETTA HVS 5A.

If there is more than one pitch on a given route it will have the adjectival grade for the whole route and each pitch will be given a technical grade, for example Charlain at Craig Arthur is given HVS 5A 4B.

We have also used stars to indicate, in our opinion, routes that are of a certain quality, this is by no means gospel as each climber's perception of a route is different.

There are a few abbreviations used in the book and they are as follows:

AO	= Abseil Off	ALT	= Alternate Lead	BA	= Bolt Anchor
BR	= Bolt Runner	FFA	= First Free Ascent	PR	= Peg Runner
S	= Soloed	TR	= Thread Runner	BB	= Bolt Belay
PB	= Peg Belay				

A word of warning, bolts have a tendency to vanish and tape and peg runners have a tendency to decay so it is advisable to check out the in-situ protection on a route before you commit yourself.

MOUNTAIN SAFETY

The very nature of our sport requires that a degree of risk must be taken to participate actively in rock climbing but by exercising a modicum of common sense, the risks can be cut down to a minimum while still allowing plenty of room for excitement. There is a local mountain rescue team in Clwyd that is on call at all times should the need arise and they have suggested the following advice:

DO	**DON'T**
Tell someone where you are	Go climbing alone
Learn First Aid	Go beyond your capabilities
Check your gear	Move anyone that falls
Note the nearest phone/houses	Move rocks/belays (unless unsafe)
Check the weather	

PHONE 999 IN THE CASE OF AN ACCIDENT
and
ASK FOR MOUNTAIN RESCUE

PROCEDURE IN CASE OF ACCIDENT

DO get assistance, preferably someone with First Aid knowledge.

DO NOT leave the person alone (unless there is no option ie. he/she will die without help).

DO ring 999 and explain that it is a crag incident, in case an ambulance is unable to get close.

DO NOT try to revive with food or drink.

DO keep the casualty warm.

DO remain as calm as possible.

Try to note any relevant detail, and write it down, ie.

- Location (with grid ref. if possible)

- Condition and any comments from the casualty
- Weather conditions
- Reason for fall
  The Mountain Rescue Team in the Clwyd area are always on the lookout for potential members. If you would like to join, contact: Clwyd Rescue Team, The Old Prison, Love Lane, Denbigh, Clwyd.

BOLTING POLICY

In August 1991 a meeting organised by the BMC was held at Llandegla village hall to try and sort out once and for all the situation regarding the bolting of routes in Clwyd.

Present at this meeting were a number of climbers from all over the area and all with a vested interest in Clwyd rock. After many hours of tempers, tantrums and trembling lower lips, an agreement was reached that did not favour any particular party but was a fair compromise to all (good old democracy).

This agreement is as follows:

1. That no electric drills are to be used in Clwyd for the placement of bolts.
2. No bolts are to be placed on or near an existing, naturally protected, route in such a way as to affect that route.
3. No further bolting at Craig y Forwen (Worlds End).
4. No bolts are to be placed at Meashafn or Pot Hole Quarry.
5. The chipping/improving of holds is not permitted.
6. No retrobolting of any routes
7. To follow the current policy statement as stipulated by the BMC for the use of in-situ equipment.

CAMPSITES

LLANGOLLEN
Is probably the best place to camp if you intend to climb in the Clwyd area. Some of the better sites are:

TOWER FARM (O.S. 212428) Hot and cold water, showers and toilets and at a very reasonable price!

WERN ISAF (O.S. 223426) All the usual facilities including a farm shop and is quite well priced (it's also halfway between the pubs and the crags, heaven).

Please note that camping below Worlds End crags is now forbidden and to do so could cause the landowner to reconsider his attitude towards climbers!

FOOD AND DRINK

After a hard day's graft upon the rock, energy supplies need to be replenished with a good brew and some serious food.

Mold

OWAIN GLYNDWR NR MEASHAFN   Pub grub, climbers welcome.
ALEX'S CHIPPY   Burgers, pizzas and chippy food.
DRUID INN, LLANFERRES.   A country pub with bar snacks.

Llangollen

PROSPECT TEA GARDEN   Go east along the road from Trevor Rocks to pick up the signposts. Not open winter and weekdays.
MAY'S PANTRY, Chapel Street A1 chocolate cake at good prices.
WYNNSTAY ARMS   Beamish!! and posh pub grub
THE GRAPES Good traditional ale house.
REGENTS STREET CHIPPY (A5)   Best priced chippy in Llan.
PIZZA AND PASTA, Chapel Street   The name says it all.
GALES WINE BAR   Good pub grub, climbers welcome.

CLIMBING SHOPS

Llansports, Berwyn Street (A5), Llangollen, Tel: 0978 860605. New route book. Open on Sundays. Noticeboard.
Ellis Brigham, Northgate Street, Chester, Tel: 0244 318311. New route book.
Camp and Climb, Brook Street, Chester, Tel: 0244 311174.
Climber and Rambler, Pont y Pair, Betws y Coed, Tel: 069 02 555/631. Open on Sundays.
High Sports, Wyle Cop, Shrewsbury, Tel: 0743 353239. New route book.

NEW ROUTES

To avoid any arguments, it is advisable to write your latest conquest in one of the recognised new route books or send it to the BMC directly. New route books are situated at: ELLIS BRIGHAM, Chester; HIGH SPORT, Shrewsbury; LLANSPORTS, Llangollen; PETE'S EATS, Llanberis.

MAESHAFN

O.S. Map 117   GR 214615

by Gary Dickinson

SITUATION AND CHARACTER

This well established crag, approximately 3 miles south-west of the town of Mold, is a firm favourite with the local climbers by virtue of its quick drying nature, good solid rock and an abundance of excellent routes in all the grades. With its relatively easy access and west facing aspect it is a must for a pleasant summer evening's climbing. The quarry consists of three main sections between 10 and 20m high, the Amphitheatre, the Main Wall and the White Wall, with two smaller buttress that are slightly hidden away amongst the trees - the Hidden Buttress and the Holly Buttress.

The use of bolts at Maeshafn is strictly against the policy agreed by the B.M.C. and local climbers (see access section, Bolting). The crag has a history of vanishing bolts, so, anybody who places bolts here is liable to find them missing on their next visit to the crag!

ACCESS AND APPROACH

To get to the quarry, follow the A494 Mold bypass towards Ruthin as far as the village of Gwernymynedd. Carry on up the hill to the Rainbow garage and turn left immediately before the garage heading towards the Owain Glyndwr public house. When you get to the pub, don't stop, turn right and go along the road for about a quarter of a mile to a bungalow on the right and, 100m further on, a farm on the left. Just after the bungalow is a dirt track on the right. Park on the side of the road and walk, through a gate, up the muddy dirt track passing some farm buildings on the left, through another gate and into a field where the Main wall of the quarry comes into view. Follow the Main wall down to the right through a small pass and you will see a stile. Cross this to reach the Amphitheatre area.

The routes start at the right-hand end of the quarry and are described from right to left as one is facing the quarry, starting with the Amphitheatre and ending at the White Wall.

IMPORTANT

The quarry is owned by Mr W.Thomas the owner of the farm visible on the left of the track. Permission must be sought from him before climbing on the crag. As with all access it is only possible to climb with the good will of the owner of the land. If you are requested to leave by the owner for any reason, it is strongly advised that you do so with the minimum of fuss and without an aggressive attitude.

THE AMPHITHEATRE

1. Ash Tree Scramble　　　Very Difficult　　　Pre 1974
Climb the cracks and blocks above the large ash tree on the right of the steep slab.

2. Wanderer　　　Very Severe, 4c　　　11/2/76
Ascend the corner at the right-hand side of the slab until a leftwards traverse can be made across the wall to finish on the grass terrace.

3. The Arête　　　Hard Very Severe, 5b　　　11/2/76
Climb the arête on the left of the slab for 5m or, climb the face direct over the bulge to finish directly up the centre of the wall. Slightly loose finish.

*** **4. Shattered Crack**　　　Hard Severe　　　Pre 1974
Take the obvious steep, broken crack on the left-hand side of the slab, stepping left onto the grass terrace to finish.

5. The Bulger　　　E1 5b　　　1975
A technical route with good protection. Start just left of Shattered Crack at a rightwards leaning corner. Climb the corner and steep slab to the thin crack in the bulging wall.

6. Little Finger Jam　　　Hard Very Severe, 5a　　　Pre 1974
Start below the overhang which crosses the wall at 2m. Climb the overhang to a thin crackline and follow it to the top.

7. Sling　　　Hard Severe　　　Pre 1974
A good, well protected route. Follow the flake crack, passing a PR near the top.

8. Dandy Lion　　　Hard Severe　　　22/4/90
Follow the left trending cracks between Sling and Elephant Crack for 5m, then move right to gain, and finish up the v-shaped chimney with a hawthorn tree above.

9. Elephant Crack　　　Severe　　　Pre 1974
Climb the vegetated groove to the overhang and up the body-width chimney, finishing on the left.

10. Ram Jam　　　E2 5c　　　30/9/75
Start as for Elephant Crack to the overhang then step left to beneath an obvious crack in the roof. Climb the strenuous crack on good jams.

To the left of Ram Jam is a large cave and jungle. The next routes start left of this.

11. Just Jolly   Very Severe, 4b   Pre 1974
The steep wall is split by a large crack from top to bottom. Climb the crack for a few feet until a ledge is gained, then go right and up towards the easy groove and top.

12. Vulcer   Hard Very Severe, 5a   15/4/76
Attack the steep crack of Just Jolly continuing straight up to a loose finish.

*   **13. Itsu**   E3 5b   5/1974
To the ledge on Vulcer, then move left for 2m and go up the thin crackline. A very serious undertaking!

*   **14. The Rasp**   E3 5c   29/9/75
A serious proposition.Left of Itsu is a protruding spike, use this to gain a slot and pull over onto the slab above trending leftwards to finish.

15. Das Bolt   E1 5b   14/11/85
Climb the wall direct between Blue Chrome and The Rasp, finishing up The Rasp.

16. Blue Chrome   Hard Very Severe, 5a   8/10/75
Up the blocks and cracks until a step right can be made onto the easier angled slab. Finish leftwards to the top.

17. Gorilla Waltz   Very Severe, 4b   Pre 1974
Ascend the overhanging groove at the left-hand end of the dark overgrown wall until a tree can be gained and "monkeyed up".

As one leaves the Amphitheatre towards the Main Wall Area (north) a wall can be seen on the right-hand side that is heavily overgrown. This is the Hanging Garden Wall. The plant that is smothering this rock face is called cotoneaster and it is an exceptional example of how this species quickly devours limestone. Underneath this plant there are three routes of dubious quality and it is requested that the wall is not gardened by any enthusiastic new route hunters. Leaving the Hanging Garden Wall, proceed north for a few metres until an arête marks the start of The Main Wall.

THE MAIN WALL

18. Slip   Hard Severe   Pre 1974
Climb the steep slab that trends right from the cave at its right-hand side.

*   **19.** Formidable   Hard Severe   15/8/76
Pull up on the overhanging arête that starts The Main Wall. It looks loose but it isn't really (honest).

20. Pengrail   E1 5b   21/4/76
Start 2m left of the arête at a shattered crack that trends right. Climb the steep wall using the crack with an awkward move at half height.

*   **21.** Barouche   E2 5b   10/8/75
A steep climb with just enough protection. Start on the right of a flat topped flake, Go up the thin cracks rightwards until it is possible to step left onto a small ledge. With difficulty, move right and up the cracks to good holds near the top.

*   **22.** So She Did   E2 5c   Unknown
An eliminate route takes the blank wall to the right of Knotty Problem to a good ledge, using protection on Knotty Problem, Make a bold run with a wide bridge to the top and success.

**   **23.** Knotty Problem   Hard Very Severe, 5a   26/6/75
Start in front of the flat topped flake which is home to a wild rose. Gain the top of the flake and mantle up on to a smaller ledge above. Finish by following a thin crack via some technical climbing to the top.

**   **24.** Laxix   E4 5c   8/9/75
Excellent climbing on a very sustained route. 3m left of the flat topped flake is a right-trending crack, start just right of this on small holds until the crack is reached at 4m. Finish up this.

25. Think A Moment   E4 6b   6/92
Climb the wall between Laxix and Cousin M and move directly up to finish above a grass terrace.

26. Cousin M   E5 6a   1/7/92
Start 3m right of the large right facing corner and climb the wall to gain a large ledge and a rest. Continue up more easily to finish.

The next two routes are a bit meandering and although they are the original routes their neighbours do take better lines.

27. The Secret　　　　　　　E3 5c　　　　　　　15/4/76
Climb the bulging wall 3m right of the corner to a ledge then traverse left into the corner. Move up, passing a PR, to finish.

* **28. The Corner**　　　　　　　E1 5b　　　　　　　Pre 1974
Climb the obvious corner past a roof at 5m. Move up to a PR and make a difficult traverse right to a good ledge then take the easier ground above to finish.

29. Rise To The Equation　　　　E2 5b　　　　　　　24/7/92
Climb the obvious right facing corner to make a very inelegant move right around the first roof to a rest. Continue up the corner, PR, using some airy bridging to a second bulge, which is thrutched over to gain easier ground to finish.

** **30. Calculus**　　　　　　　E3 6a　　　　　　　11/5/81
The arête to the left of the corner is climbed direct to an overhang and some good runners. Pull up on a good flake to gain easier ground to finish.

*** **31. Mathematical Workout**　　　　E3 6a　　　　　　　11/8/76
An excellent route, well protected with small wires. 2m left of the corner, a thin crack leads to an overhang and a horrible side pull. Slap, heave, thrutch and a pull leads to more amiable climbing to finish.

32. Alex's Crack　　　　　　　E6 6b　　　　　　　6/7/88
Climb the wall direct between Mathematical Workout and the Minstrel via a one finger pocket, long reach and delicate move to finish up the easier wall. (SERIOUS)

*** **33. The Minstrel**　　　　　　　E1 5b　　　　　　　11/8/76
One of the most frequently climbed routes in the quarry (and rightly so). The steep finger crack to the left of Mathematical Workout with a hard move at the bulge at half height leading to, and over, the overhang at the top.

34. Royal Plume　　　　　　　E1 6a　　　　　　　17/5/79
The thin crack left of The Minstrel to the overhang, move up and with difficulty step right onto the upper slab. Move back left across the slab and continue upwards to finish.

*   35. Flying Block   E1 5a   15/8/76
Climb the last of the four cracks starting just left of Royal Plume to the
overhang and up the easier wall above.

36. Ancillary   Severe   Pre 1974
The obvious vegetated groove at the left-hand side of the easier angled
slab to an ash tree and short wall behind.

37. Yobo   Hard Severe   Pre 1974
At the right-hand side of the easier angled slab is an arête. Climb up the
left side of the arête on thin cracks and large holds passing the ash tree
to its right.

*   38. Puppy Power   Very Severe, 4a   16/1/88
The slab is split by a series of cracks in the centre between Yobo and
Rambler. Ascend the cracks, avoiding the vegetation, towards a shallow
corner at the top.

39. Rambler   Very Difficult   Pre 1974
The vegetated groove and wall in the centre of the slab, slightly to the right
of Layback On Me.

40. Layback On Me   Very Severe, 4b   Pre 1974
At the left side of the slab is an obvious line of right trending overhangs.
Follow these to the terrace and the top.

*   41. Apex   E1 5b   8/10/75
To the left of the large slab, the walls start to get steep and serious. Apex
follows a line of weakness up a shallow groove to a thorn bush. Move right
below this and go up the slab on easier angled rock to finish.

*   42. Inspector Gadget   E4 6a   Unknown
Start at the right-hand end of the concrete plinth below a bulge and an
excellent undercut hold, a long reach is made (attempted) over the bulge
to mediocre holds beyond.

43. Moomba   E4 6a   23/9/77
A large rightward-trending flake crack starts behind a concrete slab,
Moomba takes a line 2.5m in from the left-hand end of this crack. Climb
straight up behind the concrete slab until a step left onto a small hold can
be achieved. Move up the steep wall slightly right towards better holds and
the top. Good protection is sparse.

* **44.** Brewing Up With Les Williams   E4 6a   15/3/88
Start this time on the left of the concrete plinth and climb to the bulge on good holds. Layaway the bulge to its left, passing a PR and continue direct to the top

45. Jocca   Hard Very Severe, 5a   5/74
The steep walls now appear to ease off a little at a short vertical section of rock above a cave. Ascend the wall on the right-hand side using the thin crack to gain the top.

46. Thrutch   Hard Severe   Pre 1974
To the left of Jocca is a prominent piece of rock. Start at the apex of this and pull over the roof and bulge finishing to the right with Jocca.

47. Joker   Very Difficult   Pre 1974
Starting 1m left of Thrutch, pull over the promontory of rock and climb leftwards on good holds to the slabs, passing below a small ash tree to finish.

** **48.** Main Wall Girdle   E3   25/11/75
An exciting 80m girdle that moves across the main wall from left to right taking in some fine climbing and some scary run outs.
   1)   5c.   Start as for Jocca up the delicate crackline to the top of the slab, move up and out right to descend onto a small ledge. Follow the horizontal line right to reach easier climbing and the arête. Swing round this to belay above the thorn bush on Apex.
   2)   4a.   Traverse with relative ease across the Yobo slab to a belay at the ash tree on Yobo.
   3)   5b.   Move up and right from the tree to the overhang on the Minstrel, then traverse right to the arête of Calculus. Swing around the arête to gain the large ledges of the Corner and a poor belay.
   4)   5c.   Descend to the small ledge at the end of the traverse on the Corner, then move right with great difficulty across the crackline of Laxix to gain another ledge. Move down to the mantleshelf ledge of Knotty Problem. Traverse across the steep wall to the thin crack at the top of Barouche and finish up this.

Walking from the Main Wall towards the White Wall Area (north), two small crags, hidden in the undergrowth on the right, are passed. The first is the Hidden Buttress and the second is Holly Buttress. Both crags are becoming overgrown but the routes are still worthwhile

HIDDEN and HOLLY BUTTRESSES

49. Sita   E2 5c   23/9/79
Hidden away on the Hidden Buttress is Sita. Looking at the crag, a sharp arête can be seen. Sita takes a line using a large pocket on the left of the arête to pull up onto a ledge. Continue up the left wall to finish.

50. Wilkinson Sword Edge   Very Severe, 4c   25/9/77
On the wall of the Holly Buttress, a sharp arête can be found. Climb the arête on its right-hand side to the top.

51. Holly Bush Wall   Very Difficult   Pre 1974
From the right of the holly bush, climb up the wall to above the bush and directly to the top.

* **52. Maeve**   E3 6a   1979
Start to the left of the bush on a line of rounded holds that trend right to finish above the bush. A poorly protected route.

Proceeding left (north) along the pathway past the two overgrown buttresses, a cul de sac that is bounded on its right-hand side by a large wall is reached. It is worth the effort of setting up a lower off rope at the top of the wall as the scramble up over the steep grass bank can be more unnerving than some of the routes.

WHITE WALL

53. Gantree   Hard Severe   16/8/75
In amongst the trees, at the right-hand end of the crag is a ledge with a thorn bush growing from it. Climb the slabs and small overhangs to a ledge on the arête, then go up the short wall beyond.

54. Carroll Street   Hard Very Severe, 5a   18/8/75
To the left of Gantree is a line of blocks leading up left to an overhang. Climb these to the overhang, then move rightwards to finish up the short but loose wall.

55. Fun With Teapots   E1 5a   Unknown
Start to the left of the obvious roof at a flake. Climb the flake to gain a good hold on the right above a bulge. Continue straight up easily but with poor protection. There is also a direct start over the bulge at 5b.

** **56. Odysseus**   Hard Very Severe, 5a   15/8/75
A few feet right of White Spring, the wall is broken by overhangs and

hanging corners. Follow these up to the corner and overhang of Carroll Street, then swing out left onto the steep wall which is climbed directly to the top.

57. White Spring   Hard Severe   Pre 1974
Climb the obvious groove and crack lines at the right-hand side of the wall.

58. Pussyfooting   E4 5c   Unknown
Start as for Running With The Wolf, up to the niche with the rose bush, ascend the wall behind to finish just left of a small thorn bush.

*** 59. Running With The Wolf   E2 5c   27/6/76
A technical and bold lead that requires a strong nerve. Start to the left of a prominent arête, home of a wild rose bush. Ascend into a niche on the left of the arête and, with difficulty, move left and up until a ledge is gained. Move up again to the overhang, where a good peg can be found. Step right and pull over to finish.

60. Muslim   Hard Very Severe, 5a   15/8/75
Climb the crack as for Rama to the ledge then continue straight up to the left-hand end of the overhangs.

61. Rama   Hard Severe   Pre 1974
To the right of Flotta Arête is a short crack leading to a ledge. Climb this then trend leftwards to finish up the slab.

62. Flotta Arête   Very Difficult   Pre 1974
Start on the left of the arête and climb rightwards onto it. Follow this to the top.

63. Cyclops   Hard Very Severe, 5b   18/8/75
Start as for Flotta Arête but climb the thin crack directly over the bulging wall to the top. Strenuous.

** 64. Haco   E4 5a   16/8/75
A good climb that needs a certain amount of nerve to lead. Start as for Cyclops but follow a line of strange "stuck on" holds that trend left until a good resting ledge is reached. Traverse right for a few feet to finish up the short bulging wall.

65. Pant-y-Gyrdl Wall   E2 5c   29/9/91
Start to the left of a vertical crack 1m from the right-hand end of the concrete plinth. Scale the wall via a crack and "stuck on" holds to a bush at the top. Hard to start.

66. Hot Tin Roof   E4 6a   7/10/75
A very strenuous and committing route that takes a line up the thin crack
on the steep wall to the right of the corner (El Cid).

67. El Cid   Hard Severe   Pre 1974
The corner at the right-hand side of the white wall that is now getting very
overgrown. A feeble route.

68. White Wall Traverse   E3   11/8/76
1) 5c. Start as for Hot Tin Roof to half height until an awkward traverse right
   can be made to the rest ledge on Haco. Move right to easier climbing and
   the rounded arête. Belay on the right.
2) 5b. Traverse quite easily right along the ledge below the overhang to a
   peg runner, then continue right to gain the groove of White Spring and a
   poor belay.
3) 4c. Again, move right along the same line until a swing down past the
   overhangs of Carroll Street can be made. Follow beneath the roofs until
   a ledge is gained on the far arête.

FIRST ASCENTS

Pre 1974	ASH TREE SCRAMBLE	Unknown
Pre 1974	SHATTERED CRACK	Unknown
Pre 1974	LITTLE FINGER JAM	Unknown
Pre 1974	SLING	Unknown
Pre 1974	ELEPHANT CRACK	Unknown
Pre 1974	JUST JOLLY	Unknown
Pre 1974	GORILLA WALTZ	Unknown
Pre 1974	SLIP	Unknown
Pre 1974	THE CORNER	Unknown
Pre 1974	ANCILLARY	Unknown
Pre 1974	YOBO	Unknown
Pre 1974	RAMBLER	Unknown
Pre 1974	LAYBACK ON ME	Unknown
Pre 1974	THRUTCH	Unknown
Pre 1974	JOKER	Unknown
Pre 1974	HOLLY BUSH WALL	Unknown
Pre 1974	WHITE SPRING	Unknown
Pre 1974	RAMA	Unknown
Pre 1974	FLOTTA ARÊTE	Unknown
Pre 1974	EL CID	Unknown
5/74	ITSU	S M Cathcart & G N Swindley
5/74	JOCCA	S M Cathcart, Solo
1975	THE BULGER	S M Cathcart & G N Swindley
26/6/75	KNOTTY PROBLEM	S M Cathcart & G N Swindley

10/8/75	BAROUCHE	S M Cathcart & G N Swindley
15/8/75	ODYSSEUS	S M Cathcart & G N Swindley
15/8/75	MUSLIM	S M Cathcart & G N Swindley
16/8/75	GANTREE	S M Cathcart, Solo
16/8/75	HACO	S M Cathcart & G N Swindley
18/8/75	CARROLL STREET	S M Cathcart & G N Swindley
18/8/75	CYCLOPS	S M Cathcart & G N Swindley
8/9/75	LAXIX	S M Cathcart & G N Swindley
29/9/75	THE RASP	S M Cathcart & D Johnson
30/9/75	RAM JAM	S M Cathcart & D Johnson
7/10/75	HOT TIN ROOF	S M Cathcart & G N Swindley
8/91	DIRECT START	D Johnson, Solo
	The original route started on top of a steel shed now removed.	
8/10/75	BLUE CHROME	S M Cathcart, Solo
8/10/75	APEX	S M Cathcart, Solo
25/11/75	MAIN WALL GIRDLE	S M Cathcart & G.N.Swindley
11/2/76	WANDERER	S M Cathcart & T Curtiss
11/2/76	THE ARÊTE	S M Cathcart & T Curtiss
15/4/76	VULCER	S M Cathcart & T Curtiss
15/4/76	THE SECRET	S M Cathcart & T Curtiss
21/4/76	PENGRAIL	S M Cathcart & T Curtiss
27/6/76	RUNNING WITH THE WOLF	S M Cathcart & T Curtiss
11/8/76	MATHEMATICAL WORKOUT	S M Cathcart & T Curtiss
11/8/76	THE MINSTREL	S M Cathcart & T Curtiss
11/8/76	WHITE WALL TRAVERSE	S M Cathcart & T Curtiss
15/8/76	FORMIDABLE	S M Cathcart, Solo
15/8/76	FLYING BLOCK	S M Cathcart & G N Swindley
23/9/77	MOOMBA	S M Cathcart & G N Swindley
25/9/77	WILKINSON SWORD EDGE	S M Cathcart, Solo
1979	MAEVE	T Curtiss & S M Cathcart
17/5/79	ROYAL PLUME	T Curtiss & S M Cathcart
23/9/79	SITA	S M Cathcart, Solo
11/5/81	CALCULUS	A Pollitt & P Bailey
14/11/85	DAS BOLT	D Johnson & A N Other
16/1/88	PUPPY POWER	S Williams, N Stanford & C Roberts
15/3/88	BREWING UP WITH LES WILLIAMS	D Johnson & I Waring
6/7/88	ALEX'S CRACK	D Johnson, Solo
22/4/90	DANDY LION	G Dickinson & P Lockett
29/9/91	PANT-Y-GYRDL WALL	G Dickinson & P Lockett
6/92	THINK A MOMENT	C Durkin, Unseconded
1/7/92	COUSIN M	C Durkin, Unseconded
24/7/92	RISE TO THE EQUATION	H Williams, P Lockett & G Dickinson
UNKNOWN	SO SHE DID	
UNKNOWN	INSPECTOR GADGET	
UNKNOWN	FUN WITH TEAPOTS	I Jones & S Dickaty-Dale
UNKNOWN	PUSSYFOOTING	

PANTYMWYN (DEVILS GORGE)

O.S. Map 116 GR 189643

by Gary Gibson and Gary Dickinson

SITUATION AND CHARACTER

Since the last guide was written, Pantymwyn has been transformed from a mediocre local crag into a superb sport climbing venue, albeit with a dramatic rise in grades for the new routes. The atmosphere of the gorge can seem a bit musty on first encounters but this is more than compensated for by two very good approaches and a number of first class sport routes that are climbable even when the rest of Clwyd is dripping with rain. The gorge is made up of two walls of solid limestone that are about 30m high, one being a slab and the other being a steep, overhanging wall. The slab wall tends to be a bit dirty with sparse protection and worrying run-outs but an abundance of trees to utilise as belays at the top of the wall. The overhanging wall, in contrast, is very clean, nearly always dry even when it is raining, well bolted and with lower offs added just for good measure. Because these routes are purely sport climbs they have been given a French grade alongside the conventional grades. There is a very convenient bridge spanning the gorge that proves to be a very convenient vantage point for taking photographs, or taking the mickey out of your friends.

APPROACH AND ACCESS

Dependent on the mood of the day, you can either take the quick and easy approach route or, for proper climbers, a long and leisurely walk in. For the Long and Leisurely approach, park near the Loggerheads Inn (GR 199626) on the main A494, Mold to Ruthin road, and follow the east bank of the river moving downstream through the country park until eventually (two miles further on) you should find the gorge.

The Quick and Easy approach starts from the T-Junction at the west end of the Village of Pantymwyn (GR 192646). Follow the farm access road down to the west that is marked as a public footpath, go through a gate to the bottom of the hill, then leave the road at the sharp left-hand bend and continue straight on across a stile. Follow the path for 50m and the gorge will come into view. Devils Gorge is part of Loggerheads Country Park, and as such, a lot of people come to view and take photographs of this natural wonder, so please brush your hair and wear clean tights. Swearing out loud is a no-no.

The routes on each wall are described as they are approached from the entrance to the gorge.

Rainbow over Twilight Tower Buttress. Photo: S.Swygart
M.Johnson on Caught in the Crossfire, Dinbren. Photo: G.Gibson

1. Ladywriter   Hard Severe   6/7/80
Directly below the footbridge on the left-hand side of the gorge is a deep
cut groove, ascend the groove, moving leftwards at some broken cracks
to the top edge of the slab, finishing to the left of the bush.

2. Portobello Belle   Hard Severe   Pre 1976
Start as for Ladywriter. Climb the groove and continue upwards over the
overlaps and the slab directly below the footbridge finishing on the left of
the footbridge.

3. A Brown Shade Of Lime   Very Severe, 4c   3/91
Start in the big leftward trending crack. Move out right to the bottom of the
slab, then head straight up to the right of the bridge.

*   4. Single Handed Sailor   Hard Very Severe, 4c   16/11/76
7m right of Ladywriter, climb direct to the top passing between two bushes.
Poorly protected.

**   5. Follow Me Home   E1 5a   6/7/80
Starting in the centre of the slab, below a protection bar that is at the foot
of a left trending overhang. Climb up to the bar and follow below the
overhang and small corner to the top.

**   6. Angel Of Mercy   E2 5a   6/7/80
Start as for Follow Me Home to the protection bar, then step right and over
the overhang and continue direct to the top. Bold

7. Grey Tripper   E2 5a   1984
3m right of Angel Of Mercy. Climb up to a tree then move up the slab to
a small overhang. Step right over the overlap and continue directly up to
the left of a broken rib and straight on to finish.

8. News   Very Severe, 4b   Pre 1976
Starting 3m left of the corner, ascend up to the right of a broken rib near
to the top, finishing on the right of the rib.

9. Where We Going   Hard Severe   Pre 1976
Climb the horrible slimy corner of the slab, moving on to the slab when
necessary. A dirty and grotty route.

10. Great Slab Girdle   Hard Very Severe, 5a   21/8/80
Climb Portobello Belle to the base of the upper slab, then traverse right

J Elcock on Echoes, Pantymwyn. Photo: G Gibson

across the slab for 35m to the far corner. Good rock, poor protection.

The remaining routes lie on the overhanging wall and are described as they are approached, from right to left.

11. Comfortably Numb   E4 6a   4/9/91
From under the extreme right-hand side of the first bulge encountered, below the bridge, make some awkward moves direct to a BR. Grope right to a good hold and swing around left onto the main part of the wall. Climb this past 2BRs to a BB. Lower off.

The initial undercut wall provides a superb low-level traverse at 6b and a wealth of minuscule problems.

Directly beneath the bridge lies a prominent rightward-rising line with a ramp to its right. Starting here is:

12. Communique   E4 5b   11/8/78
Start at the foot of a rightward slanting ramp, climb the ramp on underclings for 7m, then make a long reach to a good hold and continue up to a rest ledge. Take the thin crack above to a large block, finishing on the right of the footbridge. A direct start can be made below the resting ledge.

13. Uhu   E2 5c   30/7/91
Start at the foot of the ramp. Move up the ramp for 3m, then tackle the bulge directly above, BR, to a ledge, BR. Follow the rightward-rising line below the bridge past 3BRs to finish under and then on the right-hand side of the bridge.

*** 14. Bananas And Coffee   E5 6b (7a+)   24/7/92
An impressive route up the right-hand side of the main wall. The rock is good and the climbing provides only a short hard section, at the top. Follow Uhu to a small ledge over the bulge, then climb leftwards, 2BRs, through the quartz bulge onto a hanging slab, BR. Tiptoe off left to a good rest, BR, then move up to a shelf, BR, and swing merrily right to a slim groove, BR, and BB above. Lower off.

*** 15. Whats In A Word   E5 6b (7a+)   31/8/92
Another brilliant little route with technically intricate climbing, superb positions and immaculate rock. From the 5th BR on Bananas And Coffee, move up right to a shelf above the bulge, BR. A contorted sequence of moves rightwards on layaways lead to the edge of the wall from where moves straight up, BR, whilst talking to the tourists, lead to a diagonal shelf and BB.

** 16. The Ten Year Fog   E6 6b (7b+)   12/8/92
Excellent and steep with a powerful crux section and technical finish. Start
6m left of Bananas And Coffee. Climb the wall slightly rightwards via a
series of hidden boreholes, 3BRs, to the bulge, BR. Step left up a ramp to
an easing in angle, BR. Continue direct, gradually steepening, past 2BRs,
to a bulging finish and BB. Lower off.

*** 17. An Ivory Smile   E6 6c (7c)   7/9/92
The centre of the alarmingly overhung wall provides an outstanding climb
with a desperate crux sequence. Start 3m left of The Ten Year Fog. Climb
the lower wall via an overlap to a circular hole below the main bulge.
Difficult moves followed by a flying leap gain good pockets from where
moves up and then left gain a good flake. Pull up and then slightly right
before pursuing a steepening line past another hole to jugs below the
impending headwall. Climb this on the left to a BB: nine BRs.

18. Rotten Aid   A3   Pre 1976
Climb the overhanging wall 7m out from the back cave. A bang and dangle
exercise requiring supreme trust in the remaining gear.

*** 19. Grand Canyon   E5 6b (7b)   16/8/92
Superb, sustained and powerful climbing up the impressive overhanging
wall just to the right of the cave entrance. High in the E grade. Start 3m right
of the mini-cave at ground level. Climb the initial wall via a bulge to gain
the top of a series of finger ledges. Pull out right and go up via two
prominent boreholes to gain a bulge and pull leftwards to a jug. Step left
again, pull up and then move slightly rightwards through the next bulge to
buckets way above. One final hard move gains the BB: nine BRs. The pitch
overhangs 6m in its length!

* 20. Echoes   E4 6a (7a+)   17/8/92
This route gains the large mid-height cave via some hard moves. Start just
to the left of the mini-cave at ground level. Pull up and leftwards to some
good foot ledges, then climb the wall, dirty, to a steepening in angle. The
crux ensues via dynamic moves to gain the sanctuary of the cave, BB.
Lower off

Walk out of the gorge and turn left to follow the river upstream for 50m to a small
compact wall that sports a route.

21. Ripple Tank   E3 6a   24/7/92
Climb the wall past a BR to a lower off.

FIRST ASCENTS

Pre 1976	PORTOBELLO BELLE	Unknown (Named by S M C)
Pre 1976	NEWS	Unknown (Named by S M C)
Pre 1976	WHERE WE GOING	Unknown (Named by S M C)
Pre 1976	ROTTEN AID	Unknown
16/11/76	SINGLE HANDED SAILOR	S M Cathcart & G N Swindley
11/8/78	COMMUNIQUE	S M Cathcart & G N Swindley
	A Direct start has been added by S Taylor, Solo in October 1989.	
6/7/80	LADYWRITER	F R Bennett & M Hughes
6/7/80	FOLLOW ME HOME	S M Cathcart & M Hughes
6/7/80	ANGEL OF MERCY	S M Cathcart & M Hughes
21/8/80	GREAT SLAB GIRDLE	S M Cathcart, Solo
1984	GREY TRIPPER	G Griffith & C O'Keefe
3/91	A BROWN SHADE OF LIME	J Elcock & N Thomas
30/7/91	UHU	N Thomas & S Taylor
4/9/91	COMFORTABLY NUMB	N Thomas, Unseconded
24/7/92	BANANAS AND COFFEE	J Elcock, Unseconded
24/7/92	RIPPLE TANK	R Brooks, Unseconded
12/8/92	THE TEN YEAR FOG	G Gibson, Unseconded. Flashed a few days later.
16/8/92	GRAND CANYON	G Gibson, Unseconded
31/8/92	WHATS IN A WORD	G Gibson, Unseconded.
	Not climbed previously as the bolt hangers had been removed, despite what the locals say!	
17/8/92	ECHOES	J Elcock, Unseconded
7/9/92	AN IVORY SMILE	G Gibson, Unseconded

POT HOLE QUARRY (THREE SPRINGS)

O.S. Map 116 GR 192597

by Gary Dickinson

SITUATION AND CHARACTER

Pot Hole Quarry is a fantastic little crag that is both very solid and very popular. The climbing is on cracks and small pockets, all well protected and enjoyable, with plenty of belays suitable for top roping. The crag is nearly west facing and therefore tends to catch the evening sunshine so it is rare to find the quarry devoid of other climbers on a summers evening. The rock is quick to dry after rain with very little seepage from the cracks and the base of the quarry, below the face, is free from mud and grass so one does not have the hassle of twenty minute boot cleans every time you want to do a route. It is a friendly crag where you can take the children, have a picnic, sunbathe or even, as a last resort, do some climbing. The tendency, and the norm for this crag, is to stand around and gossip with climbers whom you have never met before. The quarry has two sections, the side wall and the main wall and, although the side wall does look slightly loose, the routes are all of very good quality. It is obvious which wall is which when you get to the quarry but just to clarify the issue, the main wall is the big one and the side wall is the smaller one down to the left.

ACCESS AND APPROACH

To get to Pot Hole Quarry, take the A494 from Mold towards Ruthin and about five miles south of Mold, you will come to the village of Llanferres. Go through the village, passing the Druid public house, to a lay-by on the left-hand side. Park here and walk back 200m to a marked footpath; cross the field towards a small bridge that spans the River Alun; follow the river upstream until a small tributary stream joins the main river from the left. Follow this tributary, passing two more stiles, and the quarry can be found another 100m further on.

With the crag being situated on sheep grazing land, the access here is very delicate and the farmer has requested that dogs are kept away from the area during the month of April and on a leash at all times. Lighting fires or leaving gates open are also aggravating the access situation to the crag and are strictly forbidden. It is a serious situation, that has to be handled with tact and diplomacy, if we wish to continue using this quarry in the future. The majority of the rock has been climbed upon and a variety of eliminates and space fillers have been done in the past few years. A lot of these do not warrant recording here, as one move to the left or right means that you're on another route! All the routes are described from right to left as you are facing the quarry.

THE MAIN WALL

1. Mestre — Severe — *BATS IN RESIDANCE '03* — Pre 1975
An obvious crack on the right-hand side of the blunt arête.

2. Sesto — *2ND TURTLE 04/03* — Very Difficult — *V. POLISHED! V. POUSHED!* — Pre 1975
Start on the right-hand side of the arête climbing left over the arête to finish.

3. Selva — Very Severe, 4a — Pre 1975
Take the crackline 2m left of the arête starting on the right of the large thorn bush.

4. Cristallo — *LED TURTLE 04/03* — Hard Severe — *VS 4c!* — Pre 1975
2m left of Selva. Move directly up the crack starting between two white crescent shaped marks. The right-hand one of three cracks.

5. Murren — *LED MARTIN 6/03* — Hard Severe — Pre 1975
The middle of the three finger cracks with a scoop to finish.

6. The Watzmann — *LED TURTLE 4/03* — Very Severe, 4b — Pre 1975
The left-hand one of the three finger cracks with a hard finish.

7. Tre-Fynnon — Very Severe, 4b — 29/12/90
A route that fills in the gap between Watzmann and Un-aided. It has poor protection after half height if side runners are not used.

8. Un-aided — *LED STEVE '99* — Very Severe, 4b — Pre 1975
Yet another thin crack, this time with its name scratched at the base.

9. Grizzly — *2ND STAVM '99* — Very Severe, 4c — 10/7/80
Start 1m left of Un-aided and climb a thin crack to join Un-aided at the top.
LED SIMON OCT 2001. MORE LIKE Sa. !

10. Major — Hard Very Severe, 5a — Pre 1975
1m left of Grizzly a thin crack rises to 3m, then a blank wall for 1m and then a crackline to the top.

** 11. Vetta — *2ND SIMVE '99* — Hard Very Severe, 5a — Pre 1975
A good, well protected route with some fine climbing. Start at a thin crack 2m left of Major and climb to the broken wall and ledge at half height, step left onto the smooth wall and ascend the good crack to the top.

POT HOLE QUARRY (THREE SPRINGS)

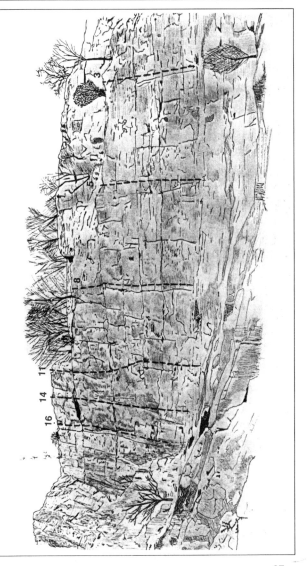

** **12. Vetta Variation**   E3 5c   6/8/78
From the ledge at half height on Vetta, ascend the wall directly above to the top.

13. Ego   E3 5c   1984
A good eliminate between Vetta and Ceba. Climb the blank looking wall on good pockets.

** **14. Ceba**   E1 5b   21/3/78
Ceba takes the crackline to the centre of the overhang with the crux moves just before the overhang. An excellent route.

** **15. Canine Meander**   E2 5b *2ND Simon Oct 2001*   12/10/84
Yet another eliminate this time between Ceba and The Dog.

*** **16. The Dog** *LED STEVE '99*   E1 5b   Pre 1975
Climb the single then twin cracks to the left of Ceba to the top either directly or using the pocketed wall at 10m. Another excellent route.

17. Right Wall   E1 5c   28/9/78
Climb the wall between The Dog and Right Angle starting on the right-hand end of the terrace in the corner. Ascend the wall on pockets until a thin crack is gained. With a good runner slightly higher, move up to the horizontal break, step left and up easier ground to the top.

18. Id   E1 5c   1984
Take the wall between Right Wall and the corner to a PR and the top.

19. Silly Lilly   E1 5b   1984
Just to the right of the corner is a left-trending crack that starts behind a small bush, follow this to the top.

20. The Right Angle   Hard Severe   Pre 1975
Climb the corner directly to the top by either bridging or an awkward layback.

21. Roger Rabbit   E1 5c   1990
Take the wall between the corner and Talking Fingers without cheating by using the other two routes.

* **22. Talking Fingers**   E2 5b   28/9/78
An obvious crackline 2.5m left of the corner with a hard move at the top. A strenuous but well protected climb.

23. Talking Legs E1 5c 28/9/78
Climb to an off balance ledge just to the left of Talking Fingers and go up the overhanging wall beyond.

24. Epitaph Very Severe, 4c Pre 1975
Climb the arête starting at a thin crack low down on the left-hand side.

25. Droggo LED MARTIN 6/03 Very Severe, 4a Pre 1975
Ascend the broken crackline between the arête and the ash tree directly.

26. Mango Hard Severe 17/6/78
Climb a crack and groove behind the ash tree to the top with a difficult move to finish. 2ND MARTIN 6/03

27. Owl Wall Severe 17/6/78
Starting on the left of the ash and sycamore trees, climb diagonally right to the top.

28. Diagonal Route E1 5a 14/7/79
Ascend Un-aided for 3m to a horizontal break, move left to the crackline of Vetta and up this to a smooth wall. Up and across to the overhang on Ceba continuing left across The Dog to Right Wall and up this to finish.

29. Main Wall Girdle E2 5c, 5a 9/8/75
1) 5c 34m. Start as for Mango for 3m until an obvious traverse line can be gained. Follow this right to the arête where a ledge is to be found. Move up to another ledge and traverse right with increasing difficulty to the corner (Right Angle) and a belay at the top.
2) 5a 17m. Move down 3m and traverse right until the top of Vetta is reached and a belay.

THE SIDE WALL

* **30. Cima** Hard Very Severe, 5a Pre 1975
A large overhang on the right-hand side of the wall is split by a finger crack. Follow this to the top.

* **31 Tosa** E1 5a 20/9/78
1m left of Cima is a white, overhanging wall with a ledge at 3m, just left of the centre, climb up to this and the easier crack above. Strenuous.

32 Burning Bush   Very Severe, 4c   20/9/78
Climb the crackline that leads to a small bush 2m left of Tosa, past the bush and up the shallow groove to the top.

33 Once Is Never Enough   Very Severe, 4c   1/90
Start below Blindfold and traverse to underneath the overlap. Pull over on the right side using a crack and a flake and continue up the slab to the top.

SECOND MARTIN 6/03.

34. Blindfold   Hard Severe   Pre 1975
Ascend the obvious large corner and wall on the left of Burning Bush.

35. Sunset   Very Difficult   Pre 1975
2m left of the corner, climb the short wall and loose looking crack to the top.

FIRST ASCENTS

Pre 1975	MESTRE	Unknown
Pre 1975	SESTO	Unknown
Pre 1975	SELVA	Unknown
Pre 1975	CRISTALLO	Unknown
Pre 1975	MURREN	Unknown
Pre 1975	THE WATZMANN	Unknown
Pre 1975	UN AIDED	Unknown
Pre 1975	MAJOR	Unknown
Pre 1975	VETTA	Unknown
Pre 1975	THE DOG	Unknown
Pre 1975	THE RIGHT ANGLE	Unknown
Pre 1975	EPITAPH	Unknown
Pre 1975	DROGGO	Unknown
Pre 1975	CIMA	Unknown
Pre 1975	BLINDFOLD	Unknown
Pre 1975	SUNSET	Unknown
9/8/75	MAIN WALL GIRDLE	S M Cathcart & G N Swindley
21/3/78	CEBA	S M Cathcart & T Curtis
17/6/78	MANGO	T Curtis, Solo
17/6/78	OWL WALL	T Curtis, Solo
6/8/78	VETTA VARIATION	S M Cathcart & G Griffiths
20/9/78	TOSA	S M Cathcart & T Curtis
20/9/78	BURNING BUSH	S M Cathcart & T Curtis
28/9/78	RIGHT WALL	S M Cathcart & T Curtis
28/9/78	TALKING FINGERS	S M Cathcart, Solo
28/9/78	TALKING LEGS	S M Cathcart, Solo
14/7/79	DIAGONAL ROUTE	S M Cathcart & M Cameron

10/7/80	GRIZZLY	S M Cathcart, Solo
1984	EGO	J Hewson & H John
1984	ID	J Hewson & H John
1984	SILLY LILLY	H John & J Hewson
12/10/84	CANINE MEANDER	I Doig & J King
1990	ROGER RABBIT	R Bennion & Co.
1/90	ONCE IS NEVER ENOUGH	A Freeman & D Romney
29/12/90	TRE-FYNNON	S Williams & A Williams

RUTHIN ESCARPMENT
(PWLLGLAS ROCKS)

O.S. Map 116 GR 122544
by Alec and Simon Williams

SITUATION AND ACCESS

Situated three miles south of Ruthin, these two tiers of west-facing limestone can be seen on the left-hand side of the road above the village of Pwllglas. Averaging about 10-12m high and running for 400m along the hillside, these small walls have the atmosphere of some of the better Yorkshire gritstone crags, with the climbing on generaly clean and solid rock. This short guide is confined to the left-hand section of the upper tier.

To reach the escarpment take the A494, from Ruthin towards Bala (south), for about three miles until you are in Pwllglas at a large layby on the left-hand side. Park here and walk back towards Ruthin for about 100m to a turning on the right. Follow this lane, passing a renovated mill, over an old railway bridge and past several houses until the road ends and a public footpath can be found on the right. Take the footpath, heading south, until the edge of the escarpment can be seen. Please do not drive cars up the road as parking there will cause annoyance to the owners of the houses and their guests thus causing potential access problems.

Although many routes have been documented along the length of the escarpment only a selection of the best have been described. The rest are left to your own imagination or are guarded by brambles. Please don't strip any of the ivy off the walls in order to create a few more climbs.

Approaching the crag across the field, the escarpment is just starting to begin. Due to the proliferation of foliage some of the routes are better reached by walking along the top of the crag and descending in. The first route lies on the first climbable, overhanging wall seen, which also sports an ivy covered pillar at its right-hand end. Below the most overhanging part is a wide groove. All the routes on the crag are described in order of approach.

1.   The Bloopers & Production No Nos   E4 6b1991
Start below the main part of the overhang. Climb the wall past 2TRs to a BR. Move leftwards up the wall to a BB and lower off.

2.   The Wee Beastie   E4 6c   14/9/86
Start slightly left of the groove and climb to the overhang, BR. Move up and left with great difficulty to a second BR and the top.

3. Green Bean   E2 6a   15/5/83
    Start at the foot of the wide groove, climb up and traverse right to the foot of a smaller groove and bolt hole. Make a hard move to enter the groove and the top.

4. The Route   Very Severe, 4c   Circa 1976
    Start below a prominent mountain ash right of Green Bean. Climb past a dodgy flake to the obvious hold, traverse right and then up to the tree.

To the right the rock becomes very overgrown. Past this there is a large flake which offers an easy descent. The next section of good rock is about 150m along to the right and is a clean, bulging buttress with two prominent horizontal bands and a deep undercut base. It is the largest buttress on the escarpment offering some of the best routes. The first route begins where a E3/4 6a is scratched into the rock just left of a rounded groove by a small stepped corner.

** 5. CCR   E3 6a   20/7/85
    Start at the stepped corner 1m left of the undercut base. Climb to a BR at 3m, move right into a shallow scoop, then up and left to a BR. Move slightly left and up to another BR, finishing over the bulge.

*   6. Old Gunks Grandads Pastime   E3 5c   30/7/90
    Start at the left-hand side of the undercut base to the right of CCR at a rounded groove. Climb this.

The next two routes both have their BRs missing.

** 7. Runner Bean   E4 6a   29/7/85
    Start at the deepest part of the undercut base, beneath some flakes. Climb up past the two sets of flakes to a long reach and a break. Move leftwards along this to a sapling, BR. Climb past a final BR up the wall (crux).

8. Summer Time Blues   E2 6b   28/5/86
    A well protected boulder problem. Start 2m in from the right-hand end of the undercut base. Climb to a BR at 5m, then up the bulge moving slightly leftwards (wire runner). Finish more easily to the top.

9. The Rock Animal Leaves His Mark   E1 5b   1/9/86
    Start to the right where the wall is less undercut. Climb the white-speckled wall moving left to a ledge. Finish up the wall via layaways on the right.

The next buttress is more easily reached from the top. Follow the path along the top of the escarpment until around 20m after stepping over a flattened fence. The trees at the base of the crag relent a bit and reveal a short sharp wall containing the only pegs found on the escarpment. The routes are described from right to left.

* **10. The Nerd**   Hard Very Severe, 5a   4/6/85
  Just to the left of where this short wall breaks down is a small overlap at the top of the wall with a BR beneath this. Climb up the wall passing the BR, overlap and PR.

** **11. Deuce Coupe**   Hard Very Severe, 5b   20/7/85
  3m to the left of The Nerd the wall contains two PRs in the top half of the wall. Climb up past these, tricky.

12. Return To The Trees   E1 5b   1/9/86
Climb up to and through the bulge 1m right of the yew tree at the top. Fight the tree to finish.

* **13. Ego Maniac**   Very Severe, 4c   12/6/85
  To the left of Deuce Coupe is a shallow groove containing a PR. Climb up to the PR, then move up and leftwards through the roof on good jugs or, alternatively, wimp out and go up the groove.

FIRST ASCENTS

1976   THE ROUTE   Ruthin School M.C.
The Route was one of twenty routes done by the schools Mountaineering Club, although the Route in fact was not finished. In their guidebook the following sentence says it all:
"Although not yet finished, it would be a travesty of appreciation to ignore the ergonomic dissipation in pursuit of this impressive corner".

15/5/83	GREEN BEAN	R Williams & A Hill
		Named after Rory's green tracksuit.
4/6/85	THE NERD	R Williams & M Brennan
12/6/85	EGO MANIAC	R Williams, Unseconded
20/7/85	CCR	R Williams & M Brennan
20/7/85	DEUCE COUPE	R Williams & M Brennan
29/7/85	RUNNER BEAN	R Williams & M Brennan
28/5/86	SUMMER TIME BLUES	R Williams & M Brennan
1/9/86	THE ROCK ANIMAL	A Hill & J Hudson
1/9/86	RETURN TO THE TREES	A Hill, Solo
14/9/86	THE WEE BEASTIE	R Williams, Unseconded
30/7/90	OLD GUNKS GRANDADS PASTIME	M Jones, Unseconded
	Mr Jones must have some very strange inspiration for his route names !	
1991	THE BLOOPERS & PRODUCTION Etc.	M Jones, Unseconded

THE EGLWYSEG VALLEY

The Eglwyseg Valley, the cream of Clwyd, consists of a selection of Limestone cliffs that run northwards for four and a half miles from the town of Llangollen. Most of the crags are of natural origin (except two) and are composed of good quality limestone that is unusually solid and pleasant to climb on, with the majority of the routes relatively clean and free from mud and debris. The protection is generally good, using cracklines for gear placements and the odd tape runner here and there. Bolts are used for a number of routes on all the crags and are placed with consideration to the guidelines of the B.M.C. and the current bolting policy agreed by them and local climbers. The rock is quick to dry after rain and, while the mountains of Snowdonia are teeming with water (and climbers), the weather here tends to be somewhat milder and drier. Because the valley runs from north to south, with all the cliffs on its eastern side, it catches the sun later on in the day, so makes for a pleasant venue for an evening's climbing during the summer months. There is a good mixture of easy through to hard routes on most of the crags with a wide variety of styles to be attempted, so it makes life a pleasure when climbing with friends of a mixed ability. The nearest main town is Llangollen, a picturesque tourist trap that straddles the River Dee, where there is an abundance of cafes and pubs, two good campsites, several petrol stations, public toilets, banks and general shopping facilities although it does tend to get a bit crowded on weekends and bank holidays.

To get to the Eglwyseg Valley, follow the A5 to the town of Llangollen. In the town there is a road bridge that spans the River Dee. Cross this and at the T-junction, turn right (east) onto the A539 and then almost immediately turn left into a small, steep side road. Follow this twisting road, the crags will soon come into view, until, after about four and a half miles you come to a ford. Look up the valley to the left-hand side and Worlds End escarpment is there in all its glory.

Access does not seem to be a problem at the moment but that does not mean that you should regard the crags, and the other users of the valley, be it walkers, farmers or anybody else for that matter, with contempt and discourtesy. They have just as much right to be there as anyone else (more so in the case of the farmers and landowners). The whole valley is a Site of Special Scientific Interest and is usually under the watchful eye of a certain number of interested parties, it is of utmost importance that any climbing restrictions are strictly adhered to. These restrictions usually involve either the nesting sites of protected birds or certain plant life and if it states in the guide or climbing press that an area is restricted to certain times of the year please observe them.

All map reference numbers are taken off the O.S. Map, sheet number 117.

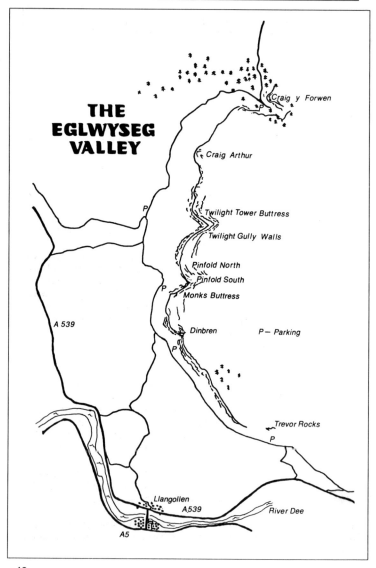

THE EGLWYSEG VALLEY

Craig y Forwen

Craig Arthur

Twilight Tower Buttress

Twilight Gully Walls

Pinfold North

Pinfold South

Monks Buttress

Dinbren

P – Parking

Trevor Rocks

Llangollen

A 539

A5

River Dee

A 539

CRAIG-Y-FORWEN (WORLDS END)

O.S. Map 117 GR 234478

by Gary Dickinson

SITUATION AND CHARACTER

This is undeniably the most popular of all of the Eglwyseg crags, possibly due to the easy approach, numerous trees at the top for belays, wealth of quality routes and the pleasant alpine atmosphere that surrounds the place. It also has the advantage of being quick to dry after a rain shower, catches the sun (when it shines) and has very little loose rock. The crag is made up of three tiers, the upper tier being the largest and most popular of the three; the lower two have a lot of loose stones at the top of the routes and can be quite hazardous for the second or belayer waiting below. The only disappointing aspect about Craig-y-Forwen is that a lot of the easier routes are getting highly polished and it can be a very unsettling experience if the rain sets in with you half way up your chosen climb! All the climbs on Craig-y-Forwen are less than 25m in length so a single rope is usually all that is needed, with protection being found using cracks and small pockets with the odd tape runner here and there, a few old pegs and an assortment of bolt runners (although further bolting would be severely frowned upon, see the notes on bolting at the front of the book). It is a good crag to go to on a warm summer's evening when the sun is on the ebb; while away a few hours on the crag followed by a pint or two afterwards at one of the local pubs, perfect.

APPROACH AND ACCESS

The easiest way to get to Craig-y-Forwen is to gain the valley road as for the rest of the Eglwyseg cliffs (see Eglwyseg introduction) and follow it for about four and a half miles until you come to a ford. Cross the stream and drive about 450m further up the hill until you come to a car park on the left-hand side. Park here and walk back down to the ford to a footpath that follows the stream uphill. Looking up at the left-hand side of the valley, Worlds End escarpment, the most northerly crag, can be seen. Follow the stream uphill, crossing a stile, until you are at the far right-hand end of the upper tier. Please do not park your car anywhere other than the proper car park as this could jeopardize the present access agreement with the landowner who, as yet, has no objections to climbers using his crag.

All routes are described from right to left as you are facing the crag. Descents are either by abseil or down any of the descent gullies mentioned in the route descriptions.

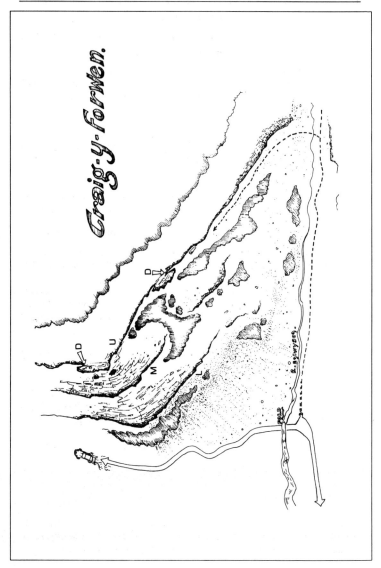

UPPER TIER

At the far right-hand end of the upper tier there is a large flake crack with a small pine tree on its left-hand side, half way up the crag.

1. Recession Blues   Very Severe, 4b   **1965-71**
Start 3m right of the flake crack, below a small overhang. Climb to the small overhang and pull through using a thin crackline to gain a ledge. Move left, then climb the easier wall above.

2. End Flake LED STEVE '99 Hard Very Difficult   **1965-71**
Layback the large flake crack to the right of the small pine tree at 3m (without using the tree root). A polished and very slippy route when damp.

3. Shelfway L.O SMILE '99 Hard Very Difficult   **1965-71**
Start at a right angled corner to the left of the pine tree. Climb diagonally right to reach the tree, then move leftwards on large ledges to the top.

To the left of the pine tree are some right trending, overhanging flake cracks.

* **4. Coltsfoot Crack**   Hard Very Severe, 5a   **1965-71**
Layback the flake cracks to gain a ledge, then follow the cracks to the top.

* **5. The Gulag Archipelago**   E3 6a   **07/91**
Start to the left of Coltsfoot Crack at a solid black slab. Climb direct to BR at 6m trending slightly right to a faint rib. Follow this via delicate moves and step back left and up a groove to finish.

Above a large boulder in the path are some left trending ledges that lead to a shattered corner near the top.

6. Right Edge   Very Severe, 4a   **1965-71**
Just right, and above the boulder are some right trending flakes. Climb diagonally right, following the flakes and cracks on their right-hand side.

7. Straight Edge   Hard Severe   **1965-71**
Take the wall between the two flake cracks to the top.

8. Left Edge   Severe   **1965-71**
Climb the left of the two flake cracks to the top.

9. Coltsfoot Corner   Severe   **1965-71**
Ascend directly up to the ledges and the loose looking corner above, or traverse in to the corner from the right and up the corner crack.

2m left of the corner is a formidable, overhanging bulge split by a white crackline at its far right end.

10. Hornbeam E3 6a 1965-71
Climb a white crack to the right of the blunt arête until it is possible to cross the path of some diagonal flake cracks. Pass the roof above the flake crack to reach a fine finger crack that leads into a v-groove. Follow this groove to finish at the top.

11. Harvey Wall Banger E1 5b 7/4/84
Climb the white smear on the left of the blunt arête until a good flake crack can be reached. Monkey up the crack, then launch yourself diagonally left to grasp a shelf below a PR. Climb past the PR and continue up the wall above to finish.

12. Hornblower E1 5b 1965-71
3m left of the arête is a steep wall with a crackline starting halfway up the face. Climb the wall to the crackline and follow it to the top. An awkward route.

13. Horny E1 5b 20/5/77
A strenuous route. Climb the start of Hornblower to a right trending flake crack. Layback this flake passing around the bulging arête to the finish of Hornbeam.

A tree that is growing horizontally out of the rock face, then a dead yew tree, are obvious landmarks for the next few routes.

14. Hornwall E1 5b 20/5/77
Start 2m right of the horizontal tree. Climb the wall to a small block and thin finger cracks above. Follow the thin cracks to a grass ledge and the top.

15. Hornbeam Wall Very Severe, 4a 1965-71
Climb the overhang on the wall to a ledge that is home to a horizontal tree. Follow the crack above, passing another tree, to finish up the wall above.

16. As Yew Like It Severe 1965-71
Ascend the shattered crack just to the right of the dead yew tree. A very pleasant climb.

17. Shabby Slab E1 5a 5/5/86
Climb the blank looking wall, 2m left of the dead yew tree, to gain some small ledges. Step right, then ascend the wall above.

18. Cornucopia   E1 5b   5/5/86
Start 3m left of the dead yew tree. Ascend a thin curving finger crack, first right, then left, to reach a grassy terrace. Climb the wall above to finish.

8m left of the dead yew tree is a prominent right-angled corner with a deep layback crack at half height and a pinnacle at its base (Twisting Corner).

*   **19. Bootlace Thread**   E4 5c   26/4/79
Climb the corner above the pinnacle for 1m, until a step right onto the slab can be made using a good handhold on the bulge above. Follow the bulge around to the right and continue to do so until you run out of rock. A direct start is possible. There is, on occasions, a thin TR on this route.

20. Twisting Corner   Hard Severe   1965-71
Layback the corner to gain a grass covered ledge, then ascend the sharp flake crack to the top.

Moving left, the walls ease off a little bit alongside some huge boulders in the path.

21. White Groove   Severe   1965-71
Start at the right-hand end of the first major boulder in the path and ascend the slightly left trending crack to the top.

22. Rich's Robbery   Severe   14/4/90
Climb the black section of the wall 2m left of the first large boulder and ascend the wall direct.

23. White Crack   Very Difficult   1965-71
Start 3m left of the first large boulder and climb the left slanting shattered crackline on good holds.

24. Scarface Groove   Difficult   1965-71
Where the black walls meet the white walls is a rather loose looking groove/corner. Climb this to the top on dubious holds.

On the path, 7m to the left, are two pinnacles perched on top of another pinnacle.

25. Gardeners Question Time   Severe   1965-71
2m right of the first pinnacle. Climb the shallow, vegetated groove via an awkward start.

26. Flakeless Groove   Hard Severe   1965-71
From the top of the second pinnacle, climb the black wall to a finger crack and follow it leftwards to the top. A harder finish can be made by stepping right around the bulge at half height.

27. Black Path   Hard Very Severe, 5a   1975
Left of the two pinnacles is a bulging wall with a small tree growing near the top. Climb the black section of wall using the faint scoops directly below the tree and climb in a nice straight line to the top. Quite steep.

28. Black Ash   Hard Very Severe, 5a   16/9/90
Climb the small layback crack to enter a fine v-groove, step left to a small ledge and continue left to finish up the groove.

* **29. Ashgrove Prelims**   Very Severe, 4c   1965-71
A well protected and enjoyable route. Take the obvious layback crack that splits the crag in a slight right-angled corner. Finishing to the left of the pine tree at the top.

30. Crackstone Rib   Hard Very Severe, 5a   21/8/77
Climb Ashgrove Prelims for 3m where a series of bold moves left on to the wall can be made. Pull up into a scoop then, move diagonally left and up to finish.

The walls now break down into a series of grass filled ramps and loose looking walls. On the left is a large chimney with an Ash tree growing from it.

* **31. Ashgrove**   Very Difficult   1965-71
Climb the body sized chimney with a large ash tree growing from it at half height. This can also be used as a descent.

* **32. Insecure**   Very Severe, 4a   1965-71
To the left of the large chimney can be found a series of blocks and a zigzag crack in the wall above. Climb the well protected blocks and crack until it is possible to traverse left on good holds to gain another vertical crack. Move up this to the top.

** **33. Incompetence**   Hard Very Difficult   1965-71
Grovel your way up the deep, left-hand crack on body jams and bum jams much to the amusement of your second, then ascend the pinnacle above.

* **34. Inspiration**   Hard Severe   1965-71
3m left of Incompetence, around a bulge, is a prominent fist sized flake crack. Climb the crack to the second crack of Inelegance and follow through to the top.

** 35. Inelegance   Very Difficult   1962
Start on the right-hand end of the bulging wall and climb the fist sized crack to reach a second crack. Follow this line trending right onto pinnacle after pinnacle to the top.

The wall to the left bulges formidably and continues to do so until a descent gully can be seen 35m away. The next four routes lie on this bulging wall.

* 36. Dead Fingers Talk   E2 6a   30/10/83
Start below a fist sized crack on the far right of the bulging wall. Ascend the crack until it is possible to step left onto the steep wall then move up to gain a finger wide flake crackline. Power up this to finish.

* 37. Dope On A Rope   E5 6a   7/4/84
Start at a scoop with a crackline above that trends diagonally right. Climb boldly up the crease and thin crack passing a PR, just left of Dead Fingers Talk.

* 38. Crystal Ship   E1 5b   1985
As the walls ease, a left curving overlap can be found above a white wall. Follow the overlap and make a step right over the roof to gain the wall above.

39. Rough Cut   Very Severe, 4a   1965-71
Take the wide, shallow groove and cracklines to the right of the descent gully (Squirm).

A large detached pillar with two descent gullies can be found on the left.

40. Squirm   Difficult   1962
Climb the overgrown gully. Best attacked armed with overalls, wellingtons and a towel!

Loose!

41. Copper Pinnacle (The Worm) ~~Hard Severe~~   4/1/64
In between the two descent gullies are a series of cracks and a groove that lead to a dead tree. Follow either crack (the left is slightly harder) to the groove and then on to the top. *LED Simon 9/03 Poor -*
V. Dirty Finish!

42. A'Cheval   Very Difficult   1962
Climb, if this is the right word, the large cave like gully that is often used as a descent.

43. Into The Fire E3 6a 4/86
1m left of the second descent gully (A'Cheval). Climb the blank looking wall to gain a thin vertical crack that is followed to the top. Sustained and serious climbing.

** **44. Fall Out** E1 5b 1965-71
2m to the left of the descent gully are some right trending, hand sized broken cracks that form the line of Fall Out. Follow these cracks up via some awkward layaways.

45. Hells Arête E3 5c 14/6/78
Take the thin finger cracks, passing some small corners and a scoop to make a step right on to the bulging arête which is followed directly to the top. Poorly protected.

Moving left again there is a large open corner that is split by some pleasant shattered cracks.

** **46. Open Book** Severe 1965-71
Climb the shattered cracks on the right wall starting on the left of an embedded spike, passing some loose looking blocks to the top. An excellent route.

** **47. J.T.P** *LED MIKE 2000* Hard Very Severe 31/1/93
Climb the large crack and blocks to the right of Open Book. Start behind the spike and follow the large cracks making an obscene move to gain a stance on the hollow sounding blocks. Layback the flakecrack above to finish.

* **48. Suicide Crack** E3 6a 16/6/75
The centre of the left wall is split by some thin finger cracks. Ascend these cracks, making an awkward move right at half height, to reach some more thin cracks that are followed up to the tree. Aptly described by its name?

** **49. Butter Arête** *2ND MIKE 2000* E2 5b *2ND Simon 9/03* 4/6/81
A good airy pitch. Climb a thin crack on the right of the arête until a step left gains the arête proper. Follow it with increasing difficulty to the top.

Moving left, around the arête, there is a small pinnacle imbedded in the ground with a young tree growing behind it.

50. Ivy Groove Very Severe, 4b 1975
Start at the right-hand end of a small pinnacle 1m left of the arête. Climb the cracks to reach a small corner which is followed to the top.

After Ivy Groove there is a large pinnacle of rock that is home to a yew tree. This is the sight of a recent rock fall and care should be taken when descending the two gullies. Left of the second gully is a lichenous, mottled wall leading to a roof split by a finger crack.

** 51. Windhover 2ND NIGE 2000 E2 5c   17/8/79
Start 2m left of the left-hand descent gully. Climb into the white groove and up to a crackline. Step right and ascend with caution up to the roof that is split by a fierce finger crack. Pull through the roof to a good hold and success.

** 52. Whim (Windy) LEAD SIMON 2000 Hard Very Severe, 5a   30/8/64
3m left of the descent gully is an obvious crackline. Climb the blocks and crack moving up and left into a shallow v-groove. Follow this groove until a step left is made onto the wall to gain another groove and the top.
SECOND SIMON 9/03.

53. Margarine Arête   Hard Very Severe, 5a   1985
Ascend the rounded arête, 5m left of the descent gully, making a step left, then back right at half height, to finish on the arête.

54. Clartum Corner   Severe   1962
Where two yew trees grow, one above the other, climb the right-hand crack and finish to the right on the arête.

55. Clartum Crack   Severe   1962
Climb either of the left-hand cracks behind the two yew trees.

From the corner moving leftwards, the walls become steep and imposing with a deep horizontal break at the base, a wave cut platform, with an elderberry tree growing from it.

* 56. Read My Lips   E5 6c   3/8/92
A good problem 1m left of the corner. Hard for the grade. Climb the wall relatively easily to the second BR over the bulge. Pass this to its right via a desperate and blind manoeuvre to gain a convenient tree.

* 57. Nurse Nurse   E5 6b   Autumn 83
Start 3m right of the elderberry tree, at a small black section of wall. Climb the short v-groove and finger flake to gain a BR below the bulging wall. Pull through the bulge to easier ground to finish.

* 58. Dr. Technical   E4 6b   14/4/84
1m right of an elderberry tree and to the left of Nurse Nurse. Climb the

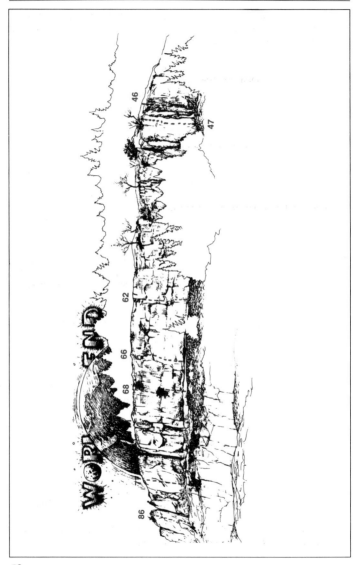

blank looking white groove to a TR, then up to a bulge with a BR sitting just below it. Move rightwards over the bulge to reach the headwall and finish up some shattered cracks.

** 59. Crystal 2ND MIKE 2cop   E1 5b   BLCODY HARD   3/12/83
Excellent clean climbing. Follow the right trending layback crack, 4m left of the elderberry tree, to reach a vertical finger crack. Move up this, passing to the left of a ledge, to finish up a short groove on the left.

A large embedded flake with a round wash hole at its lower left-hand side is a suitable landmark for the next few routes.

** 60. Titanium Man   E3 5c   20/12/83
A gem of a route with good protection and immaculate rock. Gain the top of the large flake via a wide crack, then move up some thin finger cracks and step right to a good ledge and a rest. Follow the diminutive rib, trending left to gain a PR and continue up a shallow groove, PR, to the top.

* 61. Ego Beaver   E3 6a   12/83
Technical and quite fingery for its grade. Climb the wall 1m left of Titanium Man to reach the top of the flake, then move up into the smooth scoop above, BR. Climb the tiny overlap and wall above, 2PRs, with difficulty.

62. Fossil Finish   Hard Severe   6/71
Start above a deep round wash hole at the base of the crag and 2m to the left and climb the cracks above to gain a loose wall. Continue up, moving leftwards towards the corner near the top. Finish easily up this.

63. Tripe & Landah   Hard Very Severe, 5a   19/8/80
3m left of a large embedded flake, above a second wash hole is a very thin finger crack. Climb this passing a PR to the top.

64. Brigadier Gerard   E5 6a   11/83
5m to the left of the large flake is another fine finger crack. Climb the crack passing a PR, until a move left across the bulge leads to the left-hand crackline. Soldier on using dubious holds. Good climbing, slightly superseded by:

** 65. Sisters Of The Moon   E5 6b   Spring 88
Fine wall climbing with reliable protection. Start 2m left of the Brigadier. Follow an indistinct line of holds on the featureless wall, past 2 BRs, to join and finish up the crack, as for Brigadier Gerard.

A 2m long, rectangular block in the path marks the start for the next 2 routes.

** **66. Rudolph Hess**   E7 6c   Spring 88
Probably the hardest route in the valley! Heinous. Climb the blank looking wall, starting at the right-hand end of the block, passing 2 BRs, first BR has a sling hanging from it. With extreme difficulty, gain an easing off in the angle of the rock, traverse right and go up the final crack of Brigadier Gerard.

*** **67. Shooting Star**   E4 6b   3/5/79
An important step forward in the development of the crag produced one of its best routes. Above the left end of the block is an impressive right trending crackline up the overhanging wall. Shoot up the crack, passing a wild rose bush, to reach a TR. With difficulty, move up past a PR to gain a good hold above the bulge. Pull through this and follow the crack past the left side of the overhang.

68. Cigars Of The Pharaohs   E5 6b   9/90
The wall immediately left of Shooting Star. Power up on undercuts to a BR, then trend right and upwards on more undercuts to better holds near the top, passing 2 more BRs on the way.

* **69. Yew & Me**   Hard Very Severe, 5b   8/7/81
Start below two yew trees, one above the other, and climb the wall to the first tree. Move left to finish up the easier angled slab and thin crack.

5m left of the two yew trees, the angle of the walls relent with a rounded arête and a left facing corner split by a crack.

70. Going Bad   E2 5b   20/9/78
Climb the crack and hanging pillar in the arête. Continue up the crack and wall above.

* **71. Gone Bad**   E1 5b   1965-71
2m left of Going Bad. Climb the thin groove to the right of a wild rose bush to the overhang. Move right underneath the overhang to gain a layback crack and a very exposed finish.

** **72. Intensity**   Hard Very Severe, 5a   1962
Take a line up the obvious large crack to reach a body sized crack/chimney. Forge a way up using leg and body jams. One of the very first routes to be climbed here.

Stuart Cathcart on Intensity, Craig-y-Forwen (Worlds End)

** **73. Close To The Edge** E1 5b 26/5/74
Start as for Intensity to the base of the first overhang, then traverse left for 3m to gain a v-groove at the left of the roof. Continue up more easily to the top. Can also be started directly below the v-groove at about the same grade.

74. Craznitch Crack Hard Severe 1962
Climb the large, right trending chimney that is filled with chockstones.

The wall on the left of the chimney, to the arête, now becomes dramatically overhanging. The next route begins on the front face, to the left of the arête, on a very exposed slab of rock high above the ford.

75. Jumping Jack Flash E4 5c 26/12/83
Move up the wall for 3m before traversing tentatively right around the arête to gain the base of an impressive flake, TR. Climb boldly up the flake to the top. Whether the flake stays in place whilst you do remains to be seen.

** **76. Flashdance** E4 6b 11/83
Superb technical climbing, though short lived, in a photogenic position. Start 2m left of the arête. Ascend the small ledges and thin finger crack to a PR. Pull past this to a second crack, PR, and so to the top.

* **77. Flash Harry** E4 6b 31/12/83
2m left of Flashdance is another thin finger crack that leads delicately to a small roof. Follow through, PR, then trend left to finish.

78. Christmas Spirit E1 5b 25/12/83
1m in from the left end of the slab is another finger crack. Climb this to a TR and continue up the shattered cracks and groaning flakes in the wall above.

The walls break down into a series of large gullies and chimneys that are spaced by a pleasant slabby wall. The wall is marked by a small overhang and capped by a large yew tree.

79. Wither Difficult 1962
The extremely large (2m wide) crack that is full of boulders is blocked by an aggressive looking wild rose bush. Bravely go where no person has been for quite some time!

80. Ivy Crack Severe 1962
Climb the left trending crackline, 1m left of the boulder filled gully, using body jams to half height followed by some pleasant laybacks and bridging to finish.

81. Slither   Very Severe, 4c   3/10/79
Start on the arête to the left of Ivy Crack and gain a fine finger crack that leads to an ivy covered plateau.

82. Xuxu   E1 5a   24/7/80
Start on top of the large flake and pull over the bulge on good holds to gain a good ledge. Move left to the centre of the wall and continue up passing the yew on the left.

83. Sleeping Beauty   E3 6a   1985
Start below and right of the yew tree and climb up to the overhang to clip an upturned PR on the left. Pull rightwards through the roof to join and finish with Xuxu.

84. Half and Half   Severe   1962
The prominent chimney that is full of chockstones. Ascend into the chimney until 7m up, then move on to the right wall and continue to the top.

** **85. Heart Of Darkness**   E3 5c   24/7/80
Climb the arête to the left of Half and Half in a very exposed position. Excellent climbing requiring small wire protection.

Moving left around from the arête are two large walls divided by a right slanting chimney taken by Les Elephants. These walls sport a number of small overlaps and finger cracks. The next routes can be found on these walls, starting with:-

** **86. Wasters Mall**   E4 6b   31/12/83
Technically intricate climbing. Climb the groove and wall 4m left of the blunt arête, TR and PR, moving right, then left, to gain an easier upper groove.

*** **87. Tearg Wall** ²ᴺᴼSⁱᵐᴼᴺ ²⁰⁰⁰
                                E2 5c   4/6/81
Atmospheric climbing in a superb position. Start in the centre of the first wall. Ascend the flake crack to a traverse line at 4m. Move left, then up some shattered cracks, following a right trending flake crack to reach a PR, a difficult clip if you're less than 5'8". Take the headwall direct, crux. The route can be also climbed direct, missing out the traverse at 4m.

* **88. Telegram Sam**   E3 6a   11/83
Climb the scoop and wall to the left of Tearg Wall, BR, moving left to finish up a slight crack.

89. Les Elephants   Very Severe, 4c   1962
Climb the chockstone filled chimney dividing the two walls.

*   90. Soul On Ice   E3 5c   31/12/83
Scale the vague crackline to the left of the chimney to reach a TR. Carry on in the same line to a finish on the left.

**   91. Someone Like You   E4 6a   2/7/92
A fine route up the centre of the face left of Soul On Ice. Bold. Starting at a small flake, climb the wall direct, PR, into a short right facing corner, PR. A technical finish, including a long reach gains good holds and the top.

**   92. Worlds Edge   E4 6a   8/3/84
The arête, on the left of Someone Like You, is climbed on its right-hand side to a PR, making a move right through the bulge to finish.

A number of left facing corners and large cracks, to the left of the arête, make up the next selection of climbs.

**   93. Jennifer Crack   Hard Severe   1962
A sharp, left facing corner, split by a huge crack. Climb the large, foot wedging crack that splits the corner from top to bottom.

*   94. Sting   Hard Severe   1962
To the left of Jennifer Crack is an arête with an ash tree near its top. Climb the large flake and groove on the wall to the left of the arête and tree.

95. Quill   Very Severe, 4c   5/75
1m left of the arête (with an ash tree near its top) is a good hand sized crackline that is followed to a ledge. Move off the ledge to continue up the shattered looking wall above to the top.

A good descent gully, hidden from view until you have passed it, is the next feature on this part of the crag.

96. Ash Bole (Dagga)   Severe   30/8/64
3m left of the descent gully. Climb a rather loose looking, vegetated crack on suspect rock.

*   97. Chance   E1 5b   8/3/84
Start just left of Ash Bole. Gain the break and climb the wall above to finish via a thin crack. ZND SIMON 07/04 (V. HOLLOW FLAKE!)

G Gibson on Grand Canyon, Pantymwyn. Photo: G.Gibson

*** 98. Vertical Games E4 6a 7/7/81
A superb outing. Start 4m left of the descent gully. Climb an enticing flake crack for 3m. Stand up to gain a second crack that peters out in the smooth wall above. Step right, then back left and move up gingerly to the top.

* 99. The Trick Very Severe, 5a 30/8/64
Start below a large ash tree. Climb the left trending crack to, and past, the tree to gain a fine finger crack, behind the tree. Followed this, not the tree, to the top. Also known as Durban Poison.

100. Warp Commander E1 5b 7/84
The wall and overlap to the right of the ash tree. Start on top of a large block and grab some loose looking shattered cracks to gain the wall. Move right up the shattered blocks to the overlap and ascend the wall above.

** 101. Finer Feelings E1 5b 13/5/79
Start on the top of the block, 4m left of the ash tree. Thrutch up the thin finger crack and v-groove to step right and continue up another fine crack.

102. Cathcarts Got A Brand New Brodrie E1 5b 5/7/84
2m left of the fir tree. Start below an overlap that is pulled through to gain a slight finger crack. Follow this to a petit v-groove which leads to the top.

MIDDLE TIER

Park as for the upper tier and walk back down the road to reach the ford. Follow the path upstream, crossing a stile until some remains of a dwelling are seen on the left. Walk just past these and ascend the scree slope diagonally left to reach the far right-hand end of the lower tier; scramble up the rocks and walk left for 30m to the largest section of the middle tier. All the routes are described from right to left as you are facing the rock with the easiest descent down a gully on the right-hand side. To the left of this lies a prominent yew tree at the top of the tier.

* 103. Marjoun Hard Very Severe, 5a 1965-71
Ascend the leaning crack, to the right of the tree, for 4m, then step left to join another crack. This leads to the top.

104. Mr Flay Very Severe, 4a 1975
Takes the orange, lichen covered crack and wall to the right of the tree.

D Kerr on Worlds Edge, Craig-y-Forwen. Photo: D Kerr

105. Desist (Slim Chance)   Very Severe, 4a   30/8/64
3m left of Mr Flay is a line of thin cracks.

Moving left a large flake embedded in the ground can be seen.

106. Cake Walk   Very Difficult   1962
Move up the crack, to the right of the flake, to a small grass terrace and ascend the crack beyond.

107. Handjam   Severe   1962
To the left of the flake is a shattered crack. Climb up this in a totally unexciting fashion.

108. Layback With Me   Hard Severe   1965-71
Layback the obvious crack: a well protected and pleasant climb.

109. Rumble   Difficult   1962
5m left of Handjam. Shuffle up the large crack passing a loose looking block en-route.

110. Collette   Very Severe, 4b   8/12/91
9m left of Rumble is a large pinnacle in the ground below an overhang. Start on the left of the pinnacle and climb a series of loose flakes to a roof. Traverse left at the roof, then pull up and over, trending right to finish.

LOWER TIER

Park as for the upper tier and walk back down the road to reach the ford. Follow the path upstream, crossing a stile until some remains of a dwelling are seen on the left. Walk just past these and ascend the scree slope diagonally left to reach the far right-hand end of the lower tier.

The following routes are described from right to left facing the rock with good descents at either end and in the centre. Caution should be used when climbing on the lower tier due to the large amounts of loose material to be found at the top of the routes. It could prove quite dangerous for the belayer, second or tourists who happen to be below you!

111. Ouja Chimney   Difficult   1962
Where the tier starts to fade out and the angle of the wall eases off, is a square cut gully with a pine tree 3m away. Climb the cracks in the gully on loose holds.

112. Nose   Very Difficult   1962
Climb the two fist sized cracks to the left of the square cut gully

113. Picture Arête   Very Severe, 4c   16/7/81
2m left of the arête. Climb the wall to gain a ledge beneath a small roof.
Stepping left, gain the large crack which is followed to the top.

114. Brown Cracks   Severe   1962
Climb the cracks and loose looking blocks 4m left of the arête.

* 115. Ganjah   Severe   1965-71
Take a v-groove up to a small roof, then step left, then up, to gain another
groove. Follow this to the top.

116. Black Dog   Very Severe, 4c   1965-71
Climb the shallow groove, 1m left of Ganjah, to reach another small roof.
Step left and move up the v-groove that will take you to a small tree near
the top.

* 117. Black Out   Very Severe, 4c   12/10/80
Pad up the groove to reach some shattered cracks. Follow these cracks
passing between two small trees.

* 118. La Di Da   E2 5b   15/8/80
Climb the white groove up to a small capped roof, pulling through the roof
direct.

119. Kinky   E2 5c   Unknown
Climb up the wall on faint scoops to gain a BR, then on tiny holds, shuffle
upwards very delicately to reach some loose blocks and safety.

120. Brinkman   E2 5a   15/8/80
Take a fine crack in the centre of the wall passing a PR to reach a very
loose top.

Moving left, there is a distinctive right angled corner with an appealing flake
crack in its centre.

** 121. Pleurum   Severe   1962
Storm up the obvious layback crack with good protection.

122. Caveman Wall   E2 5b   15/8/80
Climb the steep walls 5m left of the layback crack to a small cave at 3m
and gingerly move up the wall above on doubtful rock.

*   123. Icicle Of Death   E3 5c   17/5/81
Some thin right trending cracks left again lead up to a rectangular roof at
7m. Traverse awkwardly left, under the main roof, to gain some smaller
roofs and finish up a shallow scoop to their right.

*   124. Spetsnaz   E2 5c   11/10/85
5m left of Icicle Of Death is a clean wall. Ascend the wall making an
awkward move, via a one finger pocket, past a BR to reach easier ground.

*   125. Muscle Bound   E2 5b   17/5/81
The thin crack, 2m right of the left facing v-groove with a tree growing from
it, is climbed first left, then right, passing a PR on the way.

**   126. Plasuchaf Crack   Severe   1962
Lunge up the layback crack that is the home of a small tree, 4m off the floor.

To the left of the layback Crack is a wall with a large, semi detached pillar
balanced on it and a yew tree growing at the top.

127. The Cause   Hard Very Severe, 5a   16/8/79
Climb the thin cracks just to the right of the tree.

128. Carter U.C.M.   E2 5c   8/12/91
Begin 7m left of the base of the pillar of rock. Ascend the wall with difficulty
on some ledges to a BR. Make a desperate move past this to finish up an
easier angled, but loose, slab of rock.

Follow the path on the left to a small cave low down in the wall for the next two
routes.

129. Cato   Severe   1975
Start on the right side of the cave and climb leftwards to a small bush
finishing up the groove.

130. Holly Tree Wall   Severe   1962
Ascend the wall from the left of the cave to join Cato at its final moves.

The wall gradually breaks down to become a series of grassy steps that are
useful as a descent route. The next routes are situated about 25m left of this
descent path by a flake that protrudes out of the path.

131. Hypertension   E3 5b   21/6/80
Start 1m left of flake in the path and ascend the wall to a PR in a horizontal

break. Continue up, moving rightwards up the shattered wall above. Loose.

132. Pisa   Severe   1965-71
10m left of the flake in the path is a left facing, overgrown corner. Jibber your way up the corner on loose looking blocks, passing several trees en route.

133. Sunspots   Hard Very Severe, 5a   17/5/81
Climb the arête and wall to the right of Grass.

134. Grass   Hard Very Difficult   1965-71
A very overgrown, loose looking, grass filled groove. If you feel that you want to climb this, we suggest you use ice climbing techniques!

135. Prel   E3 6a   1983
Climb the compact wall from the foot of Grass and move leftwards to join the end of the traverse of Diamond Solitaire.

*   136. Diamond   Very Severe, 5a   1965-71
Climb the loose, shattered crack to a large diamond shaped roof. Step left around the roof and up the groove to finish.

** 137. Diamond Solitaire   E2 5b   20/9/80
Climb Diamond to the roof, then traverse right to gain the end of the overhangs. Escape upwards near two trees.

138. Tree   Very Severe, 4c   1965-71
Ascend the short v-groove 4m left of Diamond Solitaire and follow it to the top.

FIRST ASCENTS

1962	INELEGANCE	H J Tinkler & J Hesketh
1962	SQUIRM	H J Tinkler & J Hesketh
1962	A'CHEVAL	H J Tinkler & J Hesketh
1962	CLARTUM CORNER	H J Tinkler & J Hesketh
1962	CLARTUM CRACK	H J Tinkler & J Hesketh
1962	INTENSITY	J Hesketh & H J Tinkler
	For a long time, this was the most difficult climb in the valley!	
1962	CRAZNITCH CRACK	J Hesketh & H J Tinkler
1962	WITHER	H J Tinkler & J Hesketh
1962	IVY CRACK	H J Tinkler & J Hesketh
1962	HALF AND HALF	J Hesketh & H J Tinkler

1962	LES ELEPHANTS	J Hesketh & H J Tinkler
1962	JENNIFER CRACK	J Hesketh & H J Tinkler
1962	STING	J Hesketh & H J Tinkler
1962	CAKE WALK	H J Tinkler & J Hesketh
1962	HANDJAM	J Hesketh & H J Tinkler
1962	RUMBLE	H J Tinkler & J Hesketh
1962	OUJA CHIMNEY	H J Tinkler & J Hesketh
1962	NOSE	H J Tinkler & J Hesketh
1962	BROWN CRACKS	J Hesketh & H J Tinkler
1962	PLEURNUM	H J Tinkler & J Hesketh
1962	PLASUCHAF CRACK	J Hesketh & H J Tinkler
1962	HOLLY TREE WALL	H J Tinkler & J Hesketh
4/1/64	COPPER PINNACLE	G Ashton & R Newcombe

Incorrectly called The Worm. This, and the next routes, were somehow given the wrong names in the last guidebook. We have given them back their original names and put their "pseudonyms" in brackets here and in the route descriptions.

30/8/64	WHIM (Windy)	R Newcombe & G Ashton
30/8/64	ASH BOLE (Dagga)	R Newcombe & G Ashton
30/8/64	THE TRICK (Durban Poison)	G Ashton & R Newcombe
30/8/64	DESIST (Slim Chance)	R Newcombe & G Ashton
31/12/65	ABANDONMENT	D Roberts & J Harwood
	FFA 11/83 (Flashdance)	J Codling
1965-71	RECESSION BLUES	Unknown
1965-71	END FLAKE	Unknown
1965-71	SHELFWAY	Unknown
1965-71	COLTSFOOT CRACK	Unknown
1965-71	RIGHT EDGE	Unknown
1965-71	STRAIGHT EDGE	Unknown
1965-71	LEFT EDGE	Unknown
1965-71	COLTSFOOT CORNER	Unknown
1965-71	HORNBEAM	Unknown
1965-71	HORNBLOWER	Unknown
1965-71	HORNBEAM WALL	Unknown
1965-71	AS YEW LIKE IT	Unknown
1965-71	TWISTING CORNER	Unknown
1965-71	WHITE GROOVE	Unknown
1965-71	WHITE CRACK	Unknown
1965-71	SCARFACE GROOVE	Unknown
1965-71	GARDENERS QUESTION TIME	Unknown
1965-71	FLAKELESS GROOVE	Unknown
1965-71	ASHGROVE PRELIMS	Unknown
1965-71	ASHGROVE	Unknown
1965-71	INSECURE	Unknown
1965-71	INCOMPETENCE	Unknown
1965-71	INSPIRATION	Unknown

1965-71	ROUGH CUT	Unknown
1965-71	FALL OUT	Unknown
1965-71	OPEN BOOK	Unknown
1965-71	GONE BAD	Unknown
1965-71	MARJOUN	Unknown
1965-71	LAYBACK WITH ME	Unknown
1965-71	GANJAH	Unknown
1965-71	BLACK DOG	Unknown
1965-71	PISA	Unknown
1965-71	GRASS	Unknown
1965-71	DIAMOND	Unknown
1965-71	TREE	Unknown
1965-71	BUSH	Unknown
6/71	FOSSIL FINISH	R Tilston, Unseconded
26/5/74	CLOSE TO THE EDGE	P Stott & M Frith
1975	BLACK PATH	S M Cathcart & G N Swindley
1975	IVY GROOVE	M Frith & P Stott
1975	MR FLAY	P Stott, Unseconded
1975	CATO	P Stott, Unseconded
5/75	QUILL	S M Cathcart & N Slaney
16/6/75	SUICIDE CRACK	S M Cathcart & N Slaney
20/5/77	HORNY	S M Cathcart & G N Swindley
20/5/77	HORNWALL	S M Cathcart & G N Swindley
21/8/77	CRACKSTONE RIB	S M Cathcart & T Curtis
14/6/78	HELLS ARÊTE	S M Cathcart & T Curtis
20/9/78	GOING BAD	S M Cathcart & J Dee
26/4/79	BOOTLACE THREAD	S M Cathcart & G N Swindley
3/5/79	SHOOTING STAR	S M Cathcart & G N Swindley
13/5/79	FINER FEELINGS	S M Cathcart & J Dee
16/8/79	THE CAUSE	S M Cathcart, Solo
17/8/79	WINDHOVER	S M Cathcart & G N Swindley
3/10/79	SLITHER	S M Cathcart, Solo
21/6/80	HYPERTENSION	S M Cathcart & T Curtis
24/7/80	XUXU	S M Cathcart & M Cameron
24/7/80	HEART OF DARKNESS	S M Cathcart & M Cameron
15/8/80	LA DI DA	S M Cathcart & J Dee
15/8/80	BRINKMAN	S M Cathcart & J Dee
15/8/80	CAVEMAN WALL	S M Cathcart & J Dee
19/8/80	TRIPE & LANDAH	P Stott & D Greenald
20/9/80	DIAMOND SOLITAIRE	S M Cathcart & J Dee
12/10/80	BLACK OUT	S M Cathcart, Solo
17/5/81	ICICLE OF DEATH	S M Cathcart & M Cameron
17/5/81	MUSCLE BOUND	S M Cathcart & M Cameron
17/5/81	SUNSPOTS	S M Cathcart & M Cameron
4/6/81	BUTTER ARÊTE	S M Cathcart & M Cameron
4/6/81	TEARG WALL	S M Cathcart & M Cameron

7/7/81	VERTICAL GAMES	P Stott & S M Cathcart
8/7/81	YEW & ME	P Stott, Unseconded
16/7/81	PICTURE ARÊTE	S M Cathcart & M Cameron
1983	PREL	S M Cathcart, P Waters & D Barber
Aut. 83	NURSE NURSE	J Codling, Unseconded
30/10/83	DEAD FINGERS TALK	J Moulding & S Cardy
11/83	BRIGADIER GERARD	S Allen & J Codling
11/83	FLASHDANCE	J Codling, Unseconded
	FFA of the old aid route Abandonment.	
11/83	TELEGRAM SAM	J Codling, Unseconded
12/83	EGO BEAVER	F Crook & G Cooper
3/12/83	CRYSTAL	F Crook, K Crook & I Barker
20/12/83	TITANIUM MAN	F Crook, K Crook & G Cooper
25/12/83	CHRISTMAS SPIRIT	F Crook & G Crook
26/12/83	JUMPING JACK FLASH	J Codling & T Bristlin
31/12/83	FLASH HARRY	J Codling & J Moulding
31/12/83	WASTERS MALL	J Codling & J Moulding
31/12/83	SOUL ON ICE	J Moulding & J Codling
8/3/84	WORLDS EDGE	S Boydon & P Harrison
8/3/84	CHANCE	P Harrison & S Boydon
7/4/84	HARVEY WALL BANGER	J Codling, Unseconded
7/4/84	DOPE ON A ROPE	J Codling & A Dope
14/4/84	DR TECHNICAL	J Moulding & S Boydon
7/84	WARP COMMANDER	P Windsor, Unseconded
5/7/84	CATHCARTS GOT A.....	P Waters, Unseconded
1985	CRYSTAL SHIP	A Windsor, Unseconded
1985	MARGARINE ARÊTE	S Cardy & A Orton
1985	SLEEPING BEAUTY	I Dunn & C Dunn
11/10/85	SPETSNAZ	D Kerr & D Woolger
4/86	INTO THE FIRE	A Price, Unseconded
5/5/86	SHABBY SLAB	L Beaumont & D Williams
5/5/86	CORNUCOPIA	L Beaumont & D Williams
Spr. 88	SISTERS OF THE MOON	A Price, Unseconded
Spr. 88	RUDOLPH HESS	M Collins, Unseconded
14/4/90	RICH'S ROBBERY	R Andrews & J Howel
9/90	CIGARS OF THE PHARAOHS	D Taylor, Unseconded
16/9/90	BLACK ASH	A Casemoney & A Thompson
7/91	GULAG ARCHIPELAGO	C Silverstone, Unseconded
8/12/91	CARTER U.C.M.	R Carter & G Dickinson
	The original first ascensionists are unknown.	
8/12/91	COLLETTE	G Dickinson & J Drinkwater
2/7/92	SOMEONE LIKE YOU	G Gibson & H Gibson
3/8/92	READ MY LIPS	G Gibson, Unseconded
	After numerous attempts on five previous days.	
31/1/93	J.T.P.	G Dickinson, J Drinkwater & P Lockett
Unknown	KINKY	

CRAIG ARTHUR

O.S. Map 117 GR 224471

by Gary Gibson

SITUATION AND CHARACTER

This large cliff, clearly visible from the A5, is easily seen when travelling up the Eglwyseg Valley, sitting on the valley's right-hand rim, the striking white limestone glinting in the sunshine. It seems fitting that this impressive cliff should sit in such an imposing position.

Without doubt, Craig Arthur is the pride of all the Clwyd limestone crags, standing proudly guarding the head of the valley. Its imposing size, some 400m in length and varying between 30m and 45m in height, combined with its undoubtedly exposed position high above distinctive scree slopes, give it an unrivalled grandeur. Coupled with this, its isolated position and climatic conditions, a wind of some form is usually blowing here, giving it the true atmosphere of a big mountain crag, with all the attendant limestone characteristics.

The rock is typical of the area, albeit on a much larger scale. For the most part the cliff is composed of areas of superb, compact grey limestone, alongside areas of slightly more friable white rock. The latter rock type does not create a major problem, since routes have either received enough traffic over the years or have been thoroughly cleaned to remove surface debris. It goes without staying that no route should be underestimated.

Unfortunately on some of the easier and more traditional routes, the line of least resistance taken tends to be the most fractured and time and/or traffic have not completely had the desired affect; where appropriate this has been mentioned in the text.

As is synonymous with the area, and limestone as a whole, the foreshortening of the cliff belies its true size and steepness; many of the climbs here prove more arduous by dint of their sustained nature than by their individual technical difficulty. Having said this, the majority of the routes are well blessed with good protection, whether natural or otherwise, giving the climber a sense of security in an exposed and atmospheric playground. The climbs, combined with their approaches, isolated environment and atmosphere, can provide a very rewarding day out.

Finally a note on prevalent weather conditions: without doubt this can be a hostile environment. To sample high winds here can be an invigorating experience whilst at the base of the cliff but, whilst engaged in the intricacies of a climb, it is not a thought worth entertaining. Normally, a wind of some sort is evident, which, during the summer months, is a very desirable commodity. Any sunshine usually catches the face after mid-day and consequently it can become unbearably hot on a calm summer's afternoon. Oppositely, with the sun out and a mellow breeze prevailing, this cliff takes on a charm of its own; an afternoon or summer evening is ideal. Choose the cliff in the depths of winter and the whole place takes on an entirely new, and not altogether wholesome, character; there is no shelter from any form of cold breeze.

APPROACH AND ACCESS

It is important when finding a parking space not to block any roads or access points for other passing vehicles and local landowners. Inconsiderate attitudes have caused problems in the past and may now do similar in the World's End region, particularly in view of recent road changes; parking facilities have since become more limited.

There are two main approaches, although a direct approach up the hillside from the small river bridge (GR 222475) below Ty Canol Farm is possible, though very steep.

1. Park carefully and approach as for World's End and walk 50m down the road from the ford to a closed gate and stile on the left side of the road; this marks the Offa's Dyke Pathway. Follow the path through the large pine forest and exit from it. Continue by following the trail alongside a rickety old fence until, after about 10 minutes, the corner of a large pine forest is reached and the edge of Craig Arthur comes into view on the hillside above to the left. From here a path has been constructed up the scree slope to the left end of the crag, approximately 20 minutes from the parking spot.

2. Park at the convenient layby below Monk's Buttress, which is used for access to this and the Pinfold Crags. Walk down the road (north) for 50m and pass through the gate on the right. Follow the gravelled road around to the left, passing just right of a cottage, onto the Offa's Dyke Pathway. Follow this as it passes below Pinfold North Buttress, through a dry valley and below the Twilight cliffs, to the southern end of Craig Arthur. Here a grassy track leads up the right-hand side of the scree fan to below the South Buttress. Alternatively, continue along the Offa's Dyke Pathway until past the northern end of the crag and double back on yourself up the well constructed scree path; approximately 30 minutes from the parking spot.

On first acquaintance this is a complex cliff, with a myriad of features which only become discernible after a number of visits. For the sake of simplicity, the cliff can be divided into four main sections, the North Wall, the Central Walls, the Nemesis Wall and the South Buttress.

The left-hand side of the North Buttress is easily identifiable by the broad shattered descent gully and the broken tiers to its left. To the right of the gully the first prominent feature is a detached pillar marking the line of Arthur's Pillar.

To the right again the cliff rears up, presenting a series of square-cut overhangs of varying sizes for quite some distance. A steep crack, Three Dimensions, marks the right-hand side of these before the buttress drops back into a shattered bay. A grey slab in the right-hand side of this, taken by Stratagem, swings round into a clean, rounded buttress split by a steep crack above a small, ground level yew tree on its left-hand side: Manikins Of Horror. The centre of the buttress is taken by Dance Of The Puppets. To the right a large yew tree nestles in the back of another bay, the bay being capped by a series of overlaps and scoops, taken by Eliminator. This bay is bounded on the right by a compact grey wall and a superb arête, the former taken by Tito and Digitron and the latter by Heaven Or Hell.

The walls now swing round to form a fine white pillar, Alpha Track Etch, before they begin to diminish in size. This shorter section of cliff, initially yellow in colour, is terminated by a slender buttress capped by impressive roofs; Ten. A large vegetated area, up which Jungle Warfare battles its way, is bounded by a grey area of compact rock standing slightly forward; Charlain and Now and Then take the groove to its right. As the cliff rears up once more, the superb clean face provides a number of excellent routes, terminated by a brilliant crack splitting the right-hand side of a blunt arête, the scene for Survival Of The Fastest.

The walls now begin to overhang alarmingly and are capped by square-cut overhangs. This superb white face, the Nemesis Wall, is bisected by black seepage lines and covered in a mixture of delicate features. Here such classics as Manic Mechanic, Smokin' Gun and Tres Hombres find their way. The right side of the wall is clearly marked by a huge sycamore tree, one of the few places to cower in the full heat of the sun. To the right again a large amphitheatre, crossed by vegetated terraces, provides an arena for a series of shorter climbs.

The huge, barrel-shaped face to the right stands out almost as a buttress disconnected from the main cliff. The central wall, taken by Delaware Slide and These Foolish Things, is bounded by an overhang-capped wall taken by Gates of the Golden Dawn and Sunny Side up Mix. The face quickly loses height to the right of this to provide another grassy gully convenient for descent.

The climbs are described from left to right as this is the usual method of approach. At its left-hand, north end, the North Buttress quickly degenerates into a series of shattered tiers and a prominent gully, the main method of descent for this area.

1. Arthur's Pillar   Very Severe   Pre 1960

An unsatisfactory climb up the prominent flake pillar to the right of the descent gully.

1) 24m. 4b. Climb a short corner 3m right of the gully, passing a break leftwards, to the foot of the pillar. Follow this, moving into a groove at the top, which then leads to a ledge and belay.

2) 9m. Move left to continue loosely to the top.

2. Monkey's Claws   E3   8/10/80

Again relatively poor. Start as for Arthur's Pillar.

1) 24m. 5b. Tread rightwards over some blocks and flakes to a ledge below a vague scoop. Move up this to an overhang, PR, and pull over via good holds on the right. Belay at a hidden bush.

2) 12m. 5c. Harrowing. Move rightwards to beneath a bulging wall and move awkwardly left to a good hold on the smooth-looking wall. Now continue direct via a thin flake crack to the top.

To the right the rock begins to steepen with a series of impressive overhangs and the start of a group of excellent routes.

** 3. The Fall and Decline   E3   2/10/77

A typically steep limestone pitch, well endowed with sound protection and gratifying holds. More strenuous than technical. Start at a small corner below a prominent square-cut corner at 6m.

1) 24m. 5c. Climb the wall past a rotten peg to gain a fine, leftward trending flake crack. Romp up this to the overlap, swing left below it, hidden PR to the left, to gain a groove. An awkward entry gains a good crack and moves right after 3m lead onto the arête, PR. Climb this and a short wall to a small ledge and old peg belay.

2) 12m. 5a. Climb the overhangs via an obvious break, old PR, quickly easing. There is a thread belay over to the left.

** 4. Le Chacal   E2   14/6/81

Another worthwhile route, similar in character to The Fall and Decline but with a shorter crux section.

1) 24m. 5c. From the foot of the leftward trending flake crack on the Fall and Decline, move right into the square cut corner and climb it using holds on the left wall to gain the roof. "Monkey" right to a PR in the break and pull over onto the yellow wall with difficulty. Climb this to some good holds, then traverse right to a small ledge complete with an old bolt and peg belay.

2) 12m. 5a. Go up the flake crack right of the stance to a small tree on the left. Move back up and right into an easy groove which leads to the top.

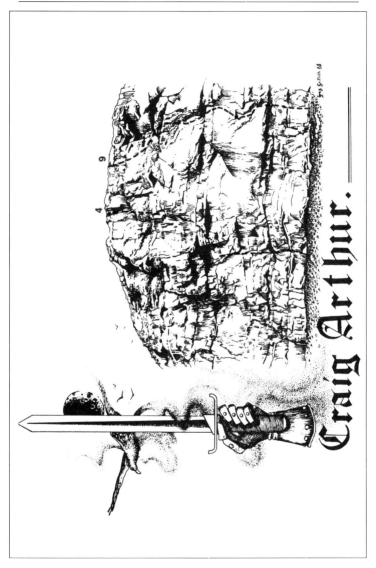

75

Roger Bennion on Le Chacal, Craig Arthur

*** 5.   A Touch Of Class   E2   13/10/80
A superb outing, meandering across the face to find the easiest line.
Nowhere desperate, with plenty of unusual and varied climbing: a classic.
Start as for La Chacal.

1)   24m. 5b. Move up to a ledge and horizontal break at 5m and from its
right-hand end, climb the compact wall to a PR bounding the left-hand side
of a white wall. Traverse tentatively right across this, PR, to gain a hidden
ramp/slab. Belay at the top of this below the roof, pegs.

2)   15m. 5b. Continue the traverse right along the break to below a steep
bottomless groove. Climb this to a TR, then swing right to a PR on the
shattered, pleasantly exposed arête. Move up this and a short wall to a tree
belay in the back of a recess.

3)   12m. 5a. Traverse left along a slim ledge onto the rounded arête and
finish up this and the short wall above, exposed.

**   6.   Back Yard Holiday   E4 6a   6/88
Good steep climbing in fine positions. The route can be split by taking a
belay at the top of the ramp/slab as for A Touch Of Class. Start 5m to the
right, below a bulge bounding the left-hand side of a smooth looking wall.
Climb up to below the bulge and make an awkward move to get established
on a base of rock, TR. Go straight up the wall above, PR on the left, to join
the traverse line of A Touch Of Class, PR. Step right and move up to a
break and old PR. Gain some undercut holds in the bulge above, BR, and
pull over it using a good hold on the right. Continue over easier rock, PR,
to finish up a slim groove above.

**   7.   Swelling Itching Brain   E5 6c   20/7/91
A very tough lower wall provides the excitement. Hard. Start 3m right of
Back Yard Holiday. Climb the lower wall direct to the break, then step left
and stand up, PR. Tackle the difficult wall on layaway holds to a distant
finger edge, BR, then extricate a pull out right onto the base of the ramp/
slab. Climb easily up this, then move left to gain a PR in the break. Pull up
through the bulge, BR, to finish up the slim groove above, PR.

At the right-hand side of the compact white wall, a prominent crack and flake
system pierce the wall.

*** 8.   One Continuous Picnic   E5 6b   8/6/91
A superb pitch, inappropriate in name and high in the grade, up the
excellent clean white wall 3m left of the prominent crack and flake system.
A fingery lower wall is coupled with a well positioned finish, luckily, with a
well earned rest in between. Start 3m left of the flake below the left-hand
end of some thorn bushes. An easy groove leads to the break from where

a series of continuously difficult moves, Rock 4, PR and BR, lead up the faint crackline and a collection of layaway holds to reach a respite below a roof, PR. Tackle the headwall directly, BR, via a layaway to a jug. Swing left to gain a good ledge and easier ground leading to the top.

** 9. Three Dimensions   E2   29/6/80

The prominent crack and flake system at the right-hand side of the wall provides excellent climbing with plentiful protection.

1) 27m. 5b. Climb a short corner and overcome a leftward trending flake overhang to a small ledge, PR. Move right and up into the crackline and continue by moving left past a large overhang, PR, to gain a bottomless groove (junction with A Touch Of Class). Climb this, TR, and swing out right in an exciting position, PR, onto a shattered arête. This leads to a tree belay in the back of a bay.

2) 12m. 5b. Move up into the corner on the left and pull out over the roof on unsound but good holds; airy.

To the right the area of compact rock ends abruptly into a recessed bay of shattered rock. As the cliff rears up again, a small yew tree at the base of the cliff provides an obvious landmark. Above and to its left, the compact grey slab gives the start for the next two routes.

10. Legacy   Hard Very Severe   28/8/76

Start to the left of the yew tree below the compact, grey slab.

1) 19m. 5a. Move up onto the foot of the slab, PR, then move down and left to a small ledge. Continue diagonally leftwards more easily, some loose rock, to a tree belay in a large bay

2) 20m. 4b. Traverse right along a horizontal break to the right-hand side of the bay. Continue up the slightly loose weakness to the top. Belay well back.

** 11. Stratagem   E2 5b   28/8/76

Very worthwhile climbing up the centre of the slab. Move up onto the slab as for Legacy, PR, and then climb pleasantly up it to a bulge at its top, PR. Move blindly leftwards through this to a horizontal break, then step right and continue up to a small tree and some large blocks. A stepped crack above leads to the top. 2ND SIMON 0704 BITCHESSY,

*** 12. Manikins Of Horror   E3 5c   29/5/76

A brilliant route featuring steep fingery climbing, excellent rock, all with the comfort of good protection. The epitome of high quality climbing. Start right of the small cave to the right of the yew tree. Pull up to a horizontal break, move left to a small corner and gain a PR above. Move carefully leftwards

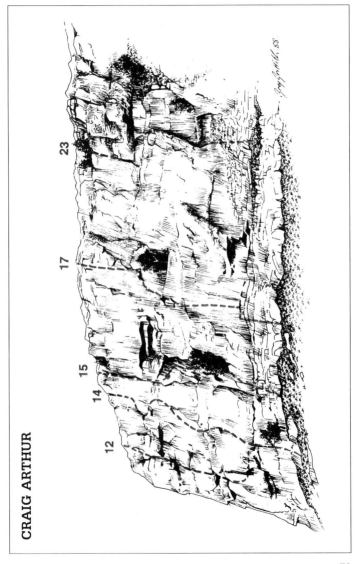

CRAIG ARTHUR

around the vague arête, onto a steep slab below the foot of a crack, PR. Climb steeply up the difficult crack, 3 PRs, to a collection of PRs at the girdle break. Move left and continue straight up past a small tree to the top.

** 13. Dance Of The Puppets   E6 6b   5/5/84
Fine direct climbing, bold in places and technical at the crux, up the centre of the slender buttress above the start of Manikins of Horror. Climb the shallow groove just to the right to gain a good pocket at 11m. Move boldly up and left to a resting place at the break, before taking the slight bulge above, right of a BR, crux, to another break, TR. Continue delicately up and right into a scoop before swinging left to a niche, PRs. Exit rightwards, TR, to a flake and finish direct.

** 14. Swlabr Link   E3   4/6/81
Superb technical face climbing gains access to an easier but classic second pitch. Described slightly out of context.
1) 24m. 6a. Follow Manikins Of Horror to its first PR and continue straight up passing a finger hole and second PR to a horizontal break. Traverse right along this, two PRs, to gain a crack leading more easily to a large ledge and tree belay.
2) 15m. 5a. Gain and climb the prominent steep crack in the bottomless groove. High in the grade but compensated for by over-abundant protection.

To the right of the yew tree, a large shattered depression is capped by a series of overhangs, hanging scoops and walls. The depression is bounded to the right by a pleasant-looking grey slabby wall and finally by an extremely inviting rounded arête.

15. Swlabr   Hard Very Severe   1969
Well worth doing for the spectacular top pitch, provided you can get your second to lead the distinctly unsafe bottom pitch. Start below and left of the yew tree.
1) 20m. 4b. Climb slightly leftwards up the degenerating wall and groove to the ivy patch and the first meaningful runner. Step left to a belay on the whitebeam tree and offer a prayer up to the gods that you will never have to do that again.
2) 15m. 5b. Up and left of the tree is a fine steep crack. Gain it via an awkward groove then stuff in the friends and go. Belay well back.

** 16. Eliminator   E4   5/9/83
Good climbing on an old aided line. Fine positions high up on the cliff. Start at a shallow corner 9m right of Swlabr.

1) 18m. Climb the shallow corner and continue leftwards over broken ground to a peg belay in a curved bay.

2) 18m. 6a. Move up to the tiered overhang and power through it, 2 PRs, into the smooth looking hanging scoop, TR. Technical climbing up this and through a bulge, PR, leads to a direct finish.

17. Tito   E1   3/5/80

A wandering route not without its share of interest. Start as for Eliminator.

1) 18m. 5b. Climb up into the shallow corner before traversing right across the steepening grey slab, PR, to a bulge, PR. Move up rather awkwardly, then step right to gain a thread belay below the left-hand end of a strip overhang.

2) 21m. 5a. Pass the overhang, via a crack on its left, to reach a sapling. Continue more easily over dubious rock to gain a large, lichen-covered scoop. This leads to the top; nowhere technical but quite intimidating.

***   18. Digitron   E2 5c   11/6/73

An outstanding pitch, with sustained difficulties, all on flawless rock. The superbly positioned crux slab at the top qualifies this as the best route of its grade in the area. Not to be missed. Start 4m left of the steep rounded arête. An easy lower wall leads to a PR where awkward moves rightwards gain a small whitebeam tree and ledge. Continue straight up passing a second peg and a small slab to an innocuous twisting crack in a bulge, PR. Overcome this directly and pass to the right of an overlap to reach the rib and a good break. Delightful climbing slightly leftwards gains a flake, hidden from below, PR, with the crux to gain a sapling and the top.

***   19. Heaven Or Hell   E5 6b   1/6/91

A suitable companion route to Digitron in style and character, although much harder. The inviting rounded arête taken direct gives a beautiful pitch, again on compacted grey limestone. Start at the right-hand side of the arête, 6m right of Digitron. Using a series of small flakes, move up to a vague pocketed ramp and make a sequence of blind moves leftwards, BR, to reach a jug at the foot of a tiny groove. Stand up on this and pull out onto the enticing arête. Follow this on its right-hand side via a succession of small flakes to a junction with Digitron at the prominent break. Step right, old PR, and make a difficult sequence of moves up the flake above the tree, BR. Step left onto the slab above and move up left via the sapling to the top, as for the final few feet of Digitron. For the best combination continue direct as for Digitron, once gained, up the superb hanging slab.

Phil Waters on Digitron, Craig Arthur

The loose recess to the right proves very uninviting and is bounded to the right by an undercut, grey pillar of more tempting limestone.

** 20. Alpha Track Etch   E6 6c   2/6/90
A brilliant, high powered pitch taking the pillar 9m to the right of Heaven or Hell. Start below the right-hand side of the low level roofs at an obvious weakness. Pull through the roofs to a slab on the right, poor PR above. Traverse leftwards on undercuts before making a very difficult move straight up past a BR to reach a short thin crack, wire protection. Ignore the scoop above and instead gain and launch up the undercut flake on the right, PR, to a semi-rest at the break. Continue directly up the slabby wall, two PRs, step left and attack the bulge above, BR and PR, to finish up an easier crack past a whitebeam tree. Peg belay.

21. Badge   E1   1965,6/4/75
Start a few feet right of Alpha Track Etch, where a shattered groove line splits the crag.
1) 21m. 5c. Pass a small overhang, PR, to enter the groove and follow it, PR, by moving first right, then back left into a large scoop. Belay here.
2) 12m. 4c. Climb the scoop, before exiting left below a bulge via a wall, all relatively easy.

The cliff now diminishes in size for a short way, yet still maintains its compact nature.

** 22. Keeping Secrets   E5 6c   2/9/91
The compact, yellow-stained wall right of Badge provides a very good route with the crux, a somewhat intense manoeuvre, at the start. Begin at a small tree below a shallow scoop. Pull up past a break to a PR and teeter frantically upwards, or slap, to gain a jug. Move out onto the flake on the left and follow it to a thin break, where the major difficulties subside. Continue up past a break, PR, to gain a prominent V-shaped groove above. Swing out left and finish up the yellow wall past a tree, exiting over to the right.

23. Scary Fairy   E3   20/7/80
An airy top pitch does little to compensate for a "spooky" first pitch. Start below an obvious flaky corner, at the left-hand end of a hollowed depression, 5m to the right of Keeping Secrets.
1) 12m. 5c. A strenuous, poorly protected start, best climbed quickly, leads to a steep and slightly easier flake and cave belay above.
2) 17m. 5b. Move left and then up into the prominent V-shaped groove. Swing pleasantly left and finish up the yellow wall past a tree, exiting over to the right.

*** 24. Ten   E6 6c   20/7/91

A superb sport climb breaching the black wall and impressive roof system right of Scary Fairy. Powerful and hard to work out. Exit directly through the lower bulge of the hollowed depression, BR, and climb the black wall, 2 BRs, to the break, BR above. Tackle the huge intimidating bulge by fierce blind moves, BR, to gain a jug above the lip, PR. Sensational final moves, BR, lead to a two bolt belay below the top of the cliff.

The cliff now returns to its former height but with an area of broken vegetated rock. This provides one very poor route, suitable more to the botanist than to the climber.

25. Jungle Warfare   Hard Very Severe   21/6/80

Appropriately named. Start below a deceptively easy looking broken scoop in a small separate pillar, at the left-hand end of a vegetated terrace and below the left-hand of the two yew trees.

1) 21m. 5a. Climb the scoop via a steepening flake crack to gain the grassy terrace. Belay behind the yew tree.

2) 15m. 5a. Climb the yew and use a good hold to get onto the wall. Move left past a large block to a small ledge and finish up a yellow groove and cracks above.

* 26. Charlain   Hard Very Severe   18/5/80

The slabby wall down and slightly forward of Jungle Warfare provides a pleasant outing. Start at the foot of the wall, 3m left of a prominent slim white groove.

1) 21m. 5a. Climb the wall via a horizontal break and PR. After a small bulge, trend gradually rightwards past a second PR onto the top of a large block. Step right and continue, slightly unsound, to a small ledge and tree belay.

2) 12m. 4b. Either climb the scrappy corner with a tree above the belay (9m) or traverse left along the terrace to gain broken cracks leading to the top; this latter method is better but for a more exciting finale, and more in keeping with the lower pitch, follow the upper reaches of Now And Then.

* 27. Now And Then   E2   21/6/80

Another enjoyable face route with an amenable but exposed finale. The lower pitch proves pleasantly sustained with protection that only appears intermittently. Start below the obvious slim white groove.

1) 21m. 5b. Pleasant climbing up the groove, PR, leads with increasing urgency to a second PR at its capping bulge. Surmount this and move rightwards rather blindly, PR above, to gain better holds leading direct to a ledge with a tree above.

2) 12m. 5a. Move up and right to a bushy whitebeam tree, then swing merrily out right along a break to gain a finishing crack in a wild situation.

The walls now begin to increase in size and steepness, the compact nature of the rock lending itself to harder routes.

* 28. Dead Man's Creek   E4 6a   5/5/84
Very good climbing up the yellow-flecked wall right of Now And Then. The lower section feels bold but the route is at the lower limit of its grade. Gain and follow the obvious flake, BR on the left, to moves slightly right and a PR. Continue direct, sustained, past an old jammed wire, until a step left and further moves up gain a ledge and peg belay - abseil off.

** 29. Punch And Judy   E5 6b   1/5/84
Named in honour of an active pair of Clwyd devotees. Superb open face climbing up the inviting grey wall to the right. Sustained and absorbing, with the crux where you least expect it. Move up the wall 5m to the right of Dead Man's Creek to gain a faded TR. Pull leftwards and then up, BR, over a bulge, to reach a thin break, PR. Mantleshelf up and then traverse delicately right past a BR, before climbing a shallow groove to easy ground. Move up, PR, and then rightwards to an easier finishing crack.

To the right the wall forms a clean and very blunt, white arête. On the right-hand side of this a thin crackline splits almost the full height of the wall, providing one of the most striking lines on the cliff.

* 30. Full Mental Jacket   E5 6c   3/7/88
Direct, though eliminate in line, with fierce and very worthwhile climbing. Start 5m right of Punch and Judy, where a flaky bulge guards entry to the crackline. Pull over the bulge to gain a small ledge, then move left and up to a PR. Pull up, BR, and continue past a thin break to gain a shallow groove by some thin moves, BR on the left. Move up the groove to good holds, then step left to reach a scoop. Step left again and then up via a groove to a ledge and peg belay - abseil off.

*** 31. Survival Of The Fastest   E4 6a   10/5/78
A Cathcart masterpiece from the late 1970s: ahead of its time for the area. An outstanding pitch taking the crackline breaching almost the full height of the wall. Sustained, well protected and thoroughly absorbing. Start, as for Full Mental Jacket, below the bulge guarding entry to the crackline. Pull over the bulge to a small ledge, then step right to below the crackline proper, PR. Straightforward at first, the crackline gradually gets tougher past 2 PRs to reach a further PR and a slight bulge with a small undercut

CRAIG ARTHUR

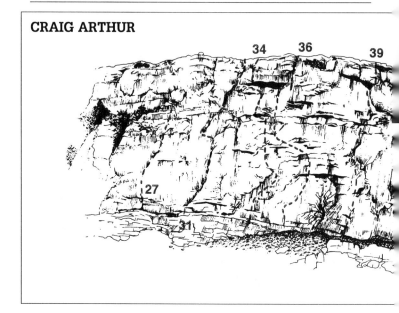

hold. Clip a BR, pull up and make an exciting swing left across onto the hanging slab via a small ledge. Stand easily up to a horizontal break, PR, pull out onto a slab and easy finishing crack on the right.

32. Survival Of The Fattest   E5 6b   1984
The very hard crux is gained by some pleasant easier climbing. Start 4m right of Survival Of The Fastest. An initial awkward bulge leads to a series of small flakes leading to the bulge at 21m. Hard moves and a "blind grope" gain an overlap which is passed to the left for a finishing crack.

The huge expansive white wall to the right, nicknamed The Nemesis Wall, gains its name from an early aid route. It gives the highest concentration of top class hard climbs in the vicinity. Superb technical, wall climbing in the lower half is perfectly contrasted with leaning grooves and exposed overhangs on the walls above. The relatively featureless lower half makes for awkward route finding on first acquaintance.

The left-hand side of the wall is formed by a long grey streak running down the face from a vegetated niche in the upper half of the cliff. A few feet to the right, a black ramp at 6m provides a noticeable feature, the start of Manic

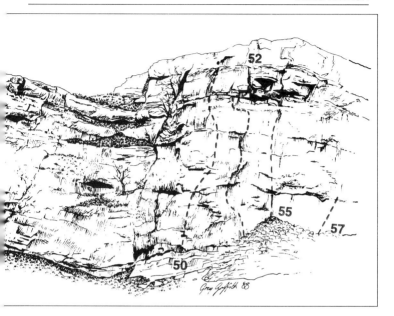

Mechanic, before the wall takes on a gleaming white appearance. Here, shallow grooves and ramps provide delicate features before the wall is bounded by a huge sycamore tree and the vague arête above.

*** 33. Friday The Thirteenth   E5   13/4/84,29/9/87
A bold and committing climb putting the nerves of most leaders to the test. Excellent. Start 3m right again below the obvious grey streak, just to the right of the bushy whitebeam tree.

    1)   24m. 6a. Move up to enter a short groove and exit leftwards to some good holds. Trend up and rightwards on a vague line to a prominent detached flake and use this with care to gain a PR on the right. Continue direct to reach a break and peg belay.

    2)   18m. 5c. Step left and follow the obvious steep groove, 3 PRs, moving right over its capping roof to a juggy final wall.

*** 34. Manic Mechanic   E5 6b   5/84
An impressive, high quality pitch breaching the entire wall in one fell swoop. Sustained but never over-technical, well protected and with an exhilarating finale. Start 3m right of the whitebeam tree marking the start

of Friday The Thirteenth. Climb direct up the black streak on a series of side pulls, BR, to gain the black ramp. From its top, trend slightly rightwards, PR on the left, into a depression, BR. Pull through the bulge, PR, to reach a break and continue up to a second break and respite. Move left and up the wall, TR, to gain the roof and pull leftwards through this, PR, in a wild position to good holds and the top.

***   35. Smokin' Gun   E6   21/5/88
A brilliant initial pitch, plum direct up the centre of the wall. A short, very technical section is followed by easier but sustained wall climbing, all on flawless rock. Start 5m right of Manic Mechanic below a shallow hanging groove.

1)   21m. 6c. Move easily up and left to gain a small ledge at the foot of the groove. Climb this to twin BRs and move desperately right onto the hanging arête and further, but easier, moves up the wall to a flake on the left, wire protection. Cross rightwards through the bulge, PR, to gain a resting place in a scoop, BR (junction with Tres Hombres). Step left onto the wall, old bolt head, and climb it to the break and peg belay.

2)   18m. 6a. Grovel into the guano-streaked niche above the belay, then traverse right around a nose, two PRs and across a smooth looking wall, PR, onto a hanging slab.Finish straight up this via 2 PRs.

***   36. Tres Hombres   E5   5/84
The final route of the superb trio on the central part of the wall. The main interest is based in the first pitch where varied fingery climbing with good protection and of a sustained nature proves extremely attractive. Start 3m right of Smokin' Gun below a pocketed crack, down and to the left of an obvious ramp.

1)   24m. 6a. Move up, at first slightly left, before moving right and then up onto the ramp, PR. From its top, TR, make tricky moves up the wall, PR, via a flake to a small bulge. This is passed to the left to reach a scoop, BR, from where a step left leads onto the wall, old bolt head. Hard moves now lead up to gain the break crossing the wall, peg and nut belay.

2)   18m. 5c. Step left into a steep groove and follow it, PR, to a roof. Move right over this and finish up the well appointed jaggy wall.

**   37. Steppin' Razor   E5 6b   24/4/88
Excellent intricate climbing. From halfway up the sycamore tree 6m to the right of Tres Hombres, swing up and left, PR and BR, to the left end of a slim roof. Go straight through this to some good flakes 3m above, pass an old PR to gain a smooth groove and second roof, PR. Pass this rightwards on good holds, PR on the hanging slab, then climb a tricky wall past a PR to finish.

* 38. Marie Antoinette   E5 6b   22/5/88
Good climbing squeezed onto the limit of the wall. Strenuous and
sustained. Start on a ledge behind the tree up which Steppin' Razor starts.
Move up and right to the blunt arête and follow this as closely as possible,
bolt and PR, and not stepping rightwards into the Big Plop. Pass a BR to
gain a break, from where fine climbing leads up the striking finger crack
to gain the roof and some old PRs. Struggle through this at a V notch, PR,
to finish.

39. The Big Plop   E3   29/5/85
The prominent hanging groove above and to the right of the large tree. A
tough entry. Start 5m to the right of the large sycamore tree, below a short
wall and tree.

1) 21m. 5b. Go up the wall and from the tree, climb slightly leftwards via
a broken crack and two further trees, to a ledge. Continue up the steep wall
above, PR, to a small ledge to the left of a bush, peg belay.

2) 15m. 6a. Enter the groove from the right and climb it with difficulty past
two PRs, until easier climbing leads to a swing right below a big roof. From
the arête, finish easily, some loose rock in places

40. The Hoax   Hard Very Severe, 5a   14/5/80
So named because ground level impressions prove deceiving; it could
also have been named tree climb! From the first tree on the Big Plop, move
up and right to follow a crack with an ash tree, PR on the left. Move right
near the top of the crack to avoid loose rock and gain the terrace. Pull up
and left from here to an old yew tree and finish up and to the right.

The upper section of the walls now become more shattered and vegetated.
This factor lends an unbalanced feeling to the next trio of routes, hence lower-
off stations have been created.

41. Voie De Bart   E4 6b   31/5/85
Often wet and unfortunately becoming a little dirty. Powerful. Start just
right of the Hoax. Gain and climb a ramp, awkward, to a bulge complete
with 2 PRs, one below and one above. A difficult sequence through this
leads to easier climbing leading rightwards to a lower-off station.

* 42. Rubberbandman   E5 6b   31/8/91
A marginally better test piece than its neighbour and slightly harder. Low
in the grade. Climb the wall 5m to the right, past a BR, to gain a slim
overhang. Pass it using layaways, BR, onto an obvious short ramp leading
to good holds, above small wire. Move up left for 3m to the lower-off
station.

** 43. Under My Thumb   E4 6b   9/6/91
An exquisite little route on impeccable rock throughout; bold to start. Climb direct up the wall 5m to the right again to a good layaway and distant BR above; a l-o-n-g clip. Pass this on the right, swing up and left past a second BR by hard moves to reach better holds. Above is a TR and lower-off station.

The walls to the right now form a series of tiers in the back of the amphitheatred bay. These provide two poor, meandering routes and two, more pleasant, short pitches.

44. Cold Finger   Hard Very Severe   20/2/78
Start just to the right of Under my Thumb.
1) 21m. 5a. Move up the black slab and trend rightwards to some small overhangs. Traverse right below these and then go up to reach the grassy terrace and tree belay on the right.
2) 15m. 4b. Move back left and climb a shattered wall and easy groove leading to the top.

45. Chopper Squad   E2 5b   27/5/91
Worthwhile. Climb the vague shallow groove 5m right of Cold Finger, RP protection, passing a bulge to gain a small ledge. Move right and then up to the terrace and the tree. Abseil off.

46. Accidents Will Happen   E1 5c   25/7/92
Climb the easy wall and difficult scarred bulge 3m right again to a small ledge. Finish direct to the tree and abseil off.

47. Octopus   Very Severe   Pre 1960
Start 2m right of Accidents Will Happen.
1) 15m. 4c. Ascend directly up the wall, old PR at 3m, to the tree. All rather loose and unpleasant.
2) 18m. 4c. Move right to tackle a broken wall to the final terrace. Move right to a tree and fight through appalling bushes above to the top; and wonder why you bothered!

To the right, as the edge of the amphitheatre swings round, the cliff forms one last impressive bastion, a fine note on which to end this superb cliff: the South Buttress. The bottom left-hand corner of the buttress forms an obvious blackened slab.

48. Scrapyard Thing   E1   1969,15/9/79
A meandering route on the extreme left-hand edge of the buttress. Some

good positions high up but some loose rock as well. Start to the left of the blackened slab, below a prominent left-facing flake above the slim overhung base.

1) 21m. 5a. Gain the flake via the overhang and climb it onto the top of a detached flake on the left - worrying.

Continue carefully up the wall, PR, and from a good hold, trend rightwards to a small tree on the wall. There is a peg belay below the overhangs.

2) 12m. 5a. Tackle the overhang from the left, 2 PRs, to a terrace. Move easily right and finish up a prominent chimney/groove.

*   49. Double Crossbones   E3   18/5/80
A good first pitch, originally the direct version, is followed by much easier climbing above. Varied and worthwhile but a little unbalanced in character. Start below the left-hand side of the blackened slab.

1) 12m. 5c. Climb direct to a thin horizontal break complete with a PR and follow this by a shallow scoop above, technical. Take a PB below the obvious overhang, or continue. The original start was up what is now These Foolish Things, before a long traverse left was made to the same stance; 5c.

2) 12m. 5a. Tackle the overhang to the right via a crack and follow the corner above to a ledge. Peg belay on the left.

3) 15m. 5a. Return to above the corner to gain the obvious prow below a larger overhang, PR. Pass the overhang to the right, all very exposed, to gain a traverse line leading right to a shattered crack and the pasture above.

**   50. Delaware Slide   E4 6a   1964,11/4/84
Fine wall climbing gradually escalating in difficulty to a well positioned crux high on the wall. Relatively well protected and more taxing to the mind than to the fingers. Climb the black wall 3m right of Double Crossbones to a good small ledge below an overlap. Move right and up through this, then continue direct through another slim overlap to the left-hand side of a broad scoop, PR in a tiny corner. Move up to some old BRs, pull out left and make some blind moves up to a break and easy ground above. Finish via an obvious shattered crack.

*** 51. These Foolish Things   E5 6b   1/6/91
A fine companion route to Delaware Slide featuring numerous difficult moves and an arduous technical crux at the top. High in quality, high in protection and high in its grade. Climb the obvious black ramp/slab just to the right, PR, to gain the slim overlap. Pull through this on the right, PR, to reach a break and continue up some thin flakes to a good small ledge.

Move awkwardly up to the next break, TR, then swing right and up into the obvious broad scoop, BR. A good rest here provides a brief respite. Exit directly up the wall above to gain good holds, step right and move up a fine flake to where the wall rears up, BR. Finish straight up past a right-veering crack.

** 52. Gates Of The Golden Dawn   E5   15/5/80,6/5/87
The central line of the buttress gives an excellent introduction to the routes hereabouts with a difficult and superbly positioned crux. Start at the left-hand end of the broken terrace, up and to the right of These Foolish Things.

1) 20m. 5b. Move out left to gain a short groove left of the initial arched wall and below the attractive orange streak. An awkward section leads to a PR, from where moves on the right via a flaky groove, PR, then back left, lead to a recess and a trio of pegs to belay on. It is possible to continue from here in one pitch.

2) 12m. 6b. Move up to a small ledge and pass a golo to reach the roof. A difficult and powerful move past 2 TRs and a PR, hard to clip for the short, gain a massive jug in an outrageous position. A short sensational layback finishes the climb.

53. The Deadly Trap   E3   22/8/77
Devious and somewhat outdated, though very impressive for its time.

1) 20m. 5b. As for Gates Of The Golden Dawn.

2) 21m. 5c. Gain the golo runner 4m above the belay and move right, TR, and reverse a short groove to a small foot ledge/break. Tiptoe carefully right past a PR to climb a steep wall past 2 PRs. Finish up a shallow groove and large flake crack.

*** 54. Sunny Side Up Mix   E6 6c   31/7/92
Brilliant climbing with a low crux section and a finish that will leave you breathless; the huge triangular prow capping the centre of the wall. Mostly in-situ gear, except where stated. Start 2m right of Gates Of The Golden Dawn and just left of a brown streak. The desperate initial wall, BR, leads to a break, PR, and extending moves, RPs, to gain a rest on the shelf above. Another hard move, BR, gains a thin break, Rock 6, from where further difficulties lead straight up, BR, to a rounded ledge and rest, thread on the left. Move up to below the jutting prow, BR, gain a good hidden hold, BR, then power through its left-hand side, BR, to an ungainly exit.

** 55. Black Poppies   E6 6c   27/5/91
Stunning face climbing incorporating a desperate crux on the lower wall with a flying roof crack. Start just to the right of the brown streak, thread

belay in the first break. Move up to the break and swing left past the thread, then pull up to the next break. Climb the wall, past a BR, to a respite and a good place to ponder the next section. Hideous moves up the wall above a PR, using a one finger pocket, lead past a second peg eventually to gain the sanctuary of a small ledge on the right. Climb the shallow groove just to the left, good wires, directly to meet the awesome roof crack. This proves a powerful and obstinate obstacle to overcome in order to reach the haven of the pastures above.

** 56. Chilean Moon   E5 6b   5/7/92
An excellent route, well worth seeking out. Well protected with in-situ gear and hence suited to the "sports climbing" enthusiast. Climb the wall 3m right of Black Poppies and power through the bulge, 2 BRs, to gain a thin break and PR. Move left and then up to the main break at a small tree, TR. Continue blindly up the shallow groove above, PR, to meet the roof and a BR. Overcoming this, BR, proves to be the crux and a suitable finale.

* 57. Chills Of Apprehension   E4 6a   31/5/85
The direct approach to the upper section of The Deadly Trap gives a good outing on the extremity of the buttress. Climb the obvious rightward-trending weakness 5m to the right, past 2 PRs and a TR, to an easing in difficulty. Move up and left to a break and follow this left before standing up below a faint groove, junction with the Deadly Trap. Climb the wall and faint groove, 2 PRs, to the wide finishing crack.

58. Lemon Kerred   E3 6b   31/8/91
A terse, technical titbit. Start 8m right of Chills Of Apprehension and climb the centre of the slight barrel-shaped wall direct, past a thread and BR, to a convenient tree with sling. A Rock 1 and 3 are useful above the bolt.

*** 59. Craig Arthur Girdle   E2   1969,12/5/79
A magnificent expedition, bring your coffee and sandwiches, with plenty of fine climbing, positions and protection. Not sustained at a high standard but with a big cliff feel and requiring a steady leader and second. Start, as for Arthur's Pillar, at the left-hand end of the cliff, below a short corner leading to the obvious detached pillar.

1) 27m. 4b. Climb the corner to gain the pillar, follow it and a groove above. From its top traverse right above the overhang to a short corner leading to a belay ledge on the right and some pegs.

2) 27m. 4b. Move right before dropping down to a bedding plane, PR. Continue right into a niche, PR, exiting right and traversing to a bay and tree belay.

3) 24m. Go across the back of the bay, before dropping down again to

reach another traverse line, PR. Follow this for 9m to a small tree beside a detached pillar, peg belay.

4) 12m. 5c. Drop down for 5m to a bunch of PRs and traverse awkwardly right, through a bay, to a ledge and tree belay.

5) 27m. 5b. Continue across to the far side of the large bay and twin bedding planes, PR. Move up past two PRs to some small trees and follow the traverse line rightwards until it becomes undercut and "impossible". Move right from a PR and clamber into the arms of a yew tree and down for a belay.

6) 18m. 5b. Traverse right across the wall to a thin bedding plane and move into a small corner. Continue across an excellent steep slab, 2 PRs, and round an arête to a small ledge. Peg belays on the right, as for Badge.

7) 27m. 5a. Traverse right, past a PR, to a large ledge and from this, PR, move down slightly and cross a steep wall, BR, to a yew tree. Struggle past this and continue to a second yew tree and belay.

8) 27m. 5a. Traverse the wall at the junction of rock and grass dropping down to an ash tree. Cross the grassy broken wall to the right to a good ledge and PR, then swing down and right. Hand-traverse into a scoop past 3 PRs and exit round and an arête to a small tree and belay.

9) 24m. 5a. Traverse easily for 3m and drop down past a PR into a prominent groove. Continue past some old bolt heads and out into a small niche. Move down below the overhang and continue along the obvious line to a good stance round the arête. Superb positions and exhilarating climbing throughout.

10) 24m. 5a. Move right past a small thorn bush to a ledge, PR. Move right to a low PR and traverse right on good holds to the terrace. Climb the shattered wall on the left to the twisted yew tree and a finishing crack on the right.

FIRST ASCENTS

Pre 1960	ARTHUR'S PILLAR	Unknown
Pre 1960	OCTOPUS	Unknown
1964	SCOUSERS	T Hurley, B Riley & D Blythe
	Free-climbed as Delaware Slide in 1984 by J Moulding, & J Codling.	
1965	BADGE	B Dearman & D Riley
	Free-climbed in 1975 by S M Cathcart & T Curtis.	
1969	SCRAPYARD THING	B Dearman & M Pedlar
	Free-climbed in 1979 by S M Cathcart	
1969	NEMESIS (A3)	T Hurley, B Riley & D Blythe

D Sarkar on Margin of Error, Compact Wall. Photo: D Kerr

Subsequently free-climbed by a host of routes on this particular wall.

1969	SWLABR	B Dearman & M Pedlar
1969	CRAIG ARTHUR GIRDLE TRAVERSE	B Dearman, D Riley & T Hurley

Free-climbed in 1979 by S M Cathcart, T Curtis & M Cameron (alts).

11/6/73	DIGITRON	S M Cathcart & G Swindley
6/4/75	BADGE	S M Cathcart & T Curtis
29/5/76	MANIKINS OF HORROR	S M Cathcart & G Swindley
28/8/76	STRATAGEM	S M Cathcart & G Swindley
28/8/76	LEGACY	S M Cathcart & G Swindley
22/8/77	THE DEADLY TRAP	S M Cathcart & N Slaney
2/10/77	THE FALL AND DECLINE	S M Cathcart & G Swindley
20/2/78	COLD FINGER	S M Cathcart & G Griffith
10/5/78	SURVIVAL OF THE FASTEST	S M Cathcart, Unseconded
3/5/80	TITO	S M Cathcart & T Curtis
14/5/80	THE BIG PLOP (1 pt. aid)	S M Cathcart & T Curtis

Originally the aided route Chota Peg by T Hurley, B Riley, D Blythe.
Completely free-climbed in 1985 by S Boydon & P Harrison.

14/5/80	THE HOAX	T Curtis & S Cathcart
15/5/80	GATES OF THE GOLDEN DAWN (1 pt. aid)	S Cathcart & G Griffith

Free climbed in 1984 by J Moulding & S Boydon
Since then a crucial hold has disappeared. This was again free
climbed in 6/5/87 at a revised grade by J Codling & J Moulding

18/5/80	DOUBLE CROSSBONES	S M Cathcart & T Curtis
18/5/80	CHARLAIN	S M Cathcart & G Griffith
21/6/80	JUNGLE WARFARE	S M Cathcart & P Stott
21/6/80	NOW AND THEN	S M Cathcart & P Stott
29/6/80	THREE DIMENSIONS	S M Cathcart & M Hughes
20/7/80	SCARY FAIRY	S M Cathcart, P Stott & F Bennett
8/10/80	MONKEY'S CLAWS	S M Cathcart & J Dee
13/10/80	A TOUCH OF CLASS	S M Cathcart & P Stott
4/6/81	SWALBR LINK	S M Cathcart & N Slaney
14/6/81	LE CHACAL	S M Cathcart & D Whitlow

Le Chacal is French for "The Jackal". Stuart nicked the route from
Paul Stott after Paul had spent a lot of time cleaning the line.

5/9/83	ELIMINATOR	J Moulding & F Stevenson
11/4/84	DELAWARE SLIDE	J Moulding & J Codling
13/4/84	FRIDAY THE THIRTEENTH	P Littlejohn & A N Other

The direct start was added on 29/9/87 by J Moulding & J Codling.

1/5/84	PUNCH AND JUDY	G Gibson, Unseconded
3/5/84	GATES OF THE GOLDEN DAWN	J Moulding & S Boyden

The first free ascent. Re-climbed in 1987 by J Codling & J Moulding
after the disappearance of a crucial hold.

5/5/84	DEAD MAN'S CREEK	G Gibson, Unseconded

G Gibson on the first ascent of Rivals, Dinbren. Photo: G Gibson

5/5/84	DANCE OF THE PUPPETS	J Codling & J Moulding
5/84	MANIC MECHANIC	J Moulding & J Codling

With rest points? Free-climbed Spring 1984 by A Pollitt

5/84	TRES HOMBRES	J Moulding, N Jowett & S Boyden
Sum. 84	SURVIVAL OF THE FATTEST	J Codling, Unseconded
29/5/85	THE BIG PLOP	S Boyden & P Harrison

The first free ascent.

31/5/85	VOIE DE BART	S Boyden & J Moulding

Named in honour of M Bartley who chose to expose himself.

31/5/85	CHILLS OF APPREHENSION	S Boyden & J Moulding
24/4/88	STEPPIN' RAZOR	J Moulding & J Codling
21/5/88	SMOKIN' GUN	J Moulding & S Cardy
22/5/88	MARIE ANTOINETTE	J Codling & J Moulding
6/88	BACK YARD HOLIDAY	P Stott, Unseconded
3/7/88	FULL MENTAL JACKET	J Moulding & J Codling
2/6/90	ALPHA TRACK ETCH	M Crocker, Unseconded
27/5/91	CHOPPER SQUAD	N Barker & G Gibson
27/5/91	BLACK POPPIES	G Gibson, Unseconded

Red-pointed past the lower, crux, section though the rest of the route was flashed.

1/6/91	HEAVEN OR HELL	G Gibson, Unseconded
1/6/91	THESE FOOLISH THINGS	G Gibson & P Gibson
8/6/91	ONE CONTINUOUS PICNIC	G Gibson, Unseconded
9/6/91	UNDER MY THUMB	G Gibson & N Barker
20/7/91	TEN	G Gibson, Unseconded

"Worked" the previous day.

20/7/91	SWELLING ITCHING BRAIN	G Gibson, Unseconded
31/8/91	LEMON KERRED	G Gibson & D Kerr
31/8/91	RUBBERBANDMAN	G Gibson, Unseconded
2/9/91	KEEPING SECRETS	G Gibson, Unseconded
5/7/92	CHILEAN MOON	G Gibson, Unseconded
25/7/92	ACCIDENTS WILL HAPPEN	G Gibson & H Williams
31/7/92	SUNNY SIDE UP MIX	G Gibson, Unseconded

THE TWILIGHT ZONE

O.S. Map 117

by Alec and Simon Williams

SITUATION AND CHARACTER

These two small and interesting buttresses, 10-15m high, host some of the best quality limestone in the valley and some good routes. The more prominent of the two buttresses is Twilight Tower which can be easily viewed from the road at Plas yn Eglwyseg (GR 216462). Twilight Tower Buttress consists of two tiers, the lower of which has routes of a low standard and hence see little traffic. The upper tier, on the other hand, incorporates some brilliant climbing on its central wall, including some wild roof climbing. Twilight Gully Walls contains some good routes with interesting climbing on smooth slabs and roofs. Some of the routes are excellent, Ten Percent Special, The Tiger Awaits and Rock Special to name but a few.

ACCESS AND APPROACH

The crags can be found in the vicinity of the second tributary valley down from the ford at World's End. Coming from the town of Llangollen, enter the valley road as for the rest of the Eglwyseg Valley (see Eglwyseg introduction) until you get to a humpback bridge at Plas yn Eglwyseg farm. Just over the bridge, the road bends sharp right and a few metres up the road from the bend there are some small pull-ins on the right. Park here or further up the road at the layby on the left. Now walk back over the bridge to where there is a public footpath sign, walk up the field on its left to where the woods start, walk or fight up through the woods until you come to a fence; get over this and the crags are then in full view in front of you. Walk up the valley in front until you reach its head and the start of the Twilight Gully Walls on your right. The Twilight Tower Buttress is off to the left along a small scree path.

TWILIGHT TOWER BUTTRESS

GR 223463

This compact buttress sits on the left flank, high up on the valley side. During the approach to the upper tier the path traverses until a short deep rightward facing chimney and cave is reached. Sloth takes the obvious layback on the left of the cave. It is possible to descend down behind the ivy covered tower on the right of the central wall, Ivy Tower Chimney, or at the left-hand end of the tier down one of several steep vegetated gullies. The routes are described on the upper tier first and from right to left as one faces the rock.

THE UPPER TIER

1. Sloth   Very Difficult   1962
This route follows the layback crack just left of the small cave.

2. Flawse   Very Difficult   6/81
Left of Sloth, climb the cracks up the front of the buttress with care.

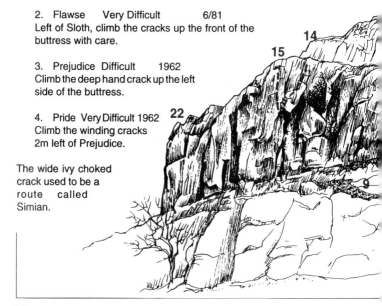

3. Prejudice Difficult   1962
Climb the deep hand crack up the left side of the buttress.

4. Pride Very Difficult 1962
Climb the winding cracks
2m left of Prejudice.

The wide ivy choked crack used to be a route called Simian.

5. To Cut A Long Story Short   Very Severe, 4c   4/81
Climb the short clean corner 2m right of a yew tree.

6. Onegin   Severe   1962
Climb the flakes and crack left of the tree.

7. Helme's Highway   Mild Severe   1962
Left of the yew tree is a shallow corner, which is climbed with a difficult mid-
section.

8. The Clearout   Very Severe, 4b   6/81
2m left of Helme's Highway is a steep crack, climb this.

*   9. Skullion   Very Severe, 4b   1980
Start at a rectangle incut below a small overhang. Climb up a flake and thin cracks to the top.

10. Cow Parsley   Very Difficult   1962
Climb up past the tree and up the right-hand chimney.

11. Ivy Tower Chimney   Very Difficult   1962
Climb past the tree and up the left-hand chimney.

12. Moncrieff   Very Difficult   1962
Climb the wide crack/chimney containing some loose blocks, just to the left of ivy covered tower.

13. Attenuation   Very Severe, 4c   7/8/81
Left of Moncrieff is a narrow wall. Climb the narrow wall and continue up the smooth short slab and groove to finish.

*   14. High Impedance   E1 5b   26/6/81
Climb easily up the large chimney to the left and position yourself under the roof facing out down the valley. Be sure to place some good gear, then make some wild moves to locate yourself in the groove above and to the top with pounding heart.

**   15. Go-A-Go-Go   E2 5b   26/6/81
Fine climbing up an airy flake line. Worth seeking out. Climb as for High Impedance to the lip of the roof, then swing left onto the steep wall to gain the excellent flake crack. Superb climbing up this leads to the top.

*** 16. Going To A Go-Go   E5 6c   28/9/92
Superb and desperate technical climbing up the front face of the pillar to the left of High Impedance. Tackle the initial bulge PR, to continue direct, 2BRs, via intricate face and 'slapping' manoeuvres to gain a good hold above an overlap (easier said than done). Clip a BR, stand up and exit rightwards through the roof to the top. The best line on the buttress.

17. Woodpigeon Crack   Hard Severe, 4a   1962
Moving round the buttress from Go-A-Go-Go there is an elder tree. Climb a groove left of the tree, then move right to a slab and large groove to finish.

*   18. Sunday Driver   Very Severe, 4c   26/6/81
Around from the bulging arête there is a crack and pocketed wall. Climb the wall and go up the slab to the top.

19. Loran   Severe, 4a   5/81
Climb the flake crack up past a yew tree, then the thin crack to safety.

20. Ruth's Ramble   Very Difficult   1962
Climb the two disjointed cracks to two dead trees, then move up into a groove to finish.

21. Sidestep   Very Severe, 4c   6/81
2m left of Ruth's Ramble there is a thin finger crack. Follow this to the V-crack and continue along the right crack until a groove is reached. This leads to the top.

*   22. Penetration Factor   Very Severe, 4c   11/5/81
Left of the steep wall of Sidestep is a widening finger crack. Follow this and continue up in a airy position to safety.

23. Inter Digital Pause   Hard Very Severe, 5a   26/6/81
Start in a scoop around the arête from Penetration Factor. Climb up the thin cracks to a hard move past a rusty peg near the top.

*   24. Funeral Corner   Hard Severe, 4a   1962
Climb the obvious corner left of Inter Digital Pause. A classic route.

25. Extension   Very Severe, 4b   6/81
Climb the obvious rounded arête on the left of Funeral Corner.

26. On Line   Severe   25/1/81
Climb the steep layback flake left again which leads to an easier V-groove and the top.

27. Fraggle Rock   Hard Very Severe, 5a   3/2/85
Near the left end of the upper tier are some thin cracks and a small overhang. Climb the cracks and carry on over the overhang.

28. Hungover   Hard Very Severe, 5b   3/2/85
The layback corner with a chockstone, round the corner from Fraggle Rock.

On recent inspection routes 26 and 27 could not be located! Feel free to find them yourself.

THE LOWER TIER

29. Terminal   Very Severe, 4c   6/81
On the right-hand side of the tier is an obvious groove with a chockstone
near the top. To its right are some thin cracks on the left of a rounded rib.
Climb these to top.

30. Open To Offa's   Very Difficult   1962
Climb the groove with a chockstone near its top.

31. Riboflavin   Severe   6/81
Climb the sharp rib right of a yew tree passing it to the right at the top.

32. Interface   Very Severe, 4b   6/81
A deep gully bounds the large pinnacle on the right, climb the wall right of
this. Interesting!

33. Pinnacle Crack   Hard Very Difficult   7/81
Climb the crack in the pinnacle to gain its summit.

TWILIGHT GULLY WALLS

GR 224461

There is only one tier with routes described on it, although a small tier set back from the main tier offers some good bouldering. This buttress is located at the head of the valley and is followed south from that point. The routes start on a small buttress to the left of the main walls. The obvious features of this crag are the curving overhangs at its start, the large detached tower some 30m right of the start of the walls and a fine smooth looking wall further to its right.

Descents are found at the left-hand end and at a steep gully containing a small tree. There are large amounts of scree at the top of these walls making it awkward for belaying and occasionally dangerous for the second, who may get showered by loose debris.

The climbs are described from left to right starting at a small buttress on the opposite side to the main walls at the head of the valley stream. The first three routes lie on the small buttress left of the head of the valley stream and opposite Shadow. 6m from the right-hand side of the buttress is a shallow groove above a short wall, the groove is taken by Bolt in the Snow.

1.   Manakin   E4 6b   1988
Boulder out the smooth wall left of Bolt in the Snow, BR (missing), past a slot to a very hard move past a PR. The difficulties then ease for the top to be gained.

2.   Bolt In The Snow   E1 5b   3/86
The wall and short groove passing a BR (missing).

3.   Jabberwocky   E2 5b   1988
Follow the unpleasant weakness a few feet right of Bolt in The Snow. Loose.

All the following routes are situated on the main wall.

4.   Shadow   E3 6a   14/8/80
At the far left-hand end of the tier is a black scoop. 5m to its right is a thin crack with a shallow groove above. Climb this faint crack, difficult, and finish up the easier groove above.

Right of Shadow towards the top of the crag there are two small whitebeam trees 5m apart. The next routes climb the walls and bulging overhangs between them.

* 5. Hungry Days   E3 5c   14/7/81
Position yourself in the middle of the slabby wall and below the groove near the top. Climb the thin crack to the overhang and traverse left across the slab to below a triangular roof. Using undercuts, gain the easy scoop and good holds out over the roof to the left. Finish easily.

* 6. Bitter Ender   E1 5b   18/6/81
Start 3m right of Hungry Days at a white painted square. Climb up and follow the leftward arching roof to its end. Move round into the shallow crack to reach the top.

** 7. Bitter Entry   E2 5c   14/7/81
Start at the white painted square. Climb the arched roof for 2m until a crack is reached, follow this through the roof to make a hard move up into safety (the top!).

** 8. Forced Entry   E3 5c   27/4/86
The leftward trending groove right of Bitter Entry past two pegs. Step right at the roof and lunge up the thin crack.

Moving right the walls relent and contain three fairly obvious grooves which provide the lines for the next trio of routes.

9. Tizer The Surpriser   Hard Very Severe, 5a   4/3/80
Climb the first of the large three grooves direct to a large dubious block halfway up the groove. Move up past the block with a hard move to finish.

10. Central Groove   Hard Severe   Unknown
Climb the middle groove directly above a white painted square to the small roof. Pull over on the right and so to the top.

11. The Pancake   Hard Severe   Unknown
Climb the right-hand of the three grooves with a thin crack at the back.

Right of The Pancake there is a large detached tower with large chockstones jammed behind it. The next routes start left of this.

12. Starting Block   Very Severe, 4b   1969
Start on the block at a white square. Climb up the arête and move left to the groove and onward to the top.

** 13. Race Riot   Hard Very Severe, 5a   23/7/81
Start as for the previous route and climb the open groove directly above.

To the right lies a prominent tower.

*   14. Twilight Chimney   Hard Severe   Unknown
Ascend the deep chimney up the left side of the tower.

15. Jittering Tower   Hard Very Severe, 5a   25/10/80
Climb the front face of the tower via a finger crack to an overhang. Move
left onto the arête and ledge, then up the wall to move finally back right into
a groove and crack. The crack can be climbed direct at a loose 5b.

16. Frejus   Hard Very Difficult   Unknown
The chimney up the right-hand side of the tower.

17. Agay   Severe   Unknown
Climb the flaked cracks in the wall behind the tower moving away from the
chimney and finishing right of a small tree.

18. Antibes   Very Severe, 4b   17/7/81
3m right of the tower is an obvious layback crack at half height. Climb up
to this and follow it to the top.

19. Running Wild   Hard Very Severe, 5a   17/7/81
Climb from the start of Antibes but instead move upwards and right into a
small v-groove. Move up the groove, then out left to the arête. Finish up
this keeping to the left of two trees.

20. Volenti   Severe   1969
Climb up a deep flake crack to a small overhang then follow the left-hand
flake to the top.

21. The Gift   Severe   1969
Start 1m right of Volenti, climb the thin crack up to an ash tree at 4m.
Traverse left to below a rotten looking yew tree climbing up and over this
to finish.

22. Zilla   Very Difficult   Unknown
This route starts below the large whitebeam tree up the left-hand of the
twin cracks. Climb this crack, then the leftward trending ramp to the top.

23. Frolic   Very Severe, 4a   Unknown
Climb the right-hand crack to the roots of the tree, then move either straight
up the wall above or to the small corner left of the small tree (the first
method is superior).

24. Roots   Very Severe, 4c   12/5/81
Start right of Frolic. Move behind the pointed flake and climb up the black slab to the roots of the tree. Move slightly right and ascend the multiple overhangs to the top.

*   25. No Grips   E2 5b   25/10/80
Start on top of a large pointed flake. Climb onto the arête and move up rightwards across the slab to a finger crack. Climb up and right onto a smaller slab, then pull over the roof on the left of a prow.

26. Missing Link   Very Severe, 4b   15/8/81
Start 5m right of the large flake beneath a square cut roof at 4m. Climb to the roof and over it on the left, then up the groove to another small triangular roof. Move over this roof and up the groove to finish. Some dubious rock.

27. The Last Fling   Very Severe, 4a   15/8/81
Start right of Missing Link. Climb the steep crack to an ash tree, then finish on the right of the sharp arête.

28. Continental Chocs   Very Severe, 4b   1969
Start at a white painted square. Climb the steep finger and hand crack to the grass filled groove and top.

29. Pagoda   Hard Very Severe, 5a   13/10/79
Start on the right of Continental Chocs at a steep white mottled wall. Climb the wall to the third crack on the right and finish up this. Hard to start.

30. Rising Champ   Hard Very Difficult   Unknown
Climb the flake and crack left of a large ash tree. Move left onto a slab and go up the flake crack to the top.

*   31. Misty Dawn   Severe   1969
Start at a white painted square, just right of the large ash tree. Climb to the deep crack and up the niche above.

32. Shakin' Stevens   Very Severe, 4b   Unknown
4m right of Misty Dawn are two thorn bushes in some chossy cracks. The route takes a line up these rotting cracks. Yuck!

*   33. Happy Valley   Very Severe, 4b   1969
Start at a white square 2m right of Shakin' Stevens. Climb up and right into a shallow groove and follow this to near the top where a move left is made

to finish. A move right at this point gives a softer option.

* 34. Rock Special   E2 5b   1/7/81
A good wall climb. To the right of Happy Valley the wall is undercut. Start
at the widest part of the undercut at the base of the wall. Pull over the bulge
(hard), traverse across the wall rightwards to an obvious mantleshelf left
of a bush. Move up and back left onto an easy angled slab and the top.

35. Howling   E1 5a   1/7/81
Start 2m right of Rock Special directly below the obvious groove at the top
of the wall. Climb the steep wall direct via layaways and thin cracks to a
groove, then on to the top.

36 Ten Percent Special   E2 5b   1/7/81
On the right of Howling is a pocketed scoop in a slab at 2m. Move into the
scoop (hard) and traverse up rightwards below the overhang into the
smooth shallow groove which is employed to gain the top. A superb route.

37. Masungi   Hard Severe   1/7/81
Climb direct to a dead yew tree and live whitebeam trees via a crack, then
fight the tree to get to the top.

38. The Avenger   Very Severe, 4b   1/7/81
Just right of Masungi is a thin crack up the wall. Climb this with increasing
difficulty.

The slabby wall right of The Avenger has been climbed direct at 5a, but the
climbs on this section of rock along to the vegetated descent gully are too short
to be credited as routes. The steep vegetated gully containing a large
whitebeam tree is an easy means of descent but if one does not realise this
from above it can appear to be a false trail.

15m right of the descent gully is a 3m tall flake of rock with a smaller flake on
its left. The next route starts on this.

39. Land Of The Fairies   E1 5b   18/3/80
Stand on the small flake and move up leftwards into the steep hanging
groove to the top.

40. Pitmungo   Severe   Unknown
Position yourself between the two flakes and climb one of the cracks to a
slab at 5m. Now step right to avoid the loose block above. Finish more
safely at the top.

41. Château   Very Severe, 4a   Unknown
Just right of the rounded arête is a white painted square. Climb from the
square up the groove and cracks to level with the largest tree, move left
of tree to finish.

42. Unite   Severe   1969
Climb the obvious deep crack to the top, if you so wish.

43. H Block   E1 5a   23/7/81
Start 1m right of Unite at a white square. Climb the groove to its top then
pull through the bulge onto the slab. Climb up the slab to the top via a
whitebeam tree.

*   44. Bay Of Pigs   E1 5b   23/7/81
Start as for H Block at the white square. Climb up rightwards across the
wall to a good crack below the roof, continue to the roof. Traverse left
across the wall and then move up the cracks to the top.

Right of Bay of Pigs is an undercut rounded arête with a tree in a crack to its
right.

*   45. The Tiger Awaits   E2 5b   23/7/81
A slightly disjointed route. Start at the foot of the crack containing the tree.
Climb up 1m, then traverse out leftwards above the undercut to climb a thin
crack in the wall. Go up this to gain the arête to below the block roof. Move
right to a good crack in the roof, which is climbed to the top and safety.

46. The Heist   Very Severe, 4c   18/3/80
Start as for the Tiger Awaits. Climb up the crack to fight through the
whitebeam tree on its right. Continue up the crack, moving around to the
right of a semi-dead yew tree. Step left of the yew tree and climb the
headwall above to the top.

47. Stay Alert Malcolm   Hard Very Severe, 5a   23/7/81
Start 6m right of The Heist at a block just left of a large ash tree. Climb
leftwards to a thin crack on the right of some white marks. Traverse right
across the smooth wall to a shallow scoop, climb this to a small roof (hard
move at top). Move right at the roof, then climb up the broken wall above
to the top.

Right of Stay Alert Malcolm is a block filled gully and large ash tree marking
the end of the crag. On its right is a small but superb smooth wall which
although it is short does in this case warrant a mention as the climbing is
excellent on top quality rock.

* **48. Hyper Medius Meets Little Finger**   E3 5c   19/4/80
Start in the centre of the small wall at a small white lichen mark. Climb up
to a good crack where the angle eases to a slab. Then utilize the small
pockets to get to the top.

FIRST ASCENTS

1962	SLOTH	H J Tinkler & J Hesketh
1962	PREJUDICE	H J Tinkler & J Hesketh
1962	PRIDE	H J Tinkler & J Hesketh
1962	ONEGIN	J Hesketh & H J Tinkler
1962	HELME'S HIGHWAY	J Hesketh & H J Tinkler
1962	COW PARSLEY	H J Tinkler & J Hesketh
1962	IVY TOWER CHIMNEY	H J Tinkler & J Hesketh
1962	MONCRIEFF	H J Tinkler & J Hesketh
1962	WOODPIGEON CRAC	J Hesketh & H J Tinkler
1962	RUTH'S RAMBLE	H J Tinkler & J Hesketh
1962	FUNERAL CORNER	J Hesketh & H J Tinkler
1962	OPEN TO OFFA'S	H J Tinkler & J Hesketh
1969	STARTING BLOCK	B Dearman
1969	VOLENTI	B Dearman
1969	THE GIFT	B Dearman
1969	CONTINENTAL CHOCS	B Dearman
1969	MISTY DAWN	B Dearman
1969	HAPPY VALLEY	B Dearman
1969	UNITE	B Dearman
1969-79	CENTRAL GROOVE	Unknown
1969-79	THE PANCAKE	Unknown
1969-79	FREJUS	Unknown
1969-79	TWILIGHT CHIMNEY	Unknown
1969-79	AGAY	Unknown
1969-79	ZILLA	Unknown
1969-79	FROLIC	Unknown
1969-79	RISING CHAMP	Unknown
1969-79	SHAKIN STEVENS	Unknown
1969-79	PITMUNGO	Unknown
1969-79	CHATEAU	Unknown
13/10/79	PAGODA	S M Cathcart & T Curtis
1980	SKULLION	S M Cathcart, Unseconded
4/3/80	TIZER THE SURPRISER	S M Cathcart, Solo
18/3/80	LAND OF THE FAIRIES	S M Cathcart & A Johnson
18/3/80	THE HEIST	S M Cathcart & A Johnson
19/4/80	HYPER MEDIUS MEETS....	S M Cathcart, Solo
14/8/80	SHADOW	S M Cathcart & J Dee
25/10/80	JITTERING TOWER	S M Cathcart & J Dee

25/10/80	NO GRIPS	S M Cathcart & J Dee
25/1/81	ON LINE	P Stott, Unseconded
4/81	TO CUT A LONG STORY	P Stott, Solo
11/5/81	PENETRATION FACTOR	P Stott & R Bennion
12/5/81	ROOTS	S M Cathcart & M Cameron
5/81	LORAN	P Stott, Solo
6/81	INTERFACE	P Stott, Solo
6/81	RIBOFLAVIN	P Stott, Solo
6/81	EXTENSION	P Stott, Solo
6/81	TERMINAL	P Stott, Solo
18/6/81	BITTER ENDER	S M Cathcart & J Dee
26/6/81	INTER DIGITAL PAUSE	P Stott & S M Cathcart
26/6/81	GO-A-GO-GO	S M Cathcart & P Stott
26/6/81	SUNDAY DRIVER	S M Cathcart & P Stott
26/6/81	HIGH IMPEDANCE	P Stott, S M Cathcart
6/81	SIDESTEP	P Stott, Solo
6/81	THE CLEAROUT	P Stott, Solo
6/81	FLAWSE	P Stott, Solo
7/81	PINNACLE CRACK	P Stott, Solo
1/7/81	ROCK SPECIAL	S M Cathcart, Solo
1/7/81	HOWLING	S M Cathcart, Solo
1/7/81	TEN PERCENT SPECIAL	S M Cathcart, Solo
1/7/81	MASUNGI	S M Cathcart, Solo
1/7/81	AVENGER	S M Cathcart, Solo
14/7/81	BITTER ENTRY	S M Cathcart & M Cameron
14/7/81	HUNGRY DAYS	S M Cathcart & M Cameron
17/7/81	ANTIBES	S M Cathcart, Solo
17/7/81	RUNNING WILD	S M Cathcart, Solo
23/7/81	THE TIGER AWAITS	S M Cathcart & M Cameron
23/7/81	BAY OF PIGS	S M Cathcart & M Cameron
23/7/81	H BLOCK	S M Cathcart & M Cameron
23/7/81	RACE RIOT	S M Cathcart & M Cameron
23/7/81	STAY ALERT MALCOLM	M Cameron & S M Cathcart
7/8/81	ATTENUATION	P Stott & S M Cathcart
15/8/81	MISSING LINK	S M Cathcart, Solo
15/8/81	THE LAST FLING	S M Cathcart, Solo
	Stuart's last route at Twilight.	
3/2/85	FRAGGLE ROCK	P Barker & A Mills
3/2/85	HUNGOVER	P Barker & A Mills
3/86	BOLT IN THE SNOW	A Price, Unseconded
27/4/86	FORCED ENTRY	D Kerr (1 rest point)
	FFA 4/88 P Harrison & S Cardy	
1988	JABBERWOCKY	Unknown
1988	MANAKIN	A Price, Unseconded
28/9/92	GOING TO A GO-GO	G Gibson, Unseconded

THE PINFOLD AREA (ROCK FARM)

O.S. Map 117

by Gary Gibson, Alec Williams and Simon Williams

SITUATION AND ACCESS

This magnificent group of crags offer the visiting climber a great variety of climbing at all grades and styles. There are open wall climbs, hand jamming cracks, sport climbs, aid climbs, wild hardman routes, new routes awaiting budding rock stars, or even those deep dark chimney grunts for the aspiring caver!! So why so quiet, who knows?

The Crags are divided into three main areas, Pinfold North, South and Monks Buttress. To reach the Pinfold Crags proceed along the valley road as for the rest of the Eglwyseg crags (read Eglwyseg introduction), until a turning, signposted Panorama, appears on your right. Follow the road around to the LEFT and after about 600m you will come to a large layby on the right near to a track: park here. Walk down the road to the gate and follow the drive up to where it crosses a river bed. From this point you can see the full grandeur of the crags in evidence, Pinfold North high on the left skyline, Pinfold South directly in front, and towering above on the right, Monks Buttress. Continue up the left bank of the stream until Pinfold South is reached. From here turn left to reach the North crag, or turn right for the Monks Buttresses.

PINFOLD SOUTH BUTTRESS

GR 222453

Walking up the path Pinfold South stands proud and tall at the head of the valley. This cluster of perfect rock sculptured into slabs, hanging grooves and strong cracklines, gives the average climber a varied collection of routes. The crag also has at its left-hand end a selection of two pitch climbs using the upper tier. Some 20m left of Lay Me Back is the Quick Tick wall and to the right of the stream the small Monkshead Buttress can be seen. The climbs are described from right to left when facing the rock, working leftwards from the stream.

1. Midnight Special   Hard Very Severe, 5b   3/4/80
Start 2m left of the tree at half height. Climb the right trending overhanging crack to a good ledge at 2m. Continue more easily up the groove above to the top.

** 2. Shoot To Thrill   E6 6b   16/8/87
Start at a niche below the smooth wall left of Midnight Special. Move up into the niche, then go up and right to a good layaway hold. Step left and move up to gain a good jug, BR, then mantleshelf and finish up a shallow groove on the right.

* 3. Banana Splits   E3 6a   Sum. 1983
Start up the smooth crack bounding the smooth wall on the left (Toccata), then move across the smooth wall to finish up the shallow groove of Shoot To Thrill.

* 4. Play To Kill   E2 5c   17/7/92
Start up Toccata for 3m, then move right and up to the overhang capping the wall. Climb through this to reach safe ground above.

** 5. Toccata   Very Severe, 5a   24/3/74
The obvious crack. Very enjoyable.

6. Devils Alternative   E1 5b   3/4/80
Climb into the niche and scoop left again and continue up the slab on good pockets to pass between two trees to gain the top. Protection in the crack on the right-hand side and small wires to the left.

7.   Alchemy   E3 6a   15/3/84
Fierce climbing up the blunt arête left of Devils Alternative, gained from
that route and finished leftwards.

*** 8.   Solo In Soho   E3 6a   3/4/80
An excellent sustained route on perfect rock. Boulder up to a PR in the
scoop, then move left at the overhang into the thin layback crack. Follow
this to the top. A direct finish has been done via the bulge at E3 6a and is
just as good: Roped Up In Runcorn.

9.   Russian Roulette   E1 5a   12/4/80
Climb the thin cracks and wall left of Solo In Soho to a small whitebeam
tree. Finish up the groove above.

10. Marander   Hard Very Severe, 4c   26/3/74
Start at a W marked on the rock. Climb up to the square cut niche, move
left to a hanging slab, awkward, to finish up the scrappy groove above.

11. Foot Loose And Fancy Free   E1 5b   29/9/80
Climb the steep crack left of the rounded arête finishing up the groove of
Marander. Strenuous.

12. Darling Rose   E3 6b   16/5/92
Start just left of Foot Loose And Fancy Free and climb a faint crack into a
tiny corner. Pull up and slightly right to climb the desperate wall, BR, to gain
good finishing holds.

*   13. Vacances Verticales   E2 5c   13/3/84
Climb the centre of the excellent grey wall, via a PR, to the top.

14. Too Many Women   E2 5c   17/7/92
Start left of Vacances Verticales and climb the wall straight to the top.

*   15. Y Corner   Very Severe, 5a   1969-74
Climb the obvious Y cracks; either crack, same grade.

** 16. Marnie   Hard Very Severe, 4c   3/9/75
Immaculate. Attack the shattered wall left of Y corner to the hanging
groove and the top. Enough protection!

17. Phallic Tower   Hard Very Severe, 5a   17/5/80
Totter up the short groove below the two trees, move right at 2m to the
arête and small pillar, then move left behind the tree to finish.

*   18. Neon Knights   E2 5b   7/4/80
An interesting technical route. Start at a small recess and climb to the
groove following it to the top.

19. Dead Or Alive   Very Severe, 4b   1/4/80
A short groove leads up to between two trees, traverse left below them to
move up and climb the slabs and walls trending right.

20. Eagles Nest Crack   Hard Severe   1962
Climb the deep chimney via a large elderberry bush and huge nest. An
awkward start, middle and finish.

*   21. E.C.V.   Very Severe, 4c   1969-74
Start at the painted letters E.C.V. Climb the short wall to a corner and follow

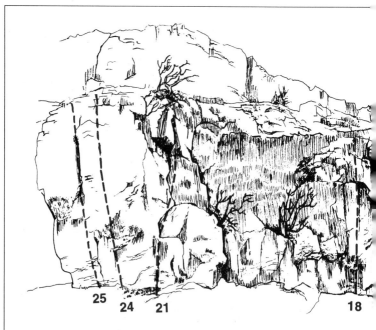

this to the overhang. Move out right to a good crack, the tree and the top; wild finish.

*   22. G.M.B.H.   E3 6a   16/5/92
A good little route. Move up E.C.V. for 3m before moving left onto the arête. A few difficult moves past a BR gains a crack and finishing groove. Abseil off from the tree.

23. Rock A Little   E2 6a   4/86
The wall right of Overhanging Crack gained from above the bulge on that route and climbed direct via 2 PRs.

**   24. Pocket Rocket   E4 6b   16/5/92
An excellent route up the front face of the buttress right of Overhanging Crack and incorporating Rock A Little. Tackle the initial bulge direct and with difficulty, BR and very blind, until on the buttress front. Climb this trending rightwards past 2PRs on the right. Abseil from the trees on the right.

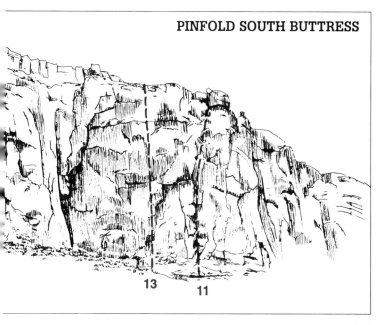

PINFOLD SOUTH BUTTRESS

13   **11**

** 25. Overhanging Crack   E1 5b   1969
Climb the obvious large crack on the block buttress wall. Large nuts help, difficult finish.

* 26. Glorious Wobblegong   E5 6b   26/5/92
Technical in its upper section. Start just left of Overhanging Crack. With difficulty gain a finger jam crack and follow it to the prominent bulge. Pull through this, BR, onto the headwall where a good hold on the right gains easier ground above.

* 27. Geralds Dilemma   Very Severe, 4c   24/3/74
Climb the corner slab to the overhang, moving onto the right wall to finish. A nice route.

The start of the two pitch routes on Pinfold South begin here.

* 28. Progressions Of Power   E3   22/8/80
A bold technical climb. Start 3m left of Geralds Dilemma.
1) 5c. Climb the delicate slab to the overhang and traverse below it to the arête on the left, with PR around to its left. Climb up the crack above to a small tree and a belay on the terrace at the foot of the obvious layback groove. The slight rib to the left can be climbed as a direct start, the Scratting Hen Start, at E4 6a.
2) 5c. Climb the fine layback groove to the overhang and then decide whether to go up the crack on its left to a poor sloping ledge and top or opt for the right-hand side at 4c.

* 29. Red Flag Day   E5   18/2/84
1) 6a. Climb a scoop, TR, onto the flake 3m left of Scratting Hen Start and move up to the bulge. Over this, 2 TRs, and up to easy ground and a belay in the corner. E3 as a pitch in its own right.
2) 6a. Climb the crease in the left wall of the layback corner via 2TRs. This was originally climbed separately as The Thin White Line.

* 30. Buster Bloodvessel   E3   17/4/80
A technical initial pitch. Start at the rightward rising line of overhangs.
1) 6a. Climb the overhang and steep wall above for 6m to a good hold and runner. Continue up to a dead yew tree and move up and left to the terrace below the upper wall. Crawl left for 9m to below a downward pointing flake and belay.
2) 5c. Establish yourself on the wall above via the downward pointing flake, then layback the crack above to a l-o-n-g reach, tree and top.

* 33. Pinfold Right-hand   Severe   1969-74

1) Climb the deep chimney and the crack above the chockstone to a belay on the widest part of the terrace.

2) Crawl left for 2m to below a roof and flying rounded arête. Stand up awkwardly to climb the roof and finish easily up the left side of the rounded arête.

34. Pinfold Left-hand   Severe   1962

Start below the deep crack found on the left side of the huge flake.

1) Climb the deep corner and crack in the chimney with a chockstone which is passable on the inside if you think you're small. Belay on the widest part of the terrace.

2) As for pitch 2 of Pinfold Right-hand.

* 35. Splitting Finger Crack   E2   16/6/79

A good route with a pleasant, but poorly protected, top pitch.

1) 5a. Start below the steep finger crack left of Pinfold Left-hand. Climb the crack to the terrace and move right to a belay at its widest part.

2) 5b. Move left to the start of the first shallow groove. Climb this and the slab above to the top. Belay well back.

36. Lay Me Back   Hard Severe   6/80

Below the obvious overhang is a layback crack, climb this to a step left onto the arête and top.

Left of Lay Me Back is a large yew tree and left again is a small buttress with one route on it.

37. Short Trip   Very Severe, 5a   4/84

Start on the right-hand side of the buttress at a short groove, just left of the tree. Climb the groove to the tree until forced left to a rib and top on flakes. The tree has engulfed the top of the route you may be relieved to know!

20m left of Lay Me Back is a smooth wall, the Quick Tick Wall. At the right end of the wall is a wide crack.

38. Celery Stick   E1 5c   18/3/84

The rib, scoop and flake 2m left of the wide crack.

39. Fingerbobs   Hard Very Severe, 5b 19/2/84

The crack and scoop just left again, TR.

PINFOLD SOUTH BUTTRESS

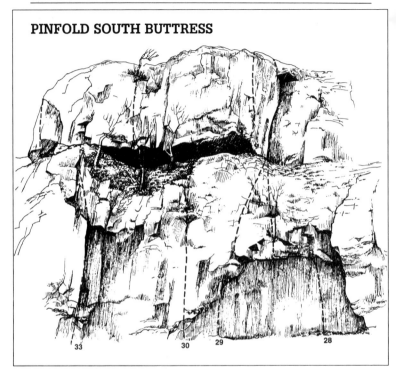

* 31. The Moving Finger   E3   18/2/84
Pleasant climbing up the slabby face 3m to the left of Buster Bloodvessel
and just right of a chimney.
1) 5c. Climb the slab rightwards via 3 TRs, now missing, and a flake to
gain a tree belay on the terrace.
2) 5c. Tackle the bulge and crack behind the tree.

32. Woolly Ramble   Very Severe   16/4/81
1) 4c. Start 2m right of the deep chimney below a tree. Climb to the tree,
move out right and follow a crack to a smooth wall. Continue up to the
terrace passing to the right of a large tree. Crawl right to belay as for
Progressions....
2) 4c. Climb the layback groove to the overhang and move right to finish.

40. Lentil Man   Hard Very Severe, 5b   18/3/84
A line of holds 2m left of Fingerbobs.

41. Pumpkin Seed   Hard Very Severe, 5b   18/3/84
A tricky start, then easier climbing just left again.

42. El Crapitan   Very Severe, 5a   18/3/84
Flake and dirty crack left again; poor!

*   43. Old Chipatti   E3 6a   19/2/84
The thin flake in the centre of the wall, gained direct. A PR has since fallen
out!

*   44. Winterhill   E3 5c   19/2/84
The shallow scoop and flake left again.

45. Pig Pen   E2 6a   19/2/84
A hard start just left leads to a rib and tree.

*   46. Crypt Tick   Hard Very Severe, 5a   18/3/84
Very pleasant climbing via a scoop just left of Pig Pen, TR.

47. Flied Lice   E1 5b   18/3/84
Thin flakes left again.

48. Toe Bitter   E2 5c   3/84
Scoop and bulges left of Flied Rice, PR. Fragile.

49. Tindaloo Trots   E2 5c   18/3/84
A mid height girdle of the wall from right to left. Fun, but don't fall off!

N.B. above the centre of the wall is a PB.

Some 60m left of the Quick Tick Wall is an obvious wide crack on a slim
buttress.

50. Gilly Flower   Hard Very Severe, 5b   3/84
The twin cracks right of the obvious wide crack, TR. Pleasant.

PINFOLD NORTH BUTTRESS

GR 220455

The crag lies at the end of the thin sheep track which begins at the left end of the Pinfold South area. The first climbable rock you come to is a small subsidiary buttress of Pinfold North which has a tiny cave at its right-hand end. To the left of this buttress is a grass slope providing an easy descent from the top of the crag, alternatively at the far left-hand end of the crag is a large partially detached flake containing two descent chimneys. Towards the centre of the crag lies an area of rock with a wildly undercut base containing some brilliant routes up the overhanging wall above, this is the Bay Area.

All the directions given assumes one is facing the rock. The routes are described from right to left.

The first route is situated on the small subsidiary buttress just to the right of the large grassy descent gully that marks the start of Pinfold North buttress.

*   1. Minnie Minor   E4 6b   16/5/92
Climb the centre of the wall, BR, keeping just right of a PR on the upper wall. Two technical sections all on immaculate rock.

2. Blister   Very Severe, 4b   16/4/79
1m right of the small cave is a block. Climb from the block via a layback into a scoop and to the top.

3. Swell   Very Severe, 4c   1969-74
Climb the crack above the cave. A difficult finish especially for the short, the tree spoils the route slightly.

*   4. Exostosis   Hard Very Severe, 5a   16/4/79
Above and left of the cave is an obvious layback flake. Gain this by using a groove and thin cracks near to the arête.

Left of Exostosis is an obvious overhang.

5. Calefaction   Very Severe, 4c   18/4/79
Climb to the overhang via a layback crack and groove. Once gained, move right, over, then back left to a crack and the top.

*   6. Centrefold   Hard Very Severe, 5b   4/84
Start in the centre of the buttress below a groove at two thirds height. Climb the groove containing a crack and so to the top.

120

7.   Frigorific   E2 5b   18/4/79
2m left of Centrefold is a small crack with an overlap at three quarter
height. Climb the crack, hard, to the overhang, then move right to a crack
and good holds. Follow the crack to the top.

8.   Auto-De-Fe   Severe   1969-74
Climb to a tree on poor holds, then climb the twin cracks to the top.

9.   Lax   Moderate   1969-74
Climb the obvious choked crack left again.

10.   Scaremonger   Very Severe, 4b   12/7/80
Start at the lowest point of the pillar containing a whitebeam tree near to
its top. Climb the flake crack to the tree.

11.   Pugilist   Hard Severe   1969-74
Left of the pillar is a chimney with a large chockstone at half height. Sweep
up this.

*   12.   Transient   Hard Very Severe, 5a   16/5/81
Start 3m left of Pugilist. Climb the thin crack to a slab on the left at 2m. Move
up the slab, step right onto the wall avoiding the tree and gain the top via
a series of good holds. A direct line at the same grade has been done up
the rib past a thread.

The buttress now swings round into a descent gully. To the left of this gully is
a large stepped overhang. Between the gully and the overhang is a slightly
vegetated thin groove with a large flake on its left near the top. The next route
takes this groove.

13.   Megalith   Hard Severe   12/11/79
Climb the thin vegetated v-groove past the tree at the top.

*   14.   Obelisks Fly High   Hard Severe   27/9/80
A good route with an exposed but slightly loose finish. Start right of the
large stepped overhang, below the obvious crack. Climb the crack to a
sloping ledge on the right, step left to a ledge on the exposed wall above
the void and follow a crack to the top. The large crack has been climbed
all the way and is very loose.

*   15.   Baby Frogs With Dirty Little Lips   E4 6b   4/6/89
Fine climbing with a technical crux. Start below the right-hand end of the
large overhang. Climb direct to the overhang and cross the wall to its right,

BR, to reach a prominent flake. A hop, skip and a jump up this, PR, lead to a short wall and the top.

** 16. Dangermouse   E5 6b   18/2/84
Brilliant climbing with a bold start and complex finish; high in the grade. Climb the vague arête to meet the left-hand end of the overhang and pull up into the bottomless groove above, situ wire. Move up, TR and PR, before exiting precariously left to attain success.

Left of the large overhang is a steep wall with a grand tree at the top.

*   17. Whispering Wall   E3 5c   17/5/80
Climb direct, following a shallow depression and intermittent cracks, moving out right into a scoop where it is possible to use a layaway above to finish.

18. Trophy   Hard Severe   19/5/79
Stand on top of some blocks to the left and climb the groove above, steep.

19. Centre Line   Very Severe, 4c   15/6/80
2m right of a large ash and holly tree is a groove at 5m. Climb straight up to the groove and top.

20. Ash Tree Ramble   Very Difficult   1969-74
A route with a certain amount of flair and character enjoyed only by a chosen few (straight jackets are optional). Climb the cracks and groove to the left of the ash and holly trees.

21. Storm Rider   E3 5c   18/5/79
2m left of the trees is a steep wall with two faint cracks. Climb the cracks and small corner to the top. A hard and committing route with just sufficient protection.

*   22. Baron Greenbach   E4 6a   16/2/84
Climb direct up the wall left of Storm Rider past PR. Fine, technical climbing.

*   23. Bagpus   E4 6a   3/5/92
Climb the thin groove just to the left of Baron Greenbach to gain some thin cracks and pull up left onto a clean, smooth looking wall. Take the right edge of this to finish on hidden jugs. High in the grade.

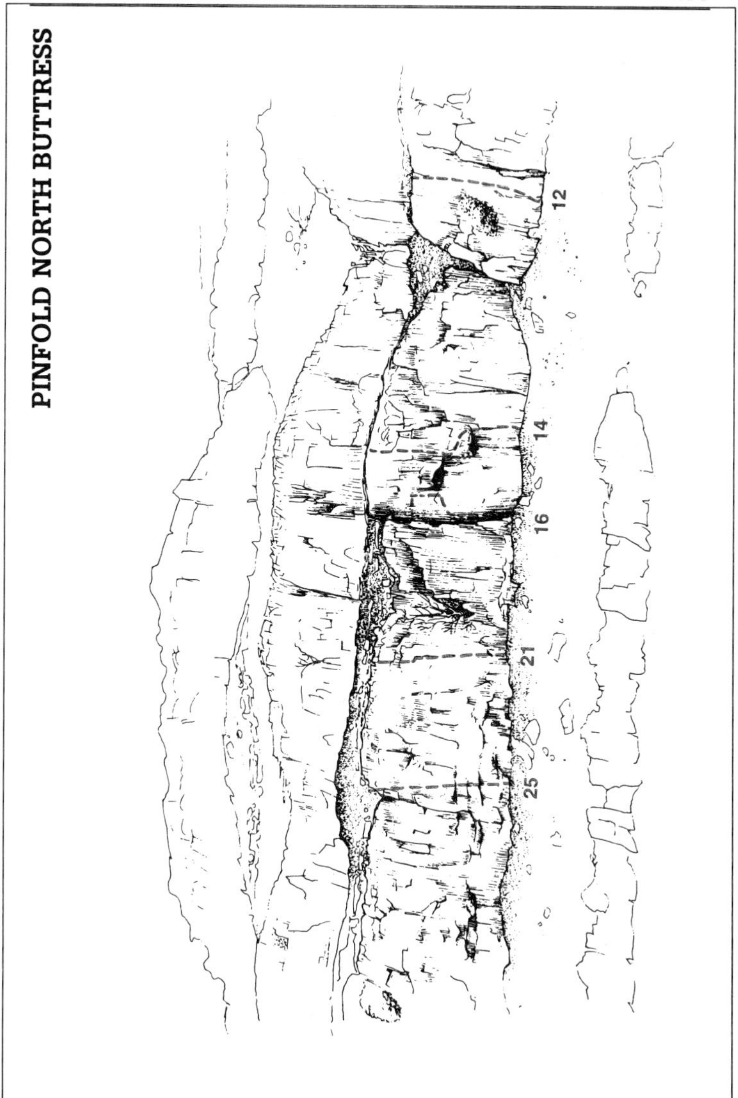
PINFOLD NORTH BUTTRESS
12
14
16
21
25

24. Poison Letter   E2 5c   21/5/79

Start below the smooth groove to the left. Climb the bulge to a good runner placement on the left at 4m, tricky. Move up the smooth groove above with increasing difficulty towards the top.

* 25. Origami Today   E3 6a   3/5/92

Worthwhile. Start 2m left of Poisoned Letter. A fingery lower wall, BR, leads to a TR and thin crack. Climb the crack on the blunt arête to the top.

26. Ornamental Art Mark 2   E4 6b   28/7/92

After the removal of much loose rock, the original line is no longer possible. A new direct start has since been added, 2.5m left of Origami Today. Tackle the initial and crux bulging wall direct to reach a prominent hanging groove. This proves much easier for the top to be gained.

* 27. The Soft Machine   E5 6b   8/4/84

The fierce bulge and gradually widening crack 5m left of Origami Today leads to a tree via a PR and two TRs.

* 28. Stress Test   E4 6b   8/7/85

Climb the bulging wall left of the Soft Machine past 2 PRs to a prominent flake, finishing direct. A sling on the second PR may need re-tying before an ascent is considered.

Left of these routes lies a slabby cracked wall. Almost in the centre of this, at its base, is a bulge with a broken pillar to its right. The next three routes share the same start.

29. Basket Case   E3 6a   18/5/79

Start in the centre of the bulge alongside a tiny grass filled crack. Climb almost direct to a sharp hand hold at 5m. Move right into a v-groove which is followed to the top.

30. Mainstay   E3 6a   11/6/79

Start as for Basket Case to the sharp hand hold at 5m and move up to easier flaky twin cracks on the left and the top.

31. King of Fools   E3 6a   11/6/79

From the sharp hold on Basket Case, traverse out left for 3m, around a sharp arête and into a yellow hanging corner above the shattered bulge.

32. Shasavaan   E1 5b   24/3/80

Climb the broken crack to the central whitebeam tree left of the bulging overhanging wall.

*   33. Wafer Way   Very Severe, 4c   17/5/80
     Left of the two large yew trees is a set of 4 cracks. Climb the right-hand
     crack to the roof and pull through on the right on good holds.

**   34. Last Fandango   E1 5b   30/5/80
     Climb the left-hand of the twin cracks to finish up the obvious steep layback
     crack.

     35. Hard Fought   E2 5b   20/4/80
     Left of the square cut overhang is a long straight thin crack left of an orange
     lichen covered wall. Climb the crack.

*   36. Friction Factor   E2 6a   5/4/84
     An excellent little route taking the centre of the barrel shaped buttress left
     of Hard Fought, PR, to a clean finishing crack.

     37. Condessa   Hard Very Severe, 5a   20/4/80
     The large yew tree at 5m has an overhanging crack running up to it. Climb
     this, difficult, then step left below the tree and climb the deep crack and
     pillar to the top.

6m left of the large yew tree on Condessa are two grooves in the upper half
of the cliff.

*   38. Spastic Spider   E2 5c   22/4/80
     Climb the bulging wall to the left of a thin crack, TR, to a slab at the foot
     of the smooth left-hand groove. Move right into the right-hand groove
     which is followed more easily to the top. A direct start can be done which
     increases the grade to E2 6a.

*   39. The Sinking, Shrinking, Shrimp E2 5c   16/2/84
     Climb the bulge as for Spastic Spider, TR, into a yellow groove. Move up
     this to its top, then traverse left across the face, TR, to a BB. Lower off.

**   40. What's Goin' On   E5 6a   5/4/84
     A fine pitch with a very bold finish since the demise of a TR. From over the
     bulge on The Sinking, Shrinking, Shrimp, traverse left onto the front face,
     BR, and go direct up this passing, tiny wire protection, to a BB. Abseil off.

***   41. Through The Grapevine   E4 6c   2/6/85
     The direct start to What's Goin' On past a situ nut and BR. Tremendous
     climbing, direct and thoroughly absorbing.

The undercut face to the left is supported by a huge block.

*** 42. Mental Transition   E4 6b   8/4/84
A magnificent route with a powerful start followed by technically immaculate climbing. Well protected. Start just right of the huge block below a steep pocketed groove above the undercut bulge. Climb the overhang, 2PR, and move intricately right into a pocketed groove. Move up and right to good holds and runners, then pursue a direct line up the steep slabby wall past a PR into a shallow scoop. Finish direct to a BB.

* 43. Demolition Man   E4 6b   17/3/84
From the block on the left of Mental Transition pull round the bulge and up to good holds. Step right and up a shallow groove, TR, to the top.

* 44. Eddie Waring Lives On   E4 6a   29/7/92
A good route with a tricky start. Begin 2m left of Demolition Man. Move up to stand on the break and pull over the bulge, BR, on small holds to gain a prominent left facing flake. Climb this, wires, before swing-ing right and up to a BB.

The wall now leads into the right-hand side of a large undercut bay with steep walls and large stepped overhangs, the Bay Area. The bay supports a few hard routes that have managed to breach the walls. In the centre of the bay the undercut narrows down to a feasible break below the overhangs.

** 45. Oxygen   E3 6a (1 pt aid)   29/4/84
A good route after a disappointing start. 5m left of Eddie Waring Lives On is a hanging groove above the undercut base. Using a BR with a hanging sling for aid, pull over the roof to gain the foot of a thin crack, PR. Climb this to its top, then traverse delicately left to a second crack. This provides a fine finale.

*** 46. Brainbox   E6 6b   18/5/92
A superb route with sustained hard climbing and sound in-situ protection. A potential classic area taking little seepage. Start 4m left of Oxygen. Using a prominent tree climb the large overhang, BR, and short difficult wall, BR, to a good jug, BR. Teeter up and left to a good flake hold, BR, then pursue a line slightly rightwards through a bulge, BR, to gain a slim groove. Pull straight up and then left to a BB.

** 47. Generation of Swine   E6 6b (1 pt aid)   4/6/89
Desperate, sustained climbing with a delicate finish starting in the centre

G Gibson on Lemon Kerred, Craig Arthur. Photo: G Gibson

of the right-hand wall of the bay. Using a Bolt for aid at the start of the route, climb the centre of the wall via a short groove and powerful bulge to a thin finishing crack. 4BRs to a BB.

**   48. Private Idaho   E6 6c   5/8/92
Superb, sustained and technical climbing after an unfortunate start. Use a BR for aid to cross the roof 4m left of Generation of Swine to gain the wall. Difficult moves up the wall above past 3BRs lead to moves slightly right, TR, into a groove. Stand up in this, TR on the left, and climb the slim groove on the right and the headwall above, BR, direct to a lower off station.

***   49. Atmospheres   E5 6a (1 pt aid)   28/7/84
A classic route of its grade taking the rightward trending line of flakes up the centre of the bay. Formerly the aid route The Bulger. Use BR for aid gain the right trending flakes and follow these past 3PRs to a resting place below an overlap. Pull out right, TR, and climb straight up to the top.

***   50. Planet Claire   E6 6b   24/5/92
A brilliant direct finish to Atmospheres incorporating its hard climbing with powerful finishing moves. Follow Atmospheres to its second PR; now step left into space and climb the undercut rib, BR, with difficulty to the roof, BR. Span the void out left to pass the roof and a wild "out there" finale. BB just above.

**   51. Killer Gorilla   E5 6b (1 pt aid)   Sum. 1985
After the aided start on Atmospheres climb direct to meet the wild overhanging crack. Climb this, 3TRs, to the top. Free climbs the Stepping Man.

Left of the last two routes is the largest single roof on the crag. The roof is split by a crack which runs parallel to the lip of the overhang. Downer (A4), an old aid route, follows this crack to a slabby niche above the lip of the roof and then follows a crack out to the right to finish up the steep wall.

    52. Another Realm   E3 5c (2 pt aid)   1/7/78
Start as for Downer. Using two nuts for aid under the roof, move out to a good hold on the lip and into the slabby niche as for Downer, PR above. Traverse out left along an obvious line for 5m, poorly protected, to a crack. Continue up leftwards to an ash tree, another tree above and up broken slabs.

To the left of the Bay Area, the front face sports a fine grey wall with a prominent hanging groove. This is the start of Pictures Of Living.

G Gibson on Hyperdrive, Dinbren. Photo: G Gibson

*   53. Slap And Tickle   E5 6b   22/7/92
A technical and direct line 5m right of Pictures Of Living. Overcome a
difficult initial bulge, BR, and move up to stand on a slim shelf below the
right-hand side of a bulge. Move up a tiny groove to a BR then take the
bulge above direct via hard blind moves to gain a jug, PR. Stand up on this
before moving left to a BB.

*   54. Dying Tonight   E4 6b   22/7/92
Another good route, short lived in difficulties. Start just on the right of
Pictures Of Living. Climb the difficult grey slab, BR, moving right past a
flake to the undercut bulge. Take this direct by a blind sequence, BR, to
gain a hanging groove, TR. Move easily up this to a BB.

*   55. Pictures Of Living   E4 6a   8/4/84
Climbs the front face of the buttress left of Another
Realm. Follow a flake and shallow groove, PR, to
move left and up onto a block. Climb the thin
crack and groove above, PR.

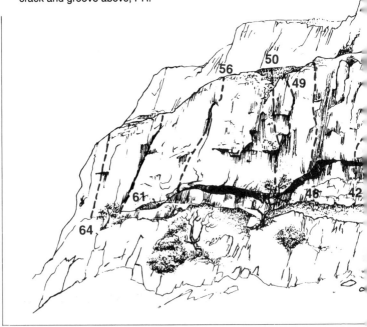

56. Mr Wobbler   E3 6a   2/6/85
From the first PR on Pictures Of Living pull into the groove above TR, and finish up its right arête.

** 57. Prickly Heat   E4 6b   13/10/91
Technical. Start at the obvious flake 4m left of the Pictures Of Living. Climb rightwards up the flake, BR, to its end then transfer left onto the face, BR. Pick a direct line up the centre of the face, BR, until holds on the left can be used to gain easier ground. A direct finish, avoiding the easier ground to the left, is E5.

PINFOLD NORTH BUTTRESS

*   **58. Physical Transaction**   E4 6b   13/10/91
Start 6m left of Prickly Heat. Climb the lower bulge with difficulty, BR, to gain a standing position above, BR. Continue direct via an awkward sequence to gain good holds and a tree.

To the left of the bulging wall is an area of grassy rock and trees.

59. Smokey Bear   E2 5b   4/7/81
Start at the beginning of the obvious large flake to the left of the vegetated area. Climb this to a good crack and a dead tree in a broken groove.

60. Non Stop   E1 5c   5/4/84
The obvious thin cracks in the wall left of Smokey Bear, TR at the top.

*   **61. Mitsuki Groove**   Hard Very Severe, 5a   26/7/79
Just left of Non Stop is a large shallow scoop split by several cracks, together with large blocks at its base. Climb the cracks from the top of the blocks with a hard move before stepping right at the top. Sustained with a loose finish.

**   **62. Space Ace**   E3 5c   9/7/81
Start as for Mitsuki Groove. Climb the groove to a traverse left, PR, at the foot of a slim groove which is followed to the top. It is possible to climb direct to the groove by the lower pocketed wall, BR, and 6a.

63. A Spaceman In The Whitehouse   E4 6a   5/4/84
Climb the faint scoop, TR, and wall left of Space Ace onto the flaked rib above. Climb this to the top.

**   **64. Unknown Feelings**   E2 5c   26/9/80
A fantastic route with good protection just when it counts. Start below the widest part of the roof and climb the wall to a ledge and thin crack below the roof. Climb the roof at its widest part to a good hold above the lip. Continue more easily up the slabs.

65. Bone Orchard   E3 5c   26/9/80
Between the start of Kinberg, on the left, and Unknown Feelings, on the right, is a tiny crack petering out at 3m. Climb the crack and move up to the ledge. From the ledge, climb to a PR in a small square corner below the tapering roof. Climb the roof and bulge, hard, to continue up the slab above.

*** 66. Atlantic Traveller   Very Severe, 4c   5/6/80
A superb route, a must for anyone visiting the area. Start as for Kinberg and climb up for 5m to the obvious traverse line along the slabby terrace below the overhangs. Finish up the cracks at their right-hand end.

*** 67. Kinberg   Very Severe, 4c   19/8/80
A brilliant route for its grade. Looking down between ones legs into the void below is not to be missed. Climb the fine overhanging corner and crack.

68. Monumental   Hard Severe   13/7/81
Left of Kinberg, above a yew tree, is an impressive prow of rock. Climb to the yew tree and continue up the groove to the left of the prow.

69. Nesting Crack   Hard Very Severe, 5a   12/4/81
8m left of Monumental is a vegetated crack, climb this. The rock is of poor quality.

* 70. Slippery Caramel   E5 6a   17/5/92
The wall to the left of Nesting Crack gives intricate climbing and a bold start to a BR. Finish direct and via a straight thin crack at the top.

** 71. A Dose of Barley Fever   E4 6a   17/5/92
The gently leaning, in all directions, arête to the left of Slippery Caramel. Take it on its right-hand side past 2BRs and some exciting moves.

* 72. Sometimes Yes, Sometimes No E3 6a   17/5/92
An excellent pitch up the thin leaning crack system in the steep wall to the right of Bold Polly. A bulge provides the crux above which is a PR. Superb rock.

73. Bold Polly   Severe   1969-74
Unknown Left of the arête is a large corner with an overhang at half height. Climb this.

74. Polytextured Finish   E3 6a   17/5/92
Climb the very compact rugosited wall 3m to the left of Bold Polly via a BR and shallow depression. The crux lies just above the bolt.

Left of Bold Polly the walls are severely undercut forming a terraced bay. On the left side of the bay is a dead tree and wild rose bush at 8m.

75. Buffoon   Very Severe, 5a   23/6/80
Climb to the dead tree and wild rose bush via the short flake crack. From there ascend the broken vegetated cracks and chimney with care.

76. Highway Hysteria   Hard Very Severe, 5a   12/6/80
Climb the thin crack and flake wall just left of a clump of trees to the lowest
ash tree. Move right below the trees to make a long reach to gain a scoop
in the slab on the right. Follow the deep crack to the top.

*   **77. Freeway Madness**   E3 5b   24/7/81
Climb Highway Hysteria to the lower ash tree. Climb above the tree, then
traverse out left across the steep slab, on pockets, to a good hold. Follow
the crack and bulge above to the top.

**   **78. Sentinel**   E1 5b   13/6/81
A fine climb with excellent protection. Just right of Bennetto is a wall with
a crack splitting it. Climb the crack following it round to the right onto a slab.
Continue over the bulge at the top of the slab.

79. Bennetto   Hard Severe   26/7/79
Climb the obvious broken corner all the way to the top.

Left of Bennetto the walls bulge forbiddingly again, with an undercut base. At
the far left end of the undercut a fine crack splits the steep wall between a
whitebeam tree and holly tree.

**   **80. Rays And Hail**   E5 6b   16/5/92
A fine open pitch up the clean white wall 5m left of Bennetto. Climb the
initially bold white wall to gain a thin crack under a bulge, small wires. Pull
through the bulge and go straight up the headwall, BR, in a fine position
to the top.

**   **81. Lurking In The Long Grass**   E4 6b   29/7/92
Good rock and protection with a single hard move. Starting 2m left of Rays
And Hail, climb the awkward lower wall, PR with sling, into a scoop. Move
up, then exit left, BR, to gain a thin flake system. Follow this, PR, direct to
the top.

**   **82. U Got Me Bugged**   E5 6b   16/5/92
Another fine, clean pitch through the large undercut and up the smooth
wall 8m left of Lurking In The Long Grass. Start below the centre of the
largest undercut. Tackle the roof, BR (ring), to gain a recess above, BR.
Pull up and right, BR, and continue up the left edge of the wall, BR, until
moves right gain good ledges and an easy finish.

**   **83. Whilst Rome Burns**   E5 6b   3/5/92
Technical face climbing up the smooth face 3m right of Stoned Roman.

Start at the extreme left-hand end of the undercut. Pull through this and up onto the wall, BR, stepping slightly right to gain the centre of the face. Proceed up this, BR, to gain a small left-facing flake, Rock 1 essential, then continue slightly rightwards to the top.

84. Stoned Roman   E1 5b   11/7/80
Below the whitebeam tree, left of the undercut, is a thin crack. Climb this to move left at the tree and finish up a slab.

85. Tweak   E1 5b   1969-74
This climbs the narrow face direct between Stoned Roman and Franko to the holly tree.

86. Franko   Hard Very Severe, 5a   26/7/79
4m left of Stoned Roman. Climb the layback crack to an awkward move to gain a grass ledge on the left. Finish up the deep crack above.

*   87. One Carlos   E5 6b   25/5/92
Intricate climbing up the wall left of Franko. Pull over the bulge just left of Franko and trend leftwards, BR, to gain a thin crack system, wires. Difficult moves up this, PR, lead to the top.

*   88. Fingernail   E1 5b   26/7/79
Left again is a steep blank wall with a curving crack and slab around the arête. Climb the crack and slab to a small hanging slab below a holly bush. Continue up the steep crack on the right, moving onto the arête near the top, slightly loose rock to finish. A far better route than it appears, with an airy finish.

89. Sayfari   Very Difficult   1969-74
Left of Fingernail is a holly bush and block corner above. Climb the slab and corner to the bush, then the corner above.

Left of Sayfari is a huge partially detached flake which marks the northern end of the crag and a descent. The right-hand descent can be ascended as a route at Difficult standard, the left-hand is not worth climbing. The face of this huge flake is split by a wide chimney filled with blocks and can be ascended at about Hard Severe but is a poor route. On the left and right of the chimney are two routes.

90. Flighting   Hard Very Severe, 5a   20/6/81
Climb to a leftward trending layback crack on the right of the chimney. Follow this around onto the right wall of the chimney and the top.

Alternatively continue straight up over the bulge after the short wall. A very loose and worrying route either way.

91. Sweet Satisfaction   Hard Severe   20/6/81
Climb the groove and layback crack left of the chimney.

The walls on the left of the descent now become short and broken. Only one route is recorded past the left descent gully.

92. Smouldering Bouldering   E3 6a   2/6/85
Climb a line 25m left of the left-hand descent gully via a smooth wall equipped with a TR and PR. Originally done without these for protection.

FIRST ASCENTS

1962	PINFOLD LEFT-HAND	H J Tinkler & J Hesketh
1962	EAGLES NEST CRACK	J Hesketh & H J Tinkler
1969	OVERHANGING CRACK	T Williams & J O'Niel
1969-74	Y CORNER	Unknown
1969-74	E.C.V.	Unknown
1969-74	PINFOLD RIGHT-HAND	
1969-74	SWELL	Unknown
1969-74	AUTO-DE-FE	Unknown
1969-74	LAX	Unknown
1969-74	SCAREMONGER	Unknown
1969-74	PUGILIST	Unknown
1969-74	ASH TREE RAMBLE	Unknown
1969-74	BOLD POLLY	Unknown
1969-74	TWEAK	Unknown
1969-74	SAYFARI	Unknown
24/3/74	TOCCATA	S M Cathcart & G N Swindley
24/3/74	GERALDS DILEMMA	S M Cathcart & G N Swindley

"He could second you up anything but at the time he would never lead. So he tried this and after a couple of hours, gave up."

26/3/74	MARANDER	S M Cathcart & G N Swindley
3/9/75	MARNIE	S M Cathcart & G N Swindley
1/7/78	ANOTHER REALM	S M Cathcart & G N Swindley
16/4/79	BLISTER	S M Cathcart, Solo
16/4/79	EXOSTOSIS	S M Cathcart, Solo
18/4/79	CALEFACTION	S M Cathcart & J Dee
18/4/79	FRIGORIFIC	S M Cathcart & J Dee
18/5/79	STORM RIDER	S M Cathcart & M Cameron
18/5/79	BASKET CASE	S M Cathcart & M Cameron
19/5/79	TROPHY	S M Cathcart, Solo

21/5/79	POISON LETTER	S M Cathcart & M Cameron
11/6/79	ORNAMENTAL ART	S M Cathcart & J Dee
11/6/79	MAINSTAY	S M Cathcart & J Dee
11/6/79	KING OF FOOLS	S M Cathcart & J Dee
16/6/79	SPLITTING FINGER CRACK	S M Cathcart & T Curtis
26/7/79	FRANKO	S M Cathcart & F R Bennett
26/7/79	FINGERNAIL	S M Cathcart & F R Bennett
26/7/79	MITZUKI GROOVE	S M Cathcart & F R Bennett
26/7/79	BENNETTO	S M Cathcart & F R Bennett
12/11/79	MEGALITH	S M Cathcart, Solo
24/3/80	SHASAVAAN	S M Cathcart, Solo
1/4/80	DEAD OR ALIVE	S M Cathcart, Solo
3/4/80	SOLO IN SOHO	S M Cathcart, Solo
3/4/80	DEVILS ALTERNATIVE	S M Cathcart, Solo
3/4/80	MIDNIGHT SPECIAL	S M Cathcart, Solo
7/4/80	NEON KNIGHTS	S M Cathcart, Solo
12/4/80	RUSSIAN ROULETTE	S M Cathcart, Solo
17/4/80	BUSTER BLOODVESSEL	S M Cathcart, Solo
20/4/80	CONDESSA	S M Cathcart, Solo
20/4/80	HARD FOUGHT	S M Cathcart, Solo
22/4/80	SPASTIC SPIDER	S M Cathcart & T Curtis
17/5/80	WAFER WAY	S M Cathcart & F R Bennett
17/5/80	WHISPERING WALL	S M Cathcart & F R Bennett
17/5/80	PHALLIC TOWER	S M Cathcart, Solo
30/5/80	LAST FANDANGO	S M Cathcart, Solo
6/80	LAY ME BACK	S M Cathcart, Solo
5/6/80	ATLANTIC TRAVELLER	S M Cathcart, Solo
12/6/80	HIGHWAY HYSTERIA	S M Cathcart, Solo
15/6/80	CENTRE LINE	S M Cathcart, Solo
23/6/80	BUFFOON	F Bennett & S M Cathcart
11/7/80	STONED ROMAN	S M Cathcart & F R Bennett
12/7/80	SCAREMONGER	S M Cathcart F R Bennett
19/8/80	KINBERG	P Stott & S M Cathcart
22/8/80	PROGRESSIONS OF POWER	S M Cathcart & T Curtis
26/8/80	UNKNOWN FEELINGS	S M Cathcart & P Stott
27/9/80	OBELISKS FLY HIGH	S M Cathcart, Solo
26/9/80	BONE ORCHARD	S M Cathcart & P Stott
29/9/80	FOOTLOOSE AND FANCY FREE	S M Cathcart, Solo
12/4/81	NESTING CRACK	S M Cathcart, Solo
16/4/81	WOOLLY RAMBLE	S M Cathcart, Solo
16/5/81	TRANSIENT	S M Cathcart & M Hughes
21/5/81	MENTAL TRANSITION	S M Cathcart, Unseconded
	FFA 8/4/84 J Codling & J Moulding	
13/6/81	SENTINEL	S M Cathcart & J Dee
20/6/81	FLIGHTING	S M Cathcart, Solo
20/6/81	SWEET SATISFACTION	S M Cathcart, Solo

4/7/81	SMOKEY BEAR	S M Cathcart & G Griffiths
9/7/81	SPACE ACE	S M Cathcart & J Dee
13/7/81	MONUMENTAL	S M Cathcart, Solo
24/7/81	FREEWAY MADNESS	S M Cathcart & P Stott
Sum. 83	BANANA SPLITS	S M Cathcart, Unseconded
16/2/84	BARON GREENBACH	N Dixon, Unseconded
16/2/84	SPASTIC SPIDER DIRECT	G Gibson, Solo
16/2/84	THE SINKING, SHRINKING...	G Gibson, Unseconded
18/2/84	SCRATTING HEN START	A Williams, A Popp & G Gibson
18/2/84	DANGERMOUSE	N Dixon, Unseconded
18/2/84	RED FLAG DAY	G Gibson & A Hudson
18/2/84	THE MOVING FINGER	A Hudson & G Gibson (alt)
19/2/84	FINGERBOBS	A Popp, Unseconded
19/2/84	OLD CHIPATTI	N Dixon & A Popp
19/2/84	WINTERHILL	A Popp & N Dixon
19/2/84	PIG PEN	A Popp, Solo
3/84	TOE BITTER	F Crook & S Smith
3/84	GILLY FLOWER	K Crook & F Crook
13/3/84	VACANCES VERTICALES	S Boyden & P Harrison
15/3/84	ALCHEMY	S Boyden & P Harrison
17/3/84	DEMOLITION MAN	J Moulding & J Codling
18/3/84	CELERY STICK	N Dixon, Solo
18/3/84	LENTIL MAN	F Crook & K Crook
18/3/84	PUMPKIN SEED	F Crook & K Crook
18/3/84	EL CRAPITAN	S Lowe, Solo
18/3/84	CRYPT TICK	B Barrett & A Popp
18/3/84	FLIED LICE	J Codling, Unseconded
18/3/84	TINDALOO TROTS	J Codling & A Popp
5/4/84	FRICTION FACTOR	F Crook & G Gibson
5/4/84	WHAT'S GOIN' ON	G Gibson & F Crook
5/4/84	NON STOP	G Gibson, Solo
5/4/84	A SPACEMAN IN THE.....	G Gibson, Solo
8/4/84	MENTAL TRANSITION FFA	J Codling & J Moulding
8/4/84	THE SOFT MACHINE	J Moulding, J Codling & P Harrison
8/4/84	PICTURES OF LIVING	J Codling, J Moulding & G Gibson
29/4/84	OXYGEN	J Codling, J Moulding & J Lockett
4/84	SHORT TRIP	F Crook & K Crook
4/84	CENTREFOLD	F Crook & K Crook
4/84	TRANSIENT DIRECT FINISH	K Crook & F Crook
28/7/84	ATMOSPHERES	J Codling & A Grondowski
2/6/85	THROUGH THE GRAPEVINE	G Gibson, Unseconded
2/6/85	MR WOBBLER	G Gibson, Unseconded
2/6/85	SMOULDERING BOULDERING	G Gibson, Solo

Later equipped with a thread and peg runner by unknowing culprits and christened 52 Devil Babies Born With Tails.

2/6/85	THE THIN WHITE LINE	G Gibson, Unseconded
8/7/85	STRESS TEST	J Codling, Unseconded
Sum. 85	KILLER GORILLA	J Moulding, Unseconded
4/86	ROCK A LITTLE	A Price, Unseconded
16/8/87	SHOOT TO THRILL	J Moulding, Solo
3/4/88	ROPED UP IN RUNCORN	D Kerr & D Sarker
4/6/89	BABY FROGS WITH......	J Moulding, J Codling, I Dring & M Mitchell
4/6/89	GENERATION OF SWINE	J Moulding, J Codling, I Dring & M Mitchell
13/10/91	PRICKLY HEAT	G Gibson, Unseconded
13/10/91	PHYSICAL TRANSACTION	G Gibson, Unseconded
3/5/92	BAGPUS	G Gibson, P Dickinson & P Lockett
3/5/92	ORIGAMI TODAY	G Gibson, Unseconded
3/5/92	WHILST ROME BURNS	G Gibson, Unseconded
16/5/92	DARLING ROSE	G Gibson & A Williams
16/5/92	G.M.B.H.	G Gibson, G Dickinson & P Lockett
16/5/92	POCKET ROCKET	G Gibson, Unseconded
16/5/92	MINNIE MINOR	G Gibson & A Williams
16/5/92	RAYS AND HAIL	G Gibson & A Williams
16/5/92	U GOT ME BUGGED	G Gibson & A Williams
17/5/92	SLIPPERY CARAMEL	G Gibson, Unseconded
17/5/92	A DOSE OF BARLEY FEVER	G Gibson, Unseconded
17/5/92	SOMETIMES YES......	G Gibson, Unseconded
17/5/92	POLYTEXTURED FINISH	G Gibson, Unseconded
18/5/92	BRAINBOX	G Gibson, Unseconded
24/5/92	PLANET CLAIRE	G Gibson, Unseconded
25/5/92	ONE CARLOS	G Gibson, Unseconded
26/5/92	GLORIOUS WOBBLEGONG	G Gibson, Unseconded
17/7/92	PLAY TO KILL	S Williams & A Williams
17/7/92	TOO MANY WOMEN	A Williams & S Williams
22/7/92	SLAP AND TICKLE	G Gibson & H Williams
22/7/92	DYING TONIGHT	G Gibson & H Williams
28/7/92	ORNAMENTAL ART MARK 2	G Gibson, Solo.
29/7/92	EDDIE WARING LIVES ON	G Gibson, P Lockett & G Dickinson
29/7/92	LURKING IN THE LONG GRASS	G Gibson, Unseconded
5/8/92	PRIVATE IDAHO	G Gibson, Unseconded

MONKSHEAD BUTTRESS

GR 222453

This is the obvious undercut bulging buttress on the far side of the stream to the start of Pinfold South buttress. Its routes are characterised by short powerful sequences with good, mainly in situ, protection. They are described from left to right.

*   1. The After Eights   E5 6c   26/5/92
    Short and hard but on perfect rock. Start 8m to the left of the tree. Tackle the widest part of the lower overhang and the very thin wall above. Two bolts and a rock 5 give comfort.

**   2. People Give Me The Eyes   E6 6c   18/5/92
    Sustained, fingery, technical, powerful! Start 3m to the right. Climb the gently leaning wall past 3BRs a flake and a mauling finale. Move right to the tree for a mode of descent.

**   3. Yankee Doodle Dandy   E6 6b   8/9/91
    The direct line to the tree, the crux area being based around the 2BRs. A rock 7 protects the start.

**   4. I Feel Like a Wog   E5 6c   8/9/91
    Start 2m right again. Move up, BR, and make grotesque moves left past a second BR to a jug, BR. Grope direct around the final bulge, PR.

    5. Yoyoyoyo   E3 6a   8/9/91
    Gain the flake 5m to the right via a difficult wall, BR, and climb it, TR, PR and friends to the top.

The next four routes, whilst on flawless rock, do suffer from seepage and bolt theft! An unfortunate occurrence, though they may have been replaced by the time you read this..

*   6. Golly Gee   E4 6b   1/9/91
    Gain and climb the first shallow groove 3m right of Yoyoyoyo past a PR high up.

*   7. Golly Gosh   E2 6a   1/9/91
    The next and more obvious shallow groove, PR high up provides a difficult entry.

* 8.   Indian Summer   E4 6b   1/9/91
  Climb the flaky wall 3m right to gain a rib, BR, and a tricky leftwards exit.

* 9.   Golly Wog   E4 6a   8/9/91
  Just to the right a thin crack splits the upper wall. Gain it direct via a bulge,
  PR.

* 10. Swiss Drum Roll   E5 6b   8/9/91
  The Final route of the wall 2m to the right and no seepage problems.

FIRST ASCENTS

1/9/91	INDIAN SUMMER	G Gibson
1/9/91	GOLLY GEE	D Kerr & G Gibson
1/9/91	GOLLY GOSH	D Kerr & G Gibson
8/9/91	GOLLY WOG	D Kerr & G Gibson

On all of the last four routes the bolt hangers were stolen by some
unknown person. All the routes were climbed without the bolts by
G Gibson on 26/5/92, solo.

8/9/91	YOYOYOYO	D Kerr & G Gibson
8/9/91	YANKEE DOODLE DANDY	G Gibson & D Kerr
8/9/91	SWISS DRUM ROLL	G Gibson, Solo
8/9/91	I FEEL LIKE A WOG	G Gibson, Solo

A route name reference to the feelings of being outcast from the
climbing world by the first ascensionist. This name became more
pertinent when all the bolt hangers were stolen in 1992.

18/5/92	PEOPLE GIVE ME THE EYES	G Gibson, Solo
26/5/92	THE AFTER EIGHTS	G Gibson, Solo

A route name reference more to the colour of the chocolate?

MONKS BUTTRESS

GR 220452

by Gary Gibson

SITUATION AND ACCESS

This imposing crag, so named for its silhouette appearance of a Monk when viewed from the approach path, stands proudly overlooking the parking place for the Pinfold cliffs. Its trio of tiers, largely undistinguishable from below, appear as one mass giving this excellent cliff a fortress-like stature.

This is an underrated and unpopular cliff with a surprisingly unusual and extremely pleasant character. The nature of the rock, a fretted and pocketed weathered limestone, is unique to the area and coupled with numerous excellent routes and magnificent airy positions make this a highly recommendable venue. It takes very little seepage in comparison to its neighbouring cliffs, dries relatively quickly and only receives the late afternoon or evening sunshine. This latter fact is an advantage for a hot summer's day or evening visit.

Whilst Monks Buttress is composed of three tiers it is only the top two which are of interest to the climber. In some instances a second pitch on the upper tier merits attention and proves consistent with its lower counterpart and is therefore described. In the higher grades this is not necessarily the case. Naturally where desired a climber can pick a suitable line at will. The layout of this barrel-shaped buttress is relatively simple yet not all of its major landmarks are easily identified from below on first acquaintance. There are two gullies, one at each end of the cliff, both providing a convenient means off the face. The main central section in between these gullies has a yellowy lichenous colour, often glowing in an evening sunset. Above this section sits a prominent single tree, again a useful means of descent for the routes arriving in its near vicinity. This area is bounded to the left by the striking zigzag crack taken by the route Beryl. Further to the right twin corners, the left-hand capped by a block overhang and to the right-hand split by a clean crack (Jibber), can be seen. The final obvious feature lies to the right of the right-hand descent gully, a slightly undercut buttress flanked by a compact wall to the right as the cliff face fizzles out; the Forgotten Buttress and Miners Wall.

The main parking space is the layby as used for the Pinfold cliffs. The best approach is then via the path up the stream bed to Pinfold South buttress and then by skirting the relatively small tier to the right of Monkshead buttress to gain the crag - a direct approach up the scree slope may seem appealing but will prove time-consuming and very tiring as well as make you unpopular with the local farmers. An alternative approach can be made by a very pleasant five minute walk across the grassy slopes from the northern end of the Alison walls of Dinbren.

The climbs are described from left to right in relation to the normal approach to the cliff from Pinfold South buttress. When approaching from Dinbren all the salient landmarks prove obvious.

1. Lucy   Very Severe, 4c   17/7/80
An unstable crack 2m left of the ash tree.

2. Wriggle Gully   Severe   1969-77
The gully above a prominent whitebeam tree 6m to the right.

*   3. Black Moments   E4 6b   4/5/92
A little gem from a small ledge at 3m just to the right, TR, climb a thin flakepulling out left, BR, into a recess - a long stretch. Finish direct and left of a tree.

4. Mainly for Pleasure   E2 5b   29/6/80
Devious but pleasant. Move rightwards up the blackened wall from the TR on Black Moments until it is possible to grasp left for the tree at the top.

To the right lies a small prominent buttress.

*   5. The Rebel   Very Severe, 4c   29/6/80
The prominent corner and flake crack on the left-hand side of the buttress. Strenuous but with good protection and the occasional hollow hold.

*   6. Sombre Music   E5 6b   15/5/92
Tackle the front face of the buttress via a thin flake, PR, to pass an overlap, BR, and short problematic headwall. Technical and fingery on good rock.

7. Second Chance   E1 5b   1/6/78
The steep and insecure crack 2m to the right, starting via a small corner.

8. Suspended Animation   E1 5b   9/9/85
Very enjoyable climbing up the thin flakes in the slender wall to the right. Finish past a small tree.

9. Grand Laddie   Very Difficult   1969-77
The obvious, and not so grand, cavernous chimney.

10. Amoco Cadiz   Hard Very Severe, 4c   17/3/81
Another unsound affair up the groove 2m right of Grand Laddie.

11. Only a Gesture   E1 5a   28/5/80
Pleasant. Reach a clean slabby groove 5m right again via a bulge and pull out right above a second bulge to gain the top. Escaping left beforehand is easier but spoils the continuity of the route.

The next obvious feature is a gully marking the line of:

12. Topology   Very Difficult   1969-77
Climb the gully containing a crack, with a yew tree to its left.

*   13. Cotteril's Found Another Toe   E5 6c   15/5/88
The black wall to the right of Topology. Mean. Make a long reach to clip a PR and then make an intense sequence of moves up the wall to its right past a BR to reach a thin crack, PR. Continue more easily to a BB.

14. Façade   E2 5b   24/5/80
From a small cave to the right exit leftwards to gain a steep but less troublesome crack.

**   15. Pierrepoint Pressure   E6 6b   15/5/92
A significant test-piece with a desperate, powerful crux sequence. Enter the hanging "cwm" 3m right of Façade by unobvious moves, 2BRs, to gain a good hold, BR, then move right to gain a respite below the arête, BR. Climb this past a final BR exiting leftwards to good holds and the top. Low in the grade.

*   16. The Hype   Hard Very Severe   16/8/77
An interesting route with a worthwhile top pitch. Start around the corner to the right just below and right of large ash and yew trees.
1) 15m. 5a. Climb an awkward thin crack to gain a slab. Continue up this and a steep crack in the wall to belay below an obvious corner above the terrace.
2) 15m. 5a. Move right for 5m and pull over the roof to gain a fine finishing groove.

17. Beryl   Very Severe   1969
1) 15m. 4b. Climb the obvious zigzag crack to the terrace. Belay below a steep continuation crack.
2) 10m. 4c. The corner.

The next dozen or so routes have only their lower pitches described since upper pitches are somewhat easier and out of character.

18. Tamsin   E3 6a   2/2/85
The first feature on this wall to the right is a shallow groove. Enter the
groove from the left, PR, and bridge up it before transferring right with
difficulty to reach a prominent flake. Use this to gain the terrace.

19. The Race Is On   E3 6a   10/2/84
Start 5m to the right of Tamsin. A tricky pull and step left leads to a TR.
Climb the thin flake above to a ledge, TR, and finish direct up the flake.

* 20. Catch Me If You Can   E4 6a   18/1/92
A good direct pitch with more sustained than overly technical climbing.
Start between The Race Is On and the beginning of a prominent diagonal
break. Pull up to and over a bulge to a thin crack itself leading to a small
ledge. Step up and right, over to a flake jug and continue via a tiny groove
exiting right to the terrace.

* 21. Sir Cathcart D'Eath   E3 6a   4/5/81
The original route of the wall, whilst somewhat overshadowed by its
neighbours, still proves worthwhile in its lower reaches. Follow the
diagonal break, TR, PR, to a small flake ledge. With good wires above exit
leftwards across a ramp to a flake and the terrace above.

*** 22. Screaming Lord Sutch   E5 6b   20/4/92
A superb pitch with sustained, technical and well protected climbing; the
route of the buttress. From the small flake ledge on Cathcart D'Eath, pull
straight up the wall above, BR and crux, to gain a slim bottomless groove.
Excellent climbing up this, PR, TR, lead to a terrace. Abseil from a large
tree on the right.

*** 23. Another Red Line   E4 6a   11/2/84
Another immaculate pitch providing the original and easier start to the
upper groove of Screaming Lord Sutch. Start 3m to the right and climb
short impending wall, 3TRs, to a bucket and easier ground. Move up the
arête on the left to a TR, then swing left in to the groove and follow it, PR
and TR, to the terrace.

24. Vladimir And Olga   E3 5c   12/2/84
The large depression to the right supports a tricky entry via a thin crack.
Move easily up to an overlap then pull out right to a subsidiary groove and
a tree above. A direct finish is loose and not recommended.

** 25. Iceburn   E5 6a   25/2/84
A hidden gem giving "Fiery" climbing up the innocuous hanging groove in

the right arête of the depression. Climb the vague arête right of Vladimir And Olga via a pinch grip, bold, to gain a groove. Tackle this, PR, and a bulge above, 2TRs, to gain a tree.

* **26. Up The Veil** E4 6b 20/4/92
The centre of the short, gently leaning wall to the right, 2BRs, gains a hanging groove. Climb the easy groove to the terrace.

27. The Mantilla   E3 5c 4c   14/8/81
A strenuous little pitch. Climb the steep crack to the right and pull out left
to a ledge left of a dead tree. Pull out right from a short corner above,
awkward, to easier climbing and the terrace. Walk left to a tree for a
convenient descent.

To the right a large whitebeam tree at 8m gives a focal point for the next two
routes.

28. Adam's Mistake   E3 5c   3/4/84
Gain the tree by a shallow groove right of The Mantilla. Enter the scoop
behind and exit it leftwards from a TR. Abseil from the tree over to the left.

* 29. Post Mortem Of A Football Team E3 6a   3/4/84
From the whitebeam tree step right and climb the excellent smooth-
looking wall above, BR, over a tiny bulge to a finishing crack.

30. Kinsman   Hard Severe   1969-77
Start 3m to the right of Post Mortem...
1) Climb easily up into the corner at 8m and follow the cracks above to
the terrace. Walk left along this to a tree belay where the overhangs end.
2) Climb the broken groove with a yew tree in it.

* 31. Cat In A Rat Trap   E4 6a   25/2/84
A fine varied pitch with a difficult upper section. Start 5m to the right of
Kinsmen below a black slab (sometimes wet). Climb easily up the slab until
trickier moves, TR, lead to an overhung break. Swing right and up into a
hanging yellow groove and teeter up this, PR, to reach good holds and a
tree on the right.

32. The Evader   Very Severe   28/5/80
A pleasant meandering route. Start 3m right again below a hanging block
overhang just left of the overhanging corner crack (Jibber).
1) 20m 4c. Follow a crack to a block overhang, TR, and then traverse the
wall on the left slightly downwards and then up to some twin cracks. Climb
these moving right to the top. Belay on a prominent yew tree.
2) 10m 4c. A short undercut layback crack leads past a tree to the top.

** 33. Life   E3 5c   18/9/79
Another varied and worthwhile outing with good positions. Gain the block
overhang as for Evader, PR, and pull through to the main overhang, PR.
Stride right onto the yellow wall and pull up to gain a groove and small
ledge. Stand up on this to gain a convenient tree on the left.

** 34. Edgeley   E5 6b   20/4/92
The brilliant overhanging arête to the right. From 5m up Life take a thin
crack to its conclusion the step right to below the arête proper. A powerful
sequence, PR, gains a small flake, BR, from where further extending
moves lead up to a thin crack and ledge. The tree on the left provides a
means of descent.

** 35. Jibber   E1 5b   13/4/80
A classic pitch, typical of its genre. Climb the overhanging corner, copious protection, to a belay on the terrace. Walk off to the right or finish direct up a crack via a clump of trees.

** 36. Breaking The Reality Effect   E3 6a   11/2/84
An impeccable route up the striking slabby arête. Move up onto it from the right and use a thin crack and holds to its right, TR, to gain easier ground (the original route came in from the right here after starting up the obvious unstable flake). Move up the slab to a PR then using the arête move tentatively up on small holds to a tree on the right. Either descend from this or belay at the terrace and walk off to the right.

37. Ginger Crack   Hard Very Severe, 5a   3/4/80
The loose crack above a small corner just to the right. A bulge provides a difficult but well protected crux.

38. Malevolence   Very Severe, 4c   4/4/80
The next crack to the right gains a whitebeam tree. Finish up the wall above.

39. Madonna Kebab   E1 5b   1984
Climb the slightly undercut wall right of Malevolence, TR, to semi-cleaned ledge and a tree. Finish up a faint crack in the headwall.

40. Scatological   Severe   1969-77
A dirty gully and crack right of a holly tree.

41. Smooth Hands   Severe   25/4/80
Climb a crack and left-trending overlap above a whitebeam tree right again.

* 42. Desperado   E5 6a   8/4/80
Brilliant rock on the boundary of the wall. From the tree on Smooth Hands pull up onto the "bubbly" wall and climb it, serious, to a small corner and relief. Short, excellent and exciting, an impressive lead for its day.

43. Little Deal   Hard Severe   1969-77
The two right-hand cracks of three right of Desperado. From a dead tree finish up a groove above. Loose.

To the right of Little Deal the crag deteriorates into a gully (suitable for descent) before the final buttresses rear up. The first worthwhile face has an undercut central section with two obvious grooves on its left-hand side:

THE FORGOTTEN BUTTRESS

44. Cloven Hoof   E1 5b   15/5/81
A gymnastic pull over the bulge gains the left-hand groove.

45. Codify   Very Severe, 4c   15/5/81
Climb the pleasant right-hand groove.

** **46. Memorable Strains**   E5 6b   15/5/92
The aesthetic arête of the buttress: very photogenic. Pull over the bulge right of the arête, TR, and make intricate fingery moves up a sinuous crack to gain an undercut block, small wire protection. Stand up and finish more easily via a wider crack in the arête itself.

* **47. Gigolo**   E2 5c   17/4/81
Another good route. From the horizontal tree just right of Memorable Strains continue up the crack behind past a second tree to the top. A better but slightly harder alternative climbs the thin crack just to the left.

48. Thick As A Brick   E2 5b   17/4/81
Awkward climbing up the next crack to the right gains an overhang. Finish up the crack to the left.

The walls to the right now begin to diminish in size. Numerous possibilities exist and have been done but only the best are worthy of further description. 40m to the right the series of smaller walls improve after a clump of trees masking the face. This compact area of wall has been named Miners Wall.

49. As Monk As A Skunk   E1 5b   31/8/87
The centre of first quaint little wall encountered, obvious by a wide break close top the top.

50. Coal Not Dole   E1 5b   Aut. 1984
The centre of the wall 10m to the right and just left of a small tree, PR.

51. Dig Deep   Hard Very Severe, 5a   Aut. 1984
The right-hand of two cracks in the final significant section of face. Finish via a capping overhang.

52. Curly Bit   Hard Very Severe, 5a   2/2/84
A shallow groove and nose right again.

FIRST ASCENTS

1969	BERYL	T Williams & J O Niel
1969-77	WRIGGLE GULLY	Unknown
1969-77	GRAND LADDIE	Unknown
1969-77	TOPOLOGY	Unknown
1969-77	KINSMAN	Unknown
1969-77	SCATOLOGICAL	Unknown
1969-77	LITTLE DEAL	Unknown
16/8/77	THE HYPE	S M Cathcart & G N Swindley
1/6/78	SECOND CHANCE	S M Cathcart & M Hughes
18/9/79	LIFE	S M Cathcart & M Hughes
3/4/80	GINGER CRACK	S M Cathcart, Solo
4/4/80	MALEVOLENCE	S M Cathcart, Solo
8/4/80	DESPERADO	S M Cathcart, Solo

A brave and bold event especially considering the lonely nature of these cliffs. An impressive effort.

13/4/80	JIBBERS	M Cathcart, Solo
25/4/80	FAÇADE	S M Cathcart & M Cameron
25/4/80	SMOOTH HANDS	S M Cathcart & M Cameron
28/5/80	THE EVADER	S M Cathcart & F R Bennett
28/5/80	ONLY A GESTURE	S M Cathcart & F R Bennett
29/6/80	THE REBEL	S M Cathcart, Solo
29/6/80	MAINLY FOR PLEASURE	S M Cathcart, Solo
17/7/80	LUCY	S M Cathcart, Solo
30/7/80	REALITY EFFECT	S M Cathcart & M Cameron

Later climbed by the more obvious direct line up the arête by G Gibson on 11/2/84.

17/3/81	AMOCO CADIZ	S M Cathcart & M Cameron
17/4/81	GIGOLO	S M Cathcart & J Dee
17/4/81	THICK AS A BRICK	S M Cathcart & J Dee
4/5/81	SIR CATHCART D'EATH	S M Cathcart & J Dee

Rated very highly by Cathcart but later dismantled by other suitors.

15/5/81	CLOVEN HOOF	S M Cathcart, Solo
15/5/81	CODIFY	S M Cathcart, Solo
14/8/81	THE MANTILLA	S M Cathcart & J Dee
2/2/84	CURLY BIT	D Kerr & P Evans
10/2/84	THE RACE IS ON	J Moulding, Solo

A reference by Moulding to the healthy competition around at the time - a line cleaned by Gibson and stolen after similar circumstances two weeks earlier on Dinbren.

11/2/84	ANOTHER RED LINE	G Gibson, Unseconded

Retaliation sought very abruptly by Gibson.

11/2/84	BREAKING THE REALITY EFFECT	G Gibson, Unseconded

The obvious start to Reality.

12/2/84	VLADIMIR & OLGA	G Gibson & A Hudson
25/2/84	ICEBURN	G Gibson, Unseconded
25/2/84	CAT IN A RAT TRAP	G Gibson, Unseconded
	Obvious new start climbed by Gibson in May 92	
3/4/84	ADAM'S MISTAKE	G Gibson, Unseconded
3/4/84	POST MORTEM OF.......	G Gibson, Unseconded
	Reference to Gibsons Favourite football team being relegated.	
Aut. 84	COAL NOT DOLE	S Cardy & M Snell
Aut. 84	DIG DEEP	P Harrison & S Cardy
1984	MADONNA KEBAB	S Whalley & L Taylor
	Named sometime later after an ascent by P Harrison.	
2/2/85	TAMSIN	D Kerr & P Evans
9/9/85	SUSPENDED ANIMATION	D Kerr & S Wilkie
31/8/87	AS MONK AS A SKUNK	I Dunn, Solo
15/5/88	COTTERIL'S FOUND	G Gibson, Unseconded
18/1/92	CATCH ME IF YOU CAN	G Gibson, D Kerr
20/4/92	SCREAMING LORD SUTCH	G Gibson, Unseconded
20/4/92	UP THE VEIL	G Gibson, Unseconded
	The same team relegated again! (see before)	
20/4/92	EDGELEY	G Gibson, Unseconded
	Activity rekindled with three top class routes.	
4/5/92	BLACK MOMENTS	G Gibson, Unseconded
	A thunderstorm erupted during the crux sequence!	
15/5/92	SOMBRE MUSIC	G Gibson, Unseconded
15/5/92	MEMORABLE STRAINS	G Gibson, Unseconded
15/5/92	PIERREPOINT PRESSURE	G Gibson, Unseconded
	A superb spell of activity completed, hence the "stranglehold" name.	

DINBREN CRAGS

O.S. Map 117 GR 220446 & 221445

by J Moulding

CHARACTER AND SITUATION

Dinbren is perhaps the most congenial crag in the Eglwyseg Valley, if not in the guidebook, having an open aspect and rock that is generally good to excellent. The climbs include some of the best and hardest in the area, spanning the grades from Very Difficult to E7 although, as is common with mountain limestone, there is a preponderance of harder routes, particularly on the left wing.

Because of their westerly exposure, the cliffs dry quickly after rain apart from a few stubborn seepage lines. The same prevailing westerlies can freeze the place in winter, though with luck and a north-east wind it is sometimes possible to climb shirtless on some of the frostiest winter days (if you're daft enough). The left wing gets the sun from mid-morning onwards, the right wing from early afternoon.

There are a substantial number of sport routes in the upper grades, though not all have been equipped with convenient lower off points. It is worthwhile carrying a set of wires and a few friends unless the descriptions specifically indicate otherwise. At a few salient points there are bombproof iron belay stakes about a metre in length.

APPROACH AND ACCESS

The approach from the westbound A5 in Llangollen is as follows: turn right at the main traffic lights and cross the River Dee bridge to a T-junction. Turn right then immediately left to follow the road over the canal and turn left onto Dinbren Road. After another 1km, Dinbren Crags come into view ahead. Turn right at the next T-junction (signposted to Panorama) and go about 100m, passing a cattle grid, to a possible parking place on the left. Parking is possible for a few cars below the crag at a passing place and at a nearby grassy patch, but be thoughtful about it. The approach path leads up from the bottom of the shallow valley through a cluster of trees.

The main cliff at Dinbren is divided into left and right wings by the appropriately named chimney of Soap, a distinctive feature immediately opposite the usual place of arrival. This is the starting point for route descriptions on both sections of the cliff, so the left wing routes are described from right to left. Below each main wing is a smaller escarpment, designated the middle tier. There are lower tiers as well, but the problems of poor rock are compounded by the difficulty of belaying on the scree slopes above.

151

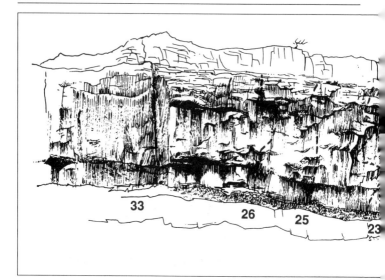

A pair of kestrels nest every year on the Left Wing, either between Silent Spirit and El Loco, or between Dr. Gonzo and The Fog. During the period April 1st to June 30th, please restrict climbing to routes at least 50m from this area.

THE LEFT WING

The principal features of the left wing are the bay from which Yale and Swansong start, the smooth pocketed wall left of Alison, the long ivy covered roof, and the chimney at the left-hand end.

1. Soap   Very Difficult   1962
The chimney in the corner, with a detour left at one third height. It can be (and is) used as a descent route, but the top section is surprisingly awkward to reverse.

2. Amadeus   Hard Very Severe, 4c   15/3/78
The unappealing broken crack just left of Soap. Serious.

3. Ice On The Motorway   E5   14/6/87
A pleasant girdle of the Fire and Ice walls starting 2m left of Soap.
1) 10m. 6a. Climb the thin wall to a break and traverse left to a belay in the deep V groove.

18 13 **DINBREN LEFT WING 1**

2) 20m. 6a. Continue left at the same height to a BR and a variety of small wires, then move slightly up to a PR. Swing down leftwards into a scoop below the bulge of Baby Crusher and a BR. Strenuous moves left lead via a long reach to a hanging groove. Finish up this.

4. Silly Games   E5 6b   22/5/88
Start just right of the large recess 6m left of Soap. Climb straight up the wall, passing two BRs and a prominent undercut.

5. Hot Stuff   E4 6a   11/4/88
Short and sweet. Start in the recess just left of Silly Games. Pull over the roof and follow a line of sideholds up the bulging wall past two BRs to gain and finish up a deep groove.

** 6. Ice   E5 6b   23/8/86
An excellent and popular route, mostly well protected. Start beneath a large yew tree. Powerful moves gain and pass the first BR to a large undercut, BR. Move slightly right and up to a hidden jug over the bulge. Pass the third bolt to better holds (good small wire) and finish more easily up the groove.

** 7. Fire   E5 6b   22/9/84

An equally good and difficult companion route to Ice. Follow Ice to the second BR, then move left, BR, and up via a tricky blind move to reach a thin crack. Climb the crack and groove to the top, then lower off the convenient horizontal branch.

* 8. Explosive Fibres   E5 6b   6/88

Similar in character to Fire and Ice, but not quite as fine. Climb to the third bolt on Ice and move left with difficulty to reach a thin crack. Finish up this.

* 9. The Planet   E5 6c   29/2/92

A difficult sequence up the wall between Fire/Ice and Fat Boys. Follow a line of 3BRs up the wall with the crux early on until blind moves high up gain a scoop. Reach holds above this before moving left to a BB.

* 10. Fat Boys   E5 6b   14/5/88

Similar in character and appearance to its neighbour, but considerably easier. Start midway between the Fire/Ice entry and a deep, roofed recess. Continuously difficult moves lead past three BRs until a PR marks an end to the difficulties. Lower off.

Left of Fat Boys is a 10 metre undercut section, bounded by the corner of Hyperdrive at its left-hand end.

* 11. Baby Crusher   E6 6b   31/5/87

Interesting and strenuous: carry a few small wires. Start 3m right of Hyperdrive at an overhanging crack. Clip a BR on the left, then move upwards and right on undercuts and pinches to an overhung block ledge and the second BR. Work into the scoop above and right, BR, to finish up the steep crack.

12. Bolt The Blue Sky   E5 6c   31/5/87

Notable for a single fierce move, which anyone from Yorkshire should be able to do statically. Start as for Baby Crusher. Undercut left to a second BR, then either leap wildly or crank effortlessly for good jugs above. Finish up the groove on the right.

** 13. Hyperdrive   E3 6a   28/8/79

The obvious steep, smooth corner. Start 2m left of the corner itself. Climb the crack to a good runner at 3m and traverse right with increasing difficulty to the corner and a PR. Ascend the corner to the bulge, PR, then either finish direct or move out right, which is considerably easier. The corner can be entered direct, increasing the grade to E4 6a.

*   14. A Different Kind of Hypertension   E3 5c   25/2/84
Very enjoyable, with a slightly scary start. Climb the thin crack 2m left of
the Hyperdrive corner to a bulge and situ wire. Step right and pull back left
into a shallow groove, TR, finishing rightwards.

*   15. Big Mouth Strikes Again   E4 6b   24/4/88
A few metres left of Hyperdrive is a wandering line with one tricky reach.
Climb boldly up and right to reach a runner placement in a flake. Make a
long stretch past a BR to ripples over the bulge, gain the recess and finish
slightly rightwards.

16. So Lucky   E3 6a   25/2/84
"Gnarly". Boulder out the crumbly wall below the big yew tree to an
undercut flake. Continue to the tree then move left to a blunt arête, PR, and
finish up it.

**   17. Melody   E4 6a   19/2/84
A pleasant line taking the blunt arête to the right of the square cut bay.
Climb the wall just right of the thin crack on small holds for about 4m. Swing
boldly right and up to a hidden hold, then back left to a short crack and good
runners. Continue up the thought-provoking arête, passing a PR, to the
dead tree. Lower off.

18. Yale   Hard Very Severe, 5a   15/3/78
The right-hand corner of the square bay. Reasonably protected, with
some unsound rock near the top.

19. Swansong   E2 6a   16/6/79
The disintegrating left-hand corner of the bay, with a frustrating start.

20. Where's The Presidents Brain? E3 5c   3/6/84
Loose and badly protected, clearly a classic of the crag. Follow the
rightward slanting flake line 2m left of Swansong to a thin crack and PR,
where the moves get harder but thankfully safer. Finish more easily.

21. Resist and Exist   E3 5c   18/11/84
Nearly as good as Where's The President's Brain, starting at the same
point. Move diagonally left onto "good" holds and climb the face via a slight
weakness to finish at the whitebeam tree.

22. Silent Spirit   Hard Very Severe 5a   15/3/78
Left of the square cut bay is a large yew tree growing a short way up the
broken wall. Scramble to the tree and pass it on the right to gain a steep
ramp. Climb this and the wall above to a whitebeam tree and the top.

*   23. El Loco   E4 6a   15/2/84
The wall and crack left of the yew tree give interesting and varied climbing with plenty of crater potential! Step off the broken flake and hand traverse nervously left to an obvious inverted pocket; brisk moves up gain a respite and the first proper runners at the foot of the crack. Struggle up this to a BR below a bulge, then launch up and left past a PR to finish direct.

*   24. Going Loco   E6 6b   4/89
A circuitous and exacting line up the wall left of El Loco, with some very technical moves. Follow El Loco to the foot of the crack before making an increasingly difficult traverse left to a BR. Move up to a good sidepull, BR, then improvise up to undercut flakes on Rhiannon. Finish more easily up and rightwards.

**   25. The Orgasmatron   E5 6b (1 pt. aid)   26/8/86
A very fine route starting from the recess about 5m left of El Loco, below a bolt. Use the bolt (or free Dinbren's first 7a move) to gain the obvious line of weakness. Follow this past a PR and TR to a rest on Rhiannon, before groping blindly right over the bulge for a memorable finale.

**   26. The Rivals   E6 6c   3/8/89
A good route up the steep wall below the roof. Start just right of a thorn bush growing out of a recess a few metres left of The Orgasmatron. Gain a good finger pocket and BR in the streaked bulge, then make some mean slaps to reach a sharp pocket, BR. Up and right is a hidden fingerhold, TR, which gives access to the jugs above. Follow the pleasant groove to the roof and step left to reach a small but stout yew tree. Lower off.

**   27. The Bandits   E7 6b   13/6/88
A powerful and sustained line at the lower limit of it's grade. Start below a drilled TR just left of Rivals. Using sidepulls and undercuts, pass the first BR and hopefully reach the second at a small undercut. Take a deep breath and overcome the fierce wall to snatch a poor rest by the third BR. Wrestle briefly with more good undercuts before finishing up the "easy" crack above, which holds perfect placements for a Friend 2 and Rock 4. Lower off a BB.

Walking left past the roof, the next obvious feature is the open corner of Alison. The area of excellent pocketed rock left of Alison is usually referred to as the Climb High wall. A belay stake above the right-hand side of the wall can be used for most of the routes on and around it.

** 28. Hot Lips   E4 6a   Spr. 84
A varied route with some spectacular situations, hard for the grade. Start
at the base of the big corner. Bridge inventively up the right wall past an
upside down but sound PR to a thin crack and good runners. Traverse
strenuously right past two TRs to a bombproof wire placement on the
arête, then before strength wanes, crank up and right to a no-hands rest
in the lichenous niche below the roof. After a suitable respite, swing out
right to an obvious jug near the lip of the overhang and go for the extremely
dead tree teetering above.

** 29. Rhiannon   E5   5/85
A superb and exciting girdle above the overhangs to the right of Alison.
Possibly the best route on the crag. A few small to medium Friends might
come in useful.
1) 10m. 6a. As for Hot Lips to a stance in the niche below the roof.
2) 12m. 6a. Follow the line of jugs and undercuts to where they fade;
move down awkwardly below a wire slot to an undercut flake line and
follow it and the continuation wall with fading strength to land in a
capacious scoop. Bolt and nut belay.
3) 12m. 6a. After moving right for 2m, step down from a good flake crack
and traverse under the bulge of The Orgasmatron, TR, to easier ground.
Balance right to finish up El Loco.

* 30. Gemma's World Direct   E4 6a   1/4/84
The steep start leads to milder climbing. Follow Hot Lips to the second TR,
then escape the difficulties via a harsh move up to good holds. Follow a
rounded crack system to a slightly loose finish. Belay on the iron spike
above the top of corner.

31. Gemma's World   E3 5c   26/4/80
A pleasant route starting 2m left of the corner. Climb direct to a big flake
at 4m then traverse into the corner (good runners). After a few moves up
the corner, move right with difficulty to good holds near the arête and
ascend the cracks above.

32. Locomotion   E5 6b   15/5/88
Start just right of Gemma's World Direct. Clip the obvious BR from the left,
then from below the roof power through via a series of jugs to a standing
position on the arête, avoiding good holds on the right. Easier climbing
leads out right above the roof to the top.

* 33. Alison   E1 5b   12/5/80
Pleasant climbing, although sometimes a bit vegetated. Follow Gemma's

World as far as the runners in the main corner, then climb it direct, carefully avoiding the vegetation. Belay on the big iron spike 5m back. It is possible to boulder out a direct start at 6a which shares most of its holds with Hot Lips.

** 34. Dreadlocks   E5 6b   16/12/83
An unrelenting string of boulder problems up the pocketed wall just left of Alison. It may be worth the potential leader's while to do Climb High first, to unlock the secret of the notorious mantleshelf move shared by both routes. Follow Alison to the big flake at 4m and then step delicately up and left to a sloping ledge and BR. Thin moves up right lead to another sloping foothold and BR. Move up a little to a leftward finger traverse which is followed past a high, rounded hold to the third BR. Using all means available (except the bolt!) stand up on the hold to reach a flake crack. Finish thoughtfully through the sinuous bulges.

*** 35. Climb High   E4 6b   9/83
The original and classic line taking the centre of the smooth wall, starting at the weakness 4m left of the corner. Go up to good ledges, left a couple of metres, then up a compact wall to a PR. Step awkwardly right into the shallow groove, BR, and climb it to good layaway holds below a rounded shelf, BR. High on the right is a smooth, rounded hold. Standing on it to reach a good flake above constitutes the crux. The most commonly used technique seems to involve dangling from the top bolt for 15 minutes until inspiration arrives. Load the crack with small wires and finish boldly straight through the bulges.

*** 36. Traction Trauma   E4 6a   3/12/83
A superb, bold problem up the left-hand side of the wall. Follow Climb High to the PR, then move left onto a faint rib and up to a BR, a hair-raising clip. Elegant, fingery moves past this gain a jug on the left and a gentler finish past a good ledge.

** 37. In Search Of Someone Silly   E5 6b   7/1/84
A fingery exercise with an unfortunately avoidable crux. Start 2m left of Climb High below a thin TR. Pass this leftwards and go via a second TR to a BR on a small slab. Trying not to detour to the right, make precarious moves direct to the base of a thin crack system which culminates in a good wire placement. To the left, a line of jugs beckons tantalisingly. Somehow reach and finish up them to a BB.

* 38. Walking With Barrence   E6 6c   8/87
A good route, making the most of the wall between In Search Of Someone

Silly and Technicolour Yawn, starting at a faint leftward leaning groove. Cruise the groove to good holds, a PR and BR. Tough moves right lead to an inhospitably overhanging groove and a second BR below a good flake. A determined reach from this will attain the jugs and easy finish of In Search....BB.

*** 39. Technicolour Yawn   E5 6a   Aut. 84
Safe, strenuous and somewhat baffling; quick thinking is prerequisite to an ascent in good style. It takes the right-hand of two lines of weakness rising, from the recess 10m left of Alison. Fire up the initial bulge past a BR to a none-rest and the second BR. Conquer the unlikely wall above via layaways and pinches to arrive at a PR and good incuts below the crack. Skirting stray dandelions, zip up the crack and lower off the BB.

* 40. I Punched Judy First   E6 6b   8/7/87
The line just left of Technicolour Yawn imparts an ugly struggle. Crank the overhang past a protruding PR and deteriorating holds to a BR above a line of undercuts. Use a layaway to snatch the downward pointing flake on the left, then a stretch from a sharp incut gains a good pocket and TR. Enter the innocuous looking crack, deal with it imperturbably and belay well back.

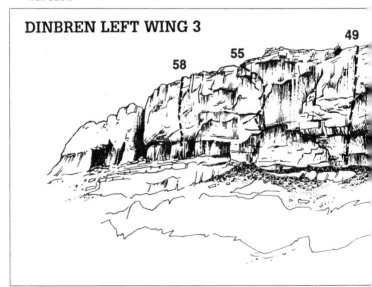

DINBREN LEFT WING 3

49

55

58

**   41. Broken Dreams   E6 6c   14/5/88
An excellent excursion, taking the line of least resistance up a smooth streaked wall. Start just right of a rose bush in the second recess left of Alison. Contrive a sequence past three BRs to good holds in a flake line. Follow the flake rightwards to a PR, then up to a TR and well deserved rest. Romp across the roof on good holds for an exhilarating finish.

**   42. Flowers Are For The Dead   E6 6c   21/5/88
A rather featureless line with a reachy start 4m left of Broken Dreams. Fight up the wall rightwards past two BRs to a good flake hold over a bulge, BR. Swing out right and climb the thin crack past a BR and small overhang to the top.

   43. Cookie King   E4 6b   5/85
Problematic. Start at the third recess left of Alison, below a bulging ramp with a PR. Clip the peg and struggle into the scoop. Surmount the steepening past another PR then move right and back left to finish up a crack in the overlap.

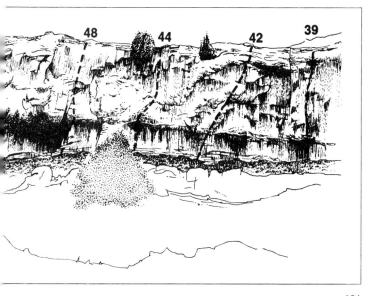

44. Kamikaze Clone   E4 6b   29/4/84
An unappealing route with a painful crux. Start 5m left of Cookie King from
a small recess with TRs in the roof. A rightward traverse past an apology
for a BR and a nasty fingerlock leads to better holds. Pull up to a PR then
trend right up a slabby wall to a delicate finishing groove.

45. Cold Turkey   E4 6b   25/12/86
Pleasant climbing in the upper section is marred by an unsound start. 4m
left of Kamikaze Clone is a recess, start just right. Cross the rotten initial
bulge rightwards to a good incut. Continue direct to a line of thin undercuts
and take the top overhang direct to finish. 3 BRs.

46. The Dinbren Sanction   E4 6a   5/85
The overhanging groove 4m right of the huge ivy covered roof requires a
fearless leader. Ascend the groove direct, moving slightly left at half
height.

* **47. Lullaby**   E5 6b   7/89
An agreeable little route starting just left of The Dinbren Sanction. Climb
the bulge and wall leftwards, BR, to gain an arched crack. Finish direct
through the bulge above.

48. Dr. Gonzo   E3 6a   13/12/83
A distinctive and reasonably protected line taking the weakness at the
right-hand end of the ivy covered roof. Pass three TRs and a hard move
at the lip to gain the wall and faint groove above.

Left of Dr. Gonzo is the expanse of rock referred to as The Ivy Roof.

** **49. The Fog**   E6 6c   5/85
The ferocious overhanging weakness at the left end of the Ivy Roof offers
an intimidating challenge. The stunted yew tree provides less support than
might be hoped, and the holds steadily diminish in usefulness as height
is gained. The TR and two PRs are scant consolation, but the overlap at
half height conceals good holds and bombproof runners. Finish easily past
the whitebeam sapling.

*** **50. Misty Vision**   E6 6c   30/5/85
Even more fun - The Fog plus added value and quality! Zoom up The Fog
to the good holds at the overlap and a shake out of sorts. Undercling the
break rightwards until below a second TR, then launch optimistically up
the headwall to fame, if not fortune.

51. Fine Feathered Fink   E6 6b   21/5/88
A difficult route 2m left of The Fog. Climb past a BR to a layaway, below and left of the second BR. Step right, all very sustained and fingery, then go up over a bulge, BR, to finish direct past a PR.

52. Stiff And Sticky   E3 6a   6/84
8m left of The Fog is an obvious problem entry leading to a big flake full of dandelions. Climb to a PR, then move strenuously right to a doubtful jug. A dynamic reach gains the flake; step right off its top and finish up the groove.

**   **53. Cured**   E6 6c/7a   21/5/88
A superb route, perhaps spoilt for those of lesser stature by the heinous crux. Start 2m left of Stiff And Sticky, underneath a short left-facing flake below the guardian overhangs. Attain a good hold and BR halfway round the first bulge without too much difficulty, before utilising a telescopic reach to gain incuts on a tiny slab. Follow the shallow scoop past a BR and overlap to the top roof and an entertaining finish.

*   **54. Train To Hell**   E4 6a (2 pts. aid)   7/4/87
Carrion for the jackals? A few metres left of Cured are two obvious parallel layback flakes about two thirds of the way up the wall. Start below these. Climb delicately up to a sharp sidehold below the roof and arrange some small wires. Judicious use of both bolts allows the first layback flake to be gained and followed to good holds. Awkward moves below the final roof lead to jugs.

*   **55. Line Of Fire**   E5 6a   30/11/83
A bold route with a certain amount of suspect rock. Start 2m left of Train To Hell below a C-shaped flake. Climb to the flake, PR, then swing up to some doubtful hanging flakes. A long reach up and right from an undercut permits entry to a hanging groove of doubtful integrity. Make it quickly to the roof and finish leftwards on good jugs.

**   **56. Bolt From The Blue**   E6 6c   1/4/84
A diverting problem, sporting continuously strenuous moves and an elusive crux. Start as for Line Of Fire. From the PR on Line Of Fire swing left from the flake and cross the leaning wall past a PR to a BR. Move quickly right and then up with some difficulty to a slanting jug at the foot of a crack. This offers an inadequate rest. Finish direct over the small roof.

** 57. Back In The Black   E6 6c   27/7/89
An illustrous challenge, being essentially Bolt From The Blue with a harder top section. Follow Bolt From The Blue to the BR and move left to a second BR. Subdue the overhanging wall, passing undercuts, to a TR below the top overlap, and the end of the difficulties.

** 58. Punishment Of Luxury   E4 6b   Spr. 1984
At the left end of the crag is a chimney. 10m right, under some bulges, is a gnarled yew tree with a discontinuous crack just right again. Avoiding the temptation to shorten the first hard moves by stepping off a block, gain the sharp pocket and handslot next to some TRs. Easier moves lead into the crack, which provides a more relaxed if occasionally grubby conclusion.

59. Hells Chimney   Difficult   Pre 1978
Climb up the back of the deep, dark chimney.

60. Tongue Pie   Hard Very Severe 4c   25/3/84
A slight pitch with little protection. From the depths of Hell's Chimney traverse above the lip of the overhang right to a thin crack near the arête. Finish straight up.

61. Hells Own Variation   Very Difficult   Pre 1978
Climb Hells Chimney and at half height, move out left to finish on top of the tower.

62. Hello Arête   Hard Very Severe 4c   12/5/80
Follow the left arête of Hells Chimney with a loose overhang to start.

63. Hell Hole   Moderate   Pre 1978
To the left of the previous routes can be found a small hidden hole that is damp, dark and depressing. Enter this (if you must) and slither to the top.

MIDDLE TIER, LEFT WING

This is the short wall below and about 60m beyond the Hell's Chimney area. The routes are described from left to right.

64. Paper Smile   Hard Very Severe, 5a   30/8/85
Delicate. Starts below the left side of a smooth compact wall on the first buttress encountered, with a PR near the centre. Balance up a shallow groove and the wall above. This and the next two routes have an iron stake belay.

*   65. The Thin Wall   E2 6a   30/8/85
A superb little route, marred only by its brevity. Climb directly up the centre
of the clean wall past a PR and situ wire. Predictably thin.

66. Goblin Girls   Hard Very Severe 5a   27/10/84
Around the buttress to the right of the Thin Wall is a hanging groove which
becomes a steep crack. Brief but sound. It is also possible to move up and
left into a groove on the blunt arête, rather harder.

67. Tangram   E1 5b   6/4/84
An attractive blunt arête 15m to the right of the last routes and past a rowan
tree. Move diagonally left up the delightful white wall then back right again
at half height where the arête narrows.

About 10m right of Tangram is a buttress with an undercut base at its right-
hand end.

68. Willy Waits For No Man   E1 5b   7/91
Climb to the left of centre up the slabby wall. Steady climbing leads to a
slight bulge that is climbed using good pockets.

69. Stein Line   E1 5b   7/91
Start in the centre of the wall and follow an obvious crack system to the top.
Ample protection.

70. Pulling Up The Daisies   E3 6a   19/6/92
Begin at the left-hand side of the buttress. A boulder problem start leads
to a ledge on the right and a bootlace TR round a small chockstone. Finish
straight up the wall.

71. Fanny Magnet   E2 5c   19/6/92
Right of the undercut buttress is a big detached pillar. A few metres right
again is an arête. Climb it direct.

THE RIGHT WING

The main features of the right wing are The Royal Arch wall, distinguished by a letter R formation, the descent gully right of Summer Solstice, and the two towers towards the right-hand end. The first tower is The Tower of Babel, the second The Babbling Tower.

72. SPC   Hard Very Severe 4c   Pre 1978
A pleasant, if abbreviated, route that is frequently used as a descent by the assured. Start just right of Soap at a short groove and ascend the wall on good holds.

73. Humble Hog   E1 5c   19/2/84
An awkward start just to the right of SPC leads to good holds and an excellent runner, then up to a flake and back left to finish.

There is an excellent and unattributed boulder problem just right of Humble Hog, involving a long stretch from a flat hold to a tiny layaway. Start from three blocks embedded in the grass. About E2 6a-ish.

* 74. Dynah Moe Hum   E4 6b   2/6/84
Rarely repeated. Start 4m right of Soap, at a water stain. Climb the faint scoop on layaways to an undercut, then move nonchalantly up and left to better holds. Thrilling.

75. Out With The New   E3 6b   8/5/88
Start 2m right of Dynah Moe Hum. Boulder out the wall to gain the obvious overlap, grope for a good jug above and pull over, then up the wall to the top.

76. Inaugural Goose Flesh   E3 6b   21/5/88
An agreeable route starting 5m right of Out With The New just past a recess. Pull over the first overhang and go up to a BR, then make a very hard stretch to a good hold above and right of the bolt. Finish direct up the short smooth wall.

77. Just Another Route Name E4 6a   10/5/88
Easier than it looks. Start 2m right of Inaugural Goose Flesh. Climb to a BR, then step left past it to improving holds and a slightly leftward finish.

78. Heinous Undercling   E5 6b   8/5/88
Start 2m right of Just Another Route Name and attack the bulging wall, BR, using undercuts and layaways to gain a flake with a BR above. Make a hard move to stand up and finish direct past a TR.

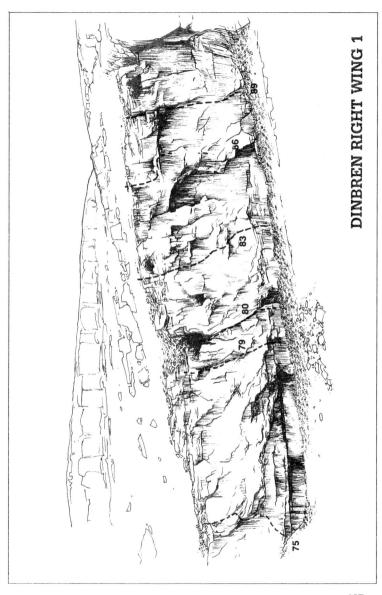

DINBREN RIGHT WING 1

To the right the undercut wall ends at a prominent crack.

79. Sarcophagus   E2 5b   12/5/79
Sarcophagus goes up a line 2m left of the crack, trending left, until a thin crack can be gained and followed to the top. Very poorly protected.

80. The Varlet   Hard Very Severe 5a   12/5/79
Climb the left trending crack to the top.

*   **81. Backs To The Wall**   E5 6b   8/5/88
A fingery route up the steep wall just right of The Varlet. Boulder up past two BRs to a poor rest. Take the bulge on the left to gain good but hidden holds and a PR, then finish direct.

82. Deadly Nightshade   E2 5b   14/5/79
The blunt and slightly loose arête on the right of The Varlet. Hard moves off the ground lead to a thin crack and so to a thorn bush. Make an awkward move around the arête towards another thorn bush and the top.

*   **83. Driller Thriller**   E4 5c   22/5/88
Pleasant but escapable climbing. Start 1m right of Deadly Nightshade. Climb straight up the fine grey wall, 2 BRs, to reach the capping bulge; struggle round this, BR, on dubious holds.

*   **84. Old Scores**   E5 6a   27/3/84
A rather contrived line but bold and entertaining. Start 6m right of Deadly Nightshade at a left-facing flake. Follow the flake until a bulge forces a difficult move, TR, to the bottom of a v-groove. Ascend the groove to a PR, step left and finish through the roof.

To the right of Old Scores, the quality of the rock improves markedly. This section is called The Royal Arch wall.

85. Pep Talk   Very Severe, 4c   Pre 1978
Start 6m left of the foot of The Royal Arch below a steep broken wall. Climb the wall passing some large blocks and finish up the groove passing a small bush.

**   **86. The Royal Arch**   E3 6a   30/8/79
A minor classic, starting at the foot of the big curving arch. Follow the arch leftwards for 8m until a vague rightward traverse line is attainable. Tread delicately right to a pinch where thin moves lead to a slot above. Move up to the roof and traverse left until it is possible to scrabble boldly into a scoop.

*   87. Blue Nine   E4 6b   4/6/88
A slightly more demanding prelude to The Royal Arch, taking a faint leftward slanting line just right. Skirmish diagonally leftwards just right of the overlap to a good jug at 5m, then step up more easily to join the parent route before the crux.

*** 88. Waltz In Black   E4 6b   6/3/84
A brilliant route on perfect rock. Start below a small leftward facing flake about 3m right of The Royal Arch. Rock on to the top of the flake with some difficulty to clip a TR on the right. Tiptoe left to a PR then, from a good flake up and left, stretch rightwards across the bulge to a small rounded ledge and a second TR. Finish up the steep groove above the roof.

*** 89. A World Of Harmony   E2 5b   30/8/79
Another fine route which starts below the far right-hand side of the long overlap. Balance bravely up the wall, small wires and a TR, to the corner crack and good runners. Step right and pull through the roof using a hidden hold.

*   90. Caught In The Crossfire   E4 6a   6/3/84
The narrow buttress right of World In Harmony. Blinkers are mandatory, but the climbing is very good, depending on the ethics employed. Disregarding the lure of the adjacent routes, pass a BR and a good wire to an unnerving finish at a small tree.

91. Death On My Tongue   E3 5c   30/8/79
Quite a serious proposition up the wavy crack 3m left of the deep corner gully.

92. Shadowplay   E1 5c   25/2/84
An eliminate past the two TRs between Death On My Tongue and the corner gully. Tunnel vision a definite advantage.

93. Let It Rip   Very Difficult   Pre 1978
The obvious green corner gully.

*   94. Return Of The Gods   E3 5c   30/8/79
The imposing but well protected crack on the right of the gully to an interesting finish. Oddly enough, most of the moves are on face holds.

*   95. Synapse Collapse   E3 5c   5/85
Interesting, with some technical moves. Start on the right arête of Return
Of The Gods. Go up the left side of the arête to ledges and a PR up and
right. Traverse right and go up into a large white scoop, PR. Finish via the
obvious crack.

96. In The Heat Of The Day   E5 6b   15/5/88
A direct start to Synapse Collapse, beginning just to the right of the arête.
The thin crack leads to an unyielding and serious bulge, above which are
some good flakes and a PR. Pull into the large scoop, PR, to finish as for
the parent route.

*   97. The Wasp Factory   E5 6b   27/7/89
A powerful concoction. Start on the right-hand side of the buttress just left
of a major hand crack. Using undercuts and layaways, climb past a PR and
a BR to twin BRs on the smooth grey headwall. Thin moves pass these to
jugs and the top.

*   98. Big Youth   Hard Very Severe, 5a   14/8/81
One of Dinbren's few classic cracks. The steep fissure 6m left of a small
rowan.

*   99. Thanks To Ellis Brigham   E2 6a   2/8/81
Good climbing up the peg scarred crack just right of Big Youth, with a hard
section at the top.

*   100. Lecherous Pig   E3 6a   6/6/84
Pleasant climbing to a subtle crux sequence at the top. Start as for Thanks
To Ellis Brigham but continue straight up the initial crack to the bulge. The
golden wall above proves trying but short-lived.

101. Summer Solstice   E1 5b   2/8/81
A good line up the flake crack just left of a rowan tree. Climb the wall to the
crack and follow it to a good hidden hold above. Finish easily up and right
into the descent gully.

Behind the small rowan tree is a polished descent gully. The back wall of this
holds two routes, both on immaculate rock.

*   102. German For Art Historians Hard Very Severe, 5b   6/3/84
Short but good. Take the thin crack 4m up the descent gully past TR,
finishing rightwards.

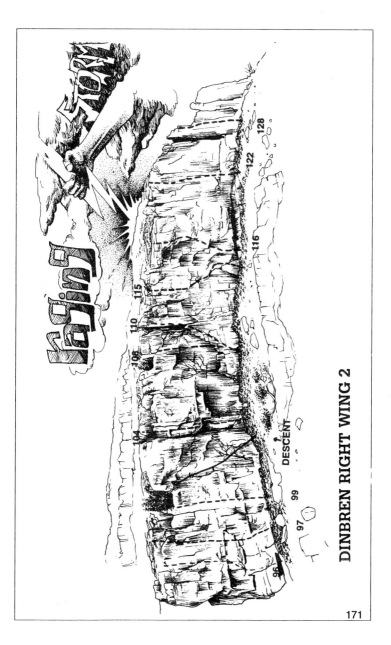

DINBREN RIGHT WING 2

*   103. Sugar Hiccup   E2 5c   6/3/84
A bold and delicate conundrum beginning 2m up the gully. Friction up and right to a good wire placement at the bulge. Step right and up to a shallow groove and short headwall.

104. Five O'Clock Shadow   Very Severe, 4c   Pre 1978
The corner rising from the foot of the descent gully.

105. Arm Worms   E4 6a   30/5/85
The unsightly fracture in the hanging arête immediately right of Five O'Clock Shadow. Obdurate, painful, and with uninspiring protection.

*   106. Quick Flash   E5 6b   10/5/88
A direct line on the buttress right of Arm Worms. A hard start leads to a good rest, BR, giving ample time to contemplate the bold finish.

107. Loosing Grasp   E2 5b   12/10/79
A frequently verdant proposition up the ragged crack in the wall just left of the big rowan tree. Mildly strenuous.

108. Wood Treatment   E3 5c   6/3/84
Start right behind the big rowan. Attack the almost protectionless wall reaching a TR. Finish reasonably. Bold.

109. Nit Nurse   E1 5b   3/84
The compact grey wall 2m right of Wood Treatment is similar to its neighbour, but minus the arboreal twiddly bits. The overlap and crack above constitute the crux, TR.

110. The Phoenix   Severe   Pre 1978
Climb the grassy ramp to the large dead yew tree and finish up the broken groove above. Highly unrecommended.

*   111. Astrola   Very Severe, 4b   12/10/79
Start below and right of the dead yew tree. Scramble up a faint crack and groove before moving up right to a good ledge and runner. Continue up the broken crack above to finish left of the whitebeam. Poorly protected.

112. The Scutters   E2 5b   12/10/79
A worthwhile route. Start at a cluster of hand size pockets 2m left of a distinctive triangular flake. Climb from the pockets up to gain a good hold at the foot of a small groove. Pull into the groove and finish up the corner above to the right of the whitebeam.

113. The Stukas   E3 5c   18/1/92
A good route. Start from the long pocket to the right of The Scutters. Climb
up to the ringbolt in the bulge, then step left and follow the thin crack to the
top.

**   114. Fighting Spirit   E4 6a   18/1/92
Fine rock and good moves, starting, once more, below the biggest pocket.
Follow The Stukas to the ringbolt, then go straight up the technical wall
past a second BR.

**   115. Combat Zone   E3 5c   3/84
A little gem, on splendid rock. Start at a large triangular flake leaning
against the cliff. From the top of the flake, go straight up to a TR and curving
undercut, then daintily left to a vague crackline. Go for the bulge, passing
a PR and a TR en route.

116. Evil Woman   E3 5c   24/8/81
Exciting. Start just right of the triangular flake at a hanging corner. Follow
the corner to a large ledge, then up the shattered bulging wall to a good
flake hold at the foot of the steep flake crack. Go up this to finish through
the exhilarating roof above.

117. Mustang Sally   E5 6c   23/5/92
Very technical, with a rather crumbly start. Halfway along the undercut to
the right of Evil Woman is a sharp fingerhold at shoulder height. Pass this
to the ledge, PR, then resolve the extremely thin wall, passing a BR and
small overlap to a bold finish.

118. Ripping Yarns   E2 6a   26/1/92
Start 9m right of Evil Woman, at the right-hand end of an undercut, at a
large flake. Climb it to a ledge, then follow the blunt and demanding arête
past a TR and flake to a convenient whitebeam.

119. Filth Faze   Very Severe, 4c   Pre 1978
Not as mangy as it looks, although that isn't saying much. Just right of
Ripping Yarns below the whitebeam tree is a shattered crackline. Do it,
passing lots of daisies.

120. Doris   Hard Very Severe, 5a   8/12/89
Very contrived, sharing many of the holds on Filth Faze. Starting as for
Filth Faze, climb the manky wall just right to a crack and follow it to the top.

121. Grooved Arête   E1 5c   3/84
The grooved arête (surprise, surprise) between Filth Faze and the clean corner 3m right. Some awkward moves. Go up the square cut groove for a few metres, until it is possible to move left onto the blunt arête. Follow it to the top.

*   122. Sally In Pink   Very Severe, 4b   11/4/80
A cracking climb taking the obvious square cut groove containing two loose looking blocks and an old yew tree.

123. Crimson Dynamo   E2 5c   3/1984
A short way right of Sally In Pink are two parallel cracks halfway up the crag. Approach them direct and finish past a whitebeam tree.

*   124. Colour Games   E1 5b   9/8/79
Low down and 5m right of Sally In Pink is a small roof with a broken, twisting crack rising from its right-hand side. Climb the crack and flake above, then finish up the pleasant slab to a stunted whitebeam tree.

** 125. Raging Storm   E3 5c   24/8/81
Splendid. Start just right of Colour Games below a line of rightward curving overlaps. Climb the wall past an obvious RP placement to the arching crack above. From the top of this make a long stride right to a line of flakes. Avoiding easier options on the right, finish direct past a small overhang.

** 126. Hydrogen   E3 5c   24/8/81
Slightly easier than Raging Storm, but just as good. Follow Raging Storm to the RP placement, then balance up and right (crux - very hard for the tiny) to a good foothold. Take the line of flakes above to the top.

To the right of Hydrogen is what appears to be a pinnacle of rock standing proud of the rest of the crag. This is the Tower of Babel.

127. The Devils Advocate   E3 5c   16/6/79
Short and sharp. To the left of the Tower Of Babel is a smooth steepening groove. Climb it with difficulty to a small tree.

128. Tower Of Babel   Very Severe, 5a   9/8/79
Start at the left-hand arête on the outside face of the tower. An awkward start leads to easy cracks and the top.

129. Babel Face   Very Severe 5a   3/84
Quite hard for the grade. The shallow groove on the front face of the tower, just to the right of the previous route.

130. Antilla   Severe   9/8/79
Barely worth the effort. Climb the slabby, vegetated groove and crack midway between the two towers.

131. Babbling Arête   Severe   13/10/91
To the left of Babbling Tower is a steep arête. Climb this using good holds on its left side.

132. Babbling Tower   Very Difficult   Pre 1978
A nice route. The large broken crack in the front face of the tower, passing a small tree near the top.

* 133. Electra Glide   E3 5c   19/6/79
A serious and sustained proposition. Start on the outside face, just left of the right arête, from a niche. Exit the niche with difficulty and move up and right to an ancient piece of bent metal. Up and left is an apparently detached block below a hanging groove. Steal bravely into the groove and follow it to the top.

* 134. Dawn Of Desire   E2 5b   19/6/79
Another scary route, taking the right arête of the tower. Boulder up past the aforementioned museum piece before moving right onto the inside wall for an easy finish. A more direct and difficult option is possible up the crack on the left of the arête past a TR, E2 5c.

135. Shaken Not Stirred   Hard Severe   Pre 1978
On the wall immediately right of The Babbling Tower is a broken groove with a PR on the right. Climb it in its entirety.

136. Chabris   Hard Very Severe, 5a   Pre 1978
The short corner to the right of Shaken Not Stirred is climbed direct.

* 137. Buccinator   E3 5c   6/8/81
A fiery little test piece. Climb the striking thin crack right of Chabris past two PRs, and make it quick.

138. Cheeky Piece   E3 5b   26/1/86
Pleasant, if a little unprotected. Start just right of Buccinator. Follow the thin, rightward trending flake line to the bulge, then up the groove to finish left of a dead yew tree.

139. Gentle Violence   E3 5c   6/8/81
This line takes the slabby wall just past a bulging arête, about 5m right of

Buccinator. Climb the short crack to a broken slab and move up to the bulge and a good runner. Climb the bulge reaching a good flake on the right and easier ground above.

140. Castella   Hard Very Difficult   Pre 1978
The obvious leftward leaning blocky groove 3m right of Gentle Violence.

141. Hamlet   Hard Severe   Pre 1978
The square cut groove just right of Castella, with which it shares the start. The moves past the dubious block to gain the foot of the groove are awkward, the rest a stroll.

142. First Graces   Hard Severe   28/4/80
An enjoyable layback flake above a small rowan sapling.

MIDDLE TIER, RIGHT WING

Walking down and right across the scree from Soap, the first feature encountered is a line of overhangs which provide quite good bouldering. 60m further on, past some smaller buttresses, the first recorded route is reached. Other routes have certainly been done in this area: it has been left to any interested parties to rediscover them.

It is advisable to be wary of sheep grazing amongst the screes above this section, as they knock down considerable amounts of rock, frequently without giving a proper warning.

143 .Subtopia   E1 5b   30/9/85
Along the top right-hand section of the first substantial buttress is a large patch of ivy. Start below and slightly right of this. Climb a short wall, a bulge and a hanging groove past a PR to finish.

144. Ice Run   E1 5b   23/9/85
Short but enjoyable. Start 6m right of Subtopia at an obvious flake crack on the left side of the next buttress. Climb it direct, past a TR.

145. Stagnation   Hard Severe   30/9/85
The central groove right of Ice Run, past a dead tree.

146. White Lightning   E1 5c   23/9/85
The clean wall on the right side of the Ice Run buttress, past a TR and an old bolt hole.

100m beyond White Lightning, and 15m past a rowan growing from the tier below, is a wall with an undercut base on the right. It holds the next two routes.

147. Fingers   Hard Very Severe, 4c   11/9/85
Climb the wall just left of centre to finish up a shallow groove.

148. Thumbs   Hard Very Severe, 5b   11/9/85
The vegetated groove to the right of Fingers, with a problem start over an undercut.

FIRST ASCENTS

1962	SOAP	H J Tinkler & J Hesketh
Pre 1978	HELLS CHIMNEY	Unknown
Pre 1978	HELLS OWN VARIATION	Unknown
Pre 1978	HELL HOLE	Unknown
Pre 1978	SPC	Unknown
Pre 1978	PEP TALK	Unknown
Pre 1978	LET IT RIP	Unknown
Pre 1978	FIVE O'CLOCK SHADOW	Unknown
Pre 1978	THE PHOENIX	Unknown
Pre 1978	FILTH FAZE	Unknown
Pre 1978	BABBLING TOWER	Unknown
Pre 1978	SHAKEN NOT STIRRED	Unknown
Pre 1978	CHABRIS	Unknown
Pre 1978	CASTELLA	Unknown
Pre 1978	HAMLET	Unknown
9/9/77	PUNISHMENT OF LUXURY	S M Cathcart & G N Swindley (1 pt)

The start of a three year period when Stuart Cathcart had the entire Eglwyseg Valley virtually to himself.

15/3/78	AMADEUS	S M Cathcart, Solo
15/3/78	YALE	S M Cathcart, Solo
15/3/78	SILENT SPIRIT	S M Cathcart, Solo
12/5/79	SARCOPHAGUS	S M Cathcart, Solo
12/5/79	THE VARLET	S M Cathcart, Solo
14/5/79	DEADLY NIGHTSHADE	S M Cathcart & J Dee
16/6/79	SWANSONG	S M Cathcart & D Johnson
16/6/79	THE DEVILS ADVOCATE	S M Cathcart & G N Swindley
19/6/79	ELECTRA GLIDE	S M Cathcart & T Curtis
19/6/79	DAWN OF DESIRE	S M Cathcart & T Curtis
9/8/79	COLOUR GAMES	S M Cathcart, Solo
9/8/79	TOWER OF BABEL	S M Cathcart, Solo
9/8/79	ANTILLA	S M Cathcart, Solo
28/8/79	HYPERDRIVE	S M Cathcart & R White

30/8/79	THE ROYAL ARCH	S M Cathcart & G N Swindley
30/8/79	A WORLD OF HARMONY	S M Cathcart & G N Swindley
30/8/79	DEATH ON MY TONGUE	S M Cathcart & G N Swindley
30/8/79	RETURN OF THE GODS	S M Cathcart & G N Swindley
12/10/79	LOOSING GRASP	S M Cathcart & R White
12/10/79	ASTROLA	S M Cathcart & R White
12/10/79	THE SCUTTERS	S M Cathcart & R White
11/4/80	SALLY IN PINK	M Cameron & S M Cathcart

The young Ms Cameron was at the bottom of the crag in a pink romper suit.

26/4/80	GEMMA'S WORLD	S M Cathcart & J Dee
28/4/80	FIRST GRACES	S M Cathcart
12/5/80	ALISON	S M Cathcart & J Dee

Named for the long suffering Mrs Cathcart.

| 12/5/80 | HELLO ARÊTE | S M Cathcart, Solo |
| 2/8/81 | THANKS TO ELLIS BRIGHAM | S M Cathcart & J Dee |

Stuart had just left the company.

2/8/81	SUMMER SOLSTICE	S M Cathcart & J Dee
6/8/81	BUCCINATOR	S M Cathcart & D Whitlow
6/8/81	GENTLE VIOLENCE	S M Cathcart & J Dee
14/8/81	BIG YOUTH	S M Cathcart, Solo
24/8/81	EVIL WOMAN	S M Cathcart & D Whitlow
24/8/81	RAGING STORM	S M Cathcart & D Whitlow
24/8/81	HYDROGEN	S M Cathcart & D Whitlow
9/83	CLIMB HIGH	S M Cathcart, P Waters & D Barker

Bolts arrive on Dinbren; the first of the modern routes, originally graded E2 6a, "or maybe a bit harder".

| 30/11/83 | LINE OF FIRE | S Allen, unseconded |

The first of a series of sporadic contributions to the valley by a talented climber. Originally E5 6a, some say it still deserves the grade.

| 3/12/83 | TRACTION TRAUMA | J Codling & J Moulding |

On an early attempt, a cross-threaded bolt runner pulled out while being used for a rest. The leader missed the gibbering second by inches and the ground by a few feet.

| 13/12/83 | DR. GONZO | J Moulding & J Codling |
| 16/12/83 | DREADLOCKS | J Codling, unseconded |

The first E5 on the crag. Needless to say, originally graded E4.

| Spr. 84 | HOT LIPS | J Codling, J Moulding & F Crook |
| Spr. 84 | PUNISHMENT OF LUXURY, FFA | |

A bone of contention. Initially freed by J Codling, by way of a long stretch from the left. This, however, avoided the essential problem and was impossible for anyone with a "normal" ape index. Free climbed direct, without recourse to the usual boulder, by S Boydon.

| 7/1/84 | IN SEARCH OF SOMEONE SILLY | G Gibson, unseconded |

15/2/84	EL LOCO	J Moulding, unseconded

Now slightly harder since some unfortunate foolishly fell on the second thread runner, which had been intended purely for decoration.

19/2/84	MELODY	G Gibson, unseconded

It is possible, though hardly advisable, to jump off from the hidden jug and live!

19/2/84	HUMBLE HOG	A Williams, Solo
25/2/84	A DIFFERENT KIND OF HYPERTENSION	G Gibson & H Carnes
25/2/84	SO LUCKY	G Gibson, unseconded

Named for the disquieting departure of a hold during the first ascent.

25/2/84	SHADOWPLAY	G Gibson & H Carnes
3/84	NIT NURSE	F Crook & I Barker
3/84	COMBAT ZONE	F Crook & I Barker
3/84	GROOVED ARÊTE	I Barker & F Crook
3/84	CRIMSON DYNAMO	F Crook & I Barker
3/84	BABEL FACE	F Crook & I Barker
6/3/84	WALTZ IN BLACK	G Gibson, A Hudson & F Crook

A Dinbren classic.

6/3/84	CAUGHT IN THE CROSSFIRE	G Gibson, A Hudson & F Crook
6/3/84	GERMAN FOR ART HISTORIANS	B Barret, A Hudson F Crook & G Gibson
6/3/84	SUGAR HICCUP	A Hudson, F Crook & G Gibson
6/3/84	WOOD TREATMENT	G Gibson & A Hudson
25/3/84	TONGUE PIE	P Harrison, unseconded
27/3/84	OLD SCORES	G Gibson, unseconded
1/4/84	GEMMA'S WORLD DIRECT	J Codling & P Gibson
1/4/84	BOLT FROM THE BLUE	J Moulding, J Lockett & J Codling

Originally done with a rest on the bolt. FFA with several yo-yos by J Monks & M Lovatt summer 29/7/84. Redpointed by J Moulding, October 1986.

6/4/84	TANGRAM	P Harrison, Solo
29/4/84	KAMIKAZE CLONE	J Codling, J Moulding & P Harrison
5/84	ALISON DIRECT START	G Gibson, unseconded
6/84	STIFF AND STICKY	J Codling, J Moulding & F Stevenson
2/6/84	DYNAH MOE HUM	J Moulding, Solo

The dents in the turf below took some time to disappear.

3/6/84	WHERE'S THE PRESIDENTS BRAIN (1 rest)	S Cardy & S Boydon

On the attempted second ascent, a well known superstar nearly met his demise as various holds and sundry runners failed simultaneously. His unprotected head came within four inches of the boulders below. FFA by S Boydon & P Harrison, summer 1984.

6/6/84	LECHEROUS PIG	P Harrison & J Moulding
Aut. 84	TECHNICOLOUR YAWN	S Allen, J Codling, J Moulding & J Lockett

Just prior to the first ascent, the leader spent some time doing the big spit, apparently due to a stomach upset. Then graded E4 and "soft" 6b, continual evolution (read "holds falling off") means that the grade has kept pace with the times. The current version has been soloed.

22/9/84	FIRE	J Codling & J Moulding
27/10/84	GOBLIN GIRLS	P Harrison & S Cardy
18/11/84	RESIST AND EXIST	P Harrison & D Kerr
5/85	RHIANNON	S Boydon & J Moulding (alts)

A naughty rest point went undeclared on the first ascent.
FFA J Moulding & J Codling (alts), July 1987.

5/85	COOKIE KING	S Boydon & S Cardy
5/85	THE DINBREN SANCTION	S Boydon, Solo
5/85	THE FOG	S Boydon, unseconded

Futuristic and probably the hardest route in Clwyd at the time. On seeing the line in 1984, one well known but misguided pundit was heard to say "won't be done for ten years".... Three attempts were necessary for success: they included one in freezing fog, hence the name, and one in a snowstorm.

5/85	SYNAPSE COLLAPSE	S Cardy & S Boydon

FFA by S Cardy on 4/7/88.

30/5/85	MISTY VISION	S Boydon, unseconded
30/5/85	ARM WORMS	S Boydon, P Harrison & J Moulding
30/8/85	THE THIN WALL	D Kerr & L Clarke
30/8/85	PAPER SMILE	D Kerr, Solo
11/9/85	FINGERS	D Kerr & D Woolgar
11/9/85	THUMBS	D Kerr & D Woolgar
23/9/85	ICE RUN	D Kerr & S Conlon
23/9/85	WHITE LIGHTNING	D Kerr & S Conlon
30/9/85	SUBTOPIA	D Kerr & S Conlon
30/9/85	STAGNATION	D Kerr, Solo
26/1/86	CHEEKY PIECE	D Kerr, Solo
23/8/86	ICE	J Codling, unseconded
26/8/86	THE ORGASMATRON	J Codling, unseconded

Named in honour of the fragrant (female) belayer. The first moves have been freed by Alan Doig, but he had to jump off as he was carrying no runners. On adding the necessary gear to his rack, he was sadly unable to repeat the feat.

25/12/86	COLD TURKEY	G Gibson, unseconded
7/4/87	TRAIN TO HELL	J Moulding & S Cardy
31/5/87	BABY CRUSHER	J Moulding & J Codling

For any outraged parents, the emphasis is intended on the second word, as in "Big Crusher".

31/5/87	BOLT THE BLUE SKY	J Moulding & J Codling
14/6/87	ICE ON THE MOTORWAY	J Codling & J Moulding (alts)

Done with several falls on an ice cold "summer" day.
FFA 8/7/1987 J Codling & G Gibson

8/7/87	I PUNCHED JUDY FIRST	G Gibson & J Codling
8/87	WALKING WITH BARRENCE	J Moulding & J Codling
11/4/88	HOT STUFF	D Kerr & A Remedios
24/4/88	BIG MOUTH STRIKES AGAIN	G Gibson, H Gibson & P Harrison
8/5/88	OUT WITH THE NEW	G Gibson, Solo
8/5/88	HEINOUS UNDERCLING	G Gibson, unseconded
8/5/88	BACKS TO THE WALL	G Gibson, unseconded
10/5/88	JUST ANOTHER ROUTE NAME	G Gibson, Solo
10/5/88	QUICK FLASH	G Gibson, Solo
14/5/88	FAT BOYS	J Codling, G Gibson & J Moulding
14/5/88	THE RIVALS	G Gibson, unseconded

A route that has caused a great deal of animosity between two of
Clwyd's keenest protagonists, Gibson and Moulding. Initially a
dubious flake was glued for the first ascent. This was later
removed, a bolt was chopped and the route recleaned and
reascended on 3/8/89 by Moulding who subsequently renamed it
Savage Henry Cranks the Rad. A grade harder at E6 6c.

14/5/88	BROKEN DREAMS	J Moulding & J Codling
15/5/88	LOCOMOTION	G Gibson, unseconded
15/5/88	IN THE HEAT OF THE DAY	G Gibson, unseconded
21/5/88	FLOWERS ARE FOR THE DEAD	G Gibson & J Codling
21/5/88	FINE FEATHERED FINK	G Gibson, unseconded
21/5/88	CURED	G Gibson, unseconded
21/5/88	INAUGURAL GOOSE FLESH	J Codling & G Gibson

Rumours that this route had been pinched by Gary Gibson were
hotly denied.

22/5/88	SILLY GAMES	G Gibson & H Gibson
22/5/88	DRILLER THRILLER	I Dunn, C Dunn & G Gibson
6/88	EXPLOSIVE FIBRES	A Walker, unseconded
4/6/88	BLUE NIN	J Moulding, Solo
13/6/88	THE BANDITS	G Gibson, unseconded

A fourth bolt, placed in the middle of the crux section of Rhiannon,
was removed by John Moulding and the route subsequently reascended by A Doig.

4/89	GOING LOCO	S Meyers, unseconded

Appropriate largesse from someone "on sabbatical" from Pen
Trwyn.

7/89	LULLABY	G Gibson, unseconded
27/7/89	BACK IN THE BLACK	J Moulding, unseconded
27/7/89	THE WASP FACTORY	J Codling & J Moulding

3/8/89	SAVAGE HENRY CRANKS THE RAD	J Moulding & J Codling

The infamous Rivals renamed. The leader's final contribution prior to totally splintering both ankles two weeks later.

8/12/89	DORIS	P Andrews & ??

The first ascensionist omitted to christen this one, so one of the authors arbitrarily named it after a toy dragon, the subject of his seven year old son's attention at the time of inspiration.

7/91	STEIN LINE	C Silverstone & P Wilson
7/91	WILLY WAITS FOR NO MAN	C Silverstone & P Wilson
13/10/91	BABBLING ARÊTE	G C Pastfield & K Davies
18/1/92	THE STUKAS	G Gibson & D Kerr
18/1/92	FIGHTING SPIRIT	G Gibson & D Kerr
26/1/92	RIPPING YARNS	G Gibson & D Kerr
29/2/92	THE PLANET	G Gibson, Unseconded
23/5/92	MUSTANG SALLY	G Gibson, unseconded
19/6/92	PULLING UP THE DAISIES	C Silverstone & P Whalley
19/6/92	FANNY MAGNET	P Whalley & C Silverstone

TREVOR ROCKS AREA

O.S. Map 117 GR 232433
by Alec and Simon Williams

CHARACTER AND SITUATION

Trevor Rocks area is the most southerly of the crags in the Eglwyseg Valley. Climbing here lies on three buttresses, all with a very different ambience from their neighbours. The crags are all ideal for taking younger climbers to, having a wide, level base and a host of climbs in different grades. They can be classed as the family crags of the Eglwyseg valley. The climbing here tends to be in the severe to lower extreme grade range and therefore doesn't have quite as intimidating an atmosphere as some of the crags in the valley. However, some of the routes do have very sparse protection and subsequently can be a bit daunting for a nervous leader. The addition of bolt runners on the newer routes tends to have eliminated some of the more worrying aspects of the climbing.

Trevor Quarry is the first and most accessible of the three, situated a short stroll up the scree slope above the parking area. Comprising of three walls of good solid rock, up to 25m in height, the quarry is very popular probably due to its amenable nature, varied difficulties and good belays.

Railway Buttress is situated within another quarry 400m to the west, but it is in fact a natural wall which was saved from the quarryman's tools. The buttress has some fine easier routes on excellent quality rock.

Compact Wall is a short, slabby shield of rock offering routes mainly in the lower extreme grade. It sits as a wall of good solid rock in a long quarry that is virtually devoid of further potential.

APPROACH AND ACCESS

The best way to approach the Trevor Rocks Area is to follow the valley road from the town of Llangollen, as you would with all the Eglwyseg crags (refer to the introduction to Eglwyseg), and follow it for one and a half miles until a turning, signposted Panorama, appears on your right. Turn here and follow the road for about a mile, ignoring a side road that drops off to the right. Continue on until a large layby on the left is reached. For Trevor Quarry, approach is made via the steep scree slope above the layby. For Compact Wall and Railway Buttress approach is along the obvious incline for about 400m leading back up the valley and along a path at the foot of the quarries. Railway Buttress is the natural buttress prominent from the rest of the quarry and Compact Wall is the shield of rock about 200m further on containing a few bolt runners.

Note: along the road from the layby is a hairpin bend with a track leading up to Trevor Quarry, although further parking is available on the bend (the walk in is less steep), vehicles should not be taken up the track from the hairpin bend as the local landowner uses this area for sheep grazing.

TREVOR QUARRY

The routes are described from right to left, the first two routes lie on the short slabby wall which is at right angles to the main steep wall.

1. Fling   Very Severe, 4b   13/2/86
Climb the slab 1m right of Lingen.

2. Lingen   Very Severe, 4b   2/77
Climb the slabby wall direct starting just right of the stepped descent. Escapable and often abseiled down by youth groups.

The next routes are situated on the desperately steep main wall.

3. White Smear   E4 5c   15/3/77
A bold and poorly protected route. On the far right end of the Main Wall is a faint crack line and white smear. Climb the crack line passing a large flat hold to make a long reach with no comfort to a difficult finish.

*   4. Trabucco   E4 6b   29/12/86
Start just left of White Smear. Climb the wall on small edges to a slim overhang. Move up direct, BR, by fingery moves and slowly improving holds to the top.

**   5. The Last Straw   E3 5c   15/3/77
Climb the obvious crack left of Trabucco with some difficult moves up to good holds above half height.

**   6. Clevor Trevor   E4 6A   4/5/92
An excellent route, typical of the wall. Start 2m left of The Last Straw. Overcome an awkward initial bulge then take a bold direct line up the grey wall to gain the overlap at a thin crack. Climb the thin crack, sometimes wet, by difficult moves on positive holds to gain larger holds and the top.

**   7. This Way To Clitheroe   E4 6a   24/8/88
Climb direct up the wall between Mud Slide Slim and Clevor Trevor past an obvious scar to reach a good break, PR. Continue direct up the smoother wall above to finish on a good ledge.

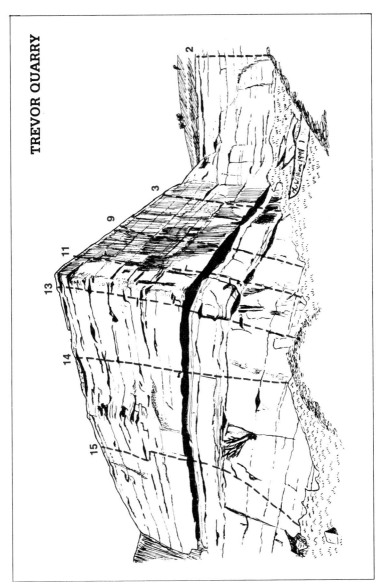

TREVOR QUARRY

* 8. Mud Slide Slim   E4 6a   29/12/86
From a "nick" on a crawl terrace, climb straight up the wall on good breaks and pass a small overlap rightward, BR, to a slim ledge, PR. Stand up with difficulty, step right finishing direct passing a situ wire.

*** 9. Any Which Way 2ND MIKE S/2000 /E2 5b   11/6/79
Start at the borehole scar below the widest part of the crawl terrace. From the terrace, pull up onto the steep main wall at a thin rightward trending crack which meets a small overhang. Follow the thin crack more or less straight to the top.

* 10. Planet Head   E3 5c   07/92
Start 3m right of the arête below a shallow groove. Climb to the terrace as for Kyani Quatsi then step right to follow the first of three leftward trending cracks to a ledge at 10m. Ascend the short blank looking wall on the right to gain a wide continuation crack and the top.

* 11. Kyani Quatsi   E2 5b   29/12/86
Gain the terrace below a shallow groove 3m right of the arête. Climb this with wires in the left wall and continue direct to a good ledge. Follow a faint crack 3m right of the arête to good holds and the top.

* 12. All Over Lancashire   E3 5c   24/4/88
A traverse of the main wall from right to left. Start as for White Smear up to the small overhang. From here follow the breakline across the wall gradually rising, to meet the arête. Finish up this.

The arête on the left of the main wall marks the start of the slab wall. Beware of the protection, it is a tad sparse!

13. The Silver Line   Hard Very Severe, 4c   5/78
The arête which separates the Main Wall and the large slabby wall climbed on its left side. Climb up the arête in a fine position, passing the crawl terrace, to a large ledge. Finish up the slab above close to the arête on good rock.

14. Dino   Very Severe, 4b   13/9/87
Start below a borehole scar, just left of Silver Line. Climb easily to the terrace, move slightly left before moving up by a slim corner. Carry straight up on easier ground. Bold for its grade. It can also be climbed direct at HVS 4c.

15. Gold Phlash   Very Severe, 4b   Pre 1977
Start 6m left of a whitebeam tree at a sloping grass ledge. Move easily rightwards to large blocks on the terrace. Gain the upper slabs at a small left facing corner, good runner, move left below small overhangs until it is possible to climb around them and up to the top. Again bold for its grade.

16. Big Splat   Hard Very Severe, 4c   12/11/92
Climb Gold Phlash to the left facing corner and attack the overhangs direct with the minimum of protection to gain the upper wall. Finishing left of a loose flake near the top.

17. Big Phlash   Very Severe, 4a   Pre 1977
Start 7m left of Gold Phlash. Climb easily to the crawl terrace to a short corner that is capped at its top. Ascend this then traverse right along a good ledge to gain and finish up a broken groove/corner. Bold.

18. Long John Silver   Very Severe, 4b   12/11/92
Climb as for Big Phlash to the short corner finishing directly up the wall above.

*   19. Blue Flash   Very Severe, 4b   16/2/86
A direct line up the slab to the finishing groove of Big Phlash.

At the far left-hand end of the wall is a large tree sitting on a triangular grassy ledge.

20. Quick Silver   Severe, 4a   12/11/92
Start 5m right of the tree by scrambling to a ledge below a sapling. Climb the slab past the sapling to the top without any protection.

21 Line Bashing   Very Severe, 4b   12/11/92
A left to right girdle of the upper slab above the crawl terrace. Start where the grass ledge meets the terrace. Follow the obvious "tramlines" to a grassy ledge at the right-hand end of the wall. Stroll along to the arête and finish up this.

RAILWAY BUTTRESS

At the left-hand end of the cliff is an obvious capped corner with an arête to the left. The routes are described rightwards from this.

1.   James The Red Engine   Hard Very Difficult   9/4/88
The arête to the left of the corner crack starting up a short crack to gain the arête.

2.   The Fat Controller   Severe   9/4/88
The corner crack, finishing direct over a small overhang. Pleasant.

3.   Thomas The Tank Engine   Severe   9/4/88
The thin slab with a crack in it to the right of the last route.

To the right are some obvious descent ledges that split the crag. The thin crack to the right of and below the ledges is Ivor The Engine (Severe).

4.   Puffing Billy   Hard Severe, 4a   9/4/88
The crack in the wall to the right of a small thorn bush that lies at one third height.

5.   The Thin Controller   Very Severe, 4a   16/4/88
The thin crack on the right side of the buttress, 2m right of Puffing Billy - poor protection.

COMPACT WALL

A good wall that the name sums up quite aptly. The routes are described from left to right as you face the crag.

6.   Thorn In My Side   Very Severe, 4b   7/5/88
The short groove to the right of the tree. Climb this, awkward, and then follow the edge of the wall past a thorn bush, ouch, to the BB on Borderline.

7.   Iron Curtain   E2 5c   16/3/86
Climb the left edge of the wall via a vague groove, 2 BRs, and then continue to Borderline's BB.

*   8.   Borderline   E2 5c   16/3/86
Immaculate climbing on superb rock. Gain and climb the obvious shallow groove, TR, moving right past an old bolt hole to a BR and an exciting finale. BB.

188

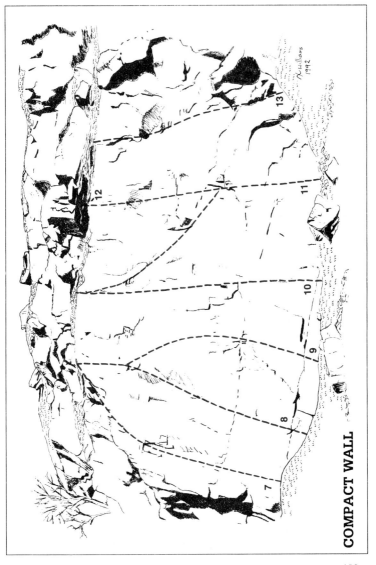

COMPACT WALL

** 9. Margin Of Error   E3 6a   5/6/86
A direct version of Borderline. Climb a short flake, slightly loose, to a PR above. Move past the PR to a BR on the right. Move up and left to join Borderline at its BR.

* 10. Checkpoint Charlie   E3 5c   5/6/86
Start right of Margin Of Error. Climb a thin flake, BR on left, over a tiny bulge and via small flakes gain and finish up the next route.

11. Over The Wall   E2 5b   16/3/86
An obvious diagonal line starting right again. Up the wall to gain the obvious ramp and follow this to a hollow flake, runners. Continue precariously to the BB.

12. The Great Escape   E2 5b   17/7/89
Start up Over The Wall and where that route goes left continue straight up, BR, over the bulge to BB.

13. I Met A Man From Mars   E2 5b   7/5/88
Climb the shallow groove, right of the last route, to a bulge, BR. Continue straight up a small crack on the left to a BB.

14. Pot Noodle, Don't Leave Home
     Without One!   Very Severe, 4b   9/4/88
The thin crack on the right side of the wall. From the overhang either finish direct or follow the crack through the overhang. Hidden thread belay well back. Either abseil off or climb the wall above to the top at around Hard Severe.

15. April Fool   Very Severe, 4b   1/4/90
The arête to the right of Compact Wall starting on its right-hand side, stepping left at the broken layer to enter a shallow groove which is followed to the top.

* 16. Try to Understand, Understand? 35m E1   5/6/86
A girdle from right to left starting up Iron Curtain.

1)   18m 5b. Start up Iron Curtain and traverse more or less at half height to join Over The Wall at the old bolt hole. Finish up this route. BB.
2)   12m 5b. Continue more or less on the same height level passing the BR on The Great Escape and moving up at the BR as for I Met A Man From Mars, continue direct to the top as for Pot Noodle...

Two more routes are recorded on a wall approximately 100m to the left of Compact Wall. A short wall has three leftward trending cracks. Betty Boop Rides Again (VS 4c) is the right-hand crack. Elmer J. Fudd (VS 4b) is the central crackline.

FIRST ASCENTS

Pre 1977	GOLD PHLASH	
Pre 1977	BIG PHLASH	
2/77	LINGEN	S M Cathcart, Solo
15/3/77	WHITE SMEAR	S M Cathcart & G N Swindley
15/3/77	THE LAST STRAW	S M Cathcart & G N Swindley
5/78	THE SILVER LINE	S M Cathcart & J Dee
11/6/79	ANY WHICH WAY	S M Cathcart & G N Swindley
13/2/86	FLING	D Kerr, Solo
16/2/86	BLUE FLASH	D Kerr & D Reynolds
16/3/86	IRON CURTAIN	D Kerr & D Reynolds
16/3/86	BORDERLINE	D Kerr & D Reynolds
16/3/86	OVER THE WALL	D Kerr & D Reynolds
5/6/86	MARGIN OF ERROR	D Kerr, Unseconded
5/6/86	TRY TO UNDERSTAND	D Kerr & M Saunders
	Additional pitches added by S Williams & C Roberts (alt.) 22/9/89	
5/6/86	CHECKPOINT CHARLIE	D Kerr & M Saunders
29/12/86	TRABUCCO	G Gibson & P Gibson
29/12/86	MUD SLIDE SLIM	G Gibson & P Gibson
29/12/86	KYANI QUATSI	P Gibson & G Gibson
13/9/87	DINO	S Williams & N Stanford
3/10/87	BETTY BOOP RIDES AGAIN	A Williams & S Williams
2/4/88	ELMER J. FUDD	S Baker & N Stanford
9/4/88	POT NOODLE, DON'T LEAVE HOME WITHOUT ONE	S Williams & C Roberts
	Direct finish on same day by C Osborne & A Williams.	
	This has got to be the daftest name in the area!	
9/4/88	JAMES THE RED ENGINE	S Williams & C Roberts
9/4/88	THE FAT CONTROLLER	S Williams & C Roberts
9/4/88	THOMAS THE TANK ENGINE	A Williams & C Osborne
9/4/88	IVOR THE ENGINE	C Osborne, A Williams & C Roberts
9/4/88	PUFFING BILLY	A Williams & C Osborne
16/4/88	THE THIN CONTROLLER	S Williams & C Roberts
24/4/88	THIS WAY TO CLITHEROE	G Gibson & H Gibson
24/4/88	ALL OVER LANCASHIRE	G Gibson, Solo
7/5/88	THORN IN MY SIDE	S Williams & C Roberts
7/5/88	I MET A MAN FROM MARS	S Williams & C Roberts
17/7/89	THE GREAT ESCAPE	S Williams & C Roberts

1/4/90	APRIL FOOL	S Williams & A Williams
4/5/92	CLEVOR TREVOR	G Gibson & H Gibson
7/92	PLANET HEAD	C Silverstone & A Picken
12/11/92	BIG SPLAT	C Silverstone, Solo
12/11/92	LONG JOHN SILVER	C Silverstone, Solo
12/11/92	QUICK SILVER	C Silverstone, Solo
12/11/92	LINE BASHING	C Silverstone, Solo

PANDY OUTCROP

O.S. Map 125 GR 195362

by Stuart Cathcart and Dave Barker

SITUATION AND ACCESS

Marked as a disused quarry on the OS Map, the crag has all the atmosphere of a small gritstone edge, perched high up above the tiny village of Pandy and a sea of trees.

The crags are visible from Pandy village looking up above the trees to the north. The crags face south and therefore dry quickly capturing any sun which may sometimes appear. The rock is a very solid igneous type, a mixture in feel to that of Llanberis Cromlech rock with all its pockets and in places similar to a Cornish granite. There is little if any loose rock. For such a small crag there is a wealth of variation from very easy slab climbs, cracks, steep easy and hard walls to wild overhanging arêtes and roofs.

The easiest approach is from the Chirk direction on the A5, following the B4500 and the pleasant Glyn Ceiriog Valley for some eight and a half miles to Pandy Village. Turn right at the old chapel, on the right just before the bridge, to follow a very narrow lane for half a mile up the River Teirw valley to where the lane opens out at a parking and turning point. Walk back up eastward via a good path for ten minutes which brings you out on the top of the crag.

The climbing is split into three areas:

The Cannon Walls are the most popular section at Pandy and justly so, sporting an interesting steep wall and large slab. This is the first area you reach on the approach. The Cannon is an obvious block which protrudes out from near the top of the crag just left of the Main Wall. Two excellent routes conquer The Cannon either side with one of the hardest routes to date climbing a superb overhanging arête to its left. The large slab sports slightly easier routes with a classic two pitch girdle at Hard Severe.

Pinnacle Walls can be found 200 yards further along the cliff top path down to the right flanked on its left by a large oak tree. Descent is down the right-hand side from above. Although only three routes are described each is worth the effort of a visit.

The Old Quarry is a short way beyond the Pinnacle walls and again only has three routes but each is excellent, two are longer than anything else at Pandy. They mainly consist of a steep wall to start with slab climbing at varying standards above.

The routes are described from left to right whilst facing the rock.

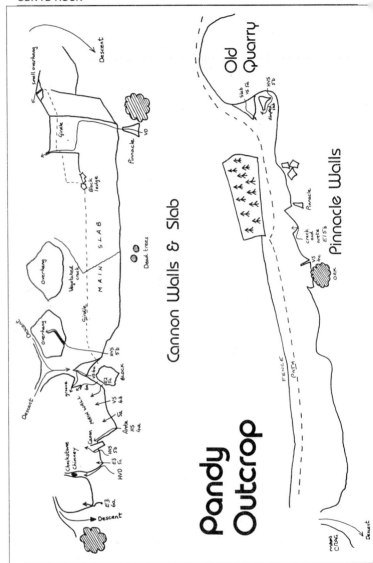

Cannon Walls & Slab

Pandy Outcrop

Pinnacle Walls

Old Quarry

194

CANNON WALLS

The routes are described from left to right facing the crag. 10m left of the cannon rock and marking the left end of the climbing is a large oak tree. Just right of the oak is a little used slabby descent.

** 1. Hovering On Eternity   E4 6a   Unknown
Climb the ever so overhanging short arête just right of the descent. Hard to start, hard to continue and hard to finish and protect but excellent for flying!

** 2. Cannon Chimney   Hard Very Difficult   Unknown
The obvious classic chimney with a chockstone.

*** 3. Bawls Like A Bull   E3 5c   Unknown
The overhanging arête on the right of Cannon Chimney proves longer than it looks but excellent throughout and good holds. Wire runner on right and PR two thirds of the way up.

** 4. Cannon Left-hand 2NOSTEVIE 4/2000   Hard Very Severe, 5b   Unknown
Start as for "Bawls Like A Bull" and climb up to the crack formed by the left-hand side of the cannon rock. Very steep and somewhat frustrating moves gain the top of the cannon, usually panting on ones belly. Finish more easily direct. Very well protected.

*** 5. Cannon Arête 2NOSTEVIE 4/2000   Hard Severe, 4a   Unknown
A real gem. Start directly below the cannon at the lowest part of the crag at an arête. Climb the arête which steepens to a crack on the right of the cannon, all on jugs.

6. ELP   E1 5a   Unknown
An eliminate which if completed properly provides excellent climbing with a tricky finish. Climb the wall direct a few feet all the way up just right of Cannon Arête, runners can be placed in that route, but not handies!!!

*** 7. Face Value   Very Severe, 4c   Unknown
For a small crag this route has a serious feel due to the lack of gear even though there are an abundance of big holds. Climb the centre of the wall with a good rest half way.

* 8. Victims   E2 5c   Unknown
Start on the small pointed block at the base of the overhanging start to the wall at a thin peg scarred crack. Climb direct to a pocket and good hold at 3m and up the wall above.

** 9. Tension Stretcher   E2 6a   Unknown
Slightly eliminate but very worthwhile combination of moves. Using pockets up the wall just right of Victims gain the smooth green scoop below and overhang. Pull over the overhang and up the wall on the left of the arête.

10. Lightning Groove   Very Severe, 4c   Unknown
Climb the wide layback crack just right of Tension Stretcher to the descent ledge. Step left into the obvious green groove which is followed to its top and the rounded arête above.

11. Villeta   Moderate   Unknown
The first of the slab routes climbing a wide crack up from the base of the descent to the left-hand side of the left-hand block which sticks out from the top of the slab.

* 12. Blue Thunder 2ND STEVE 4/2000 Hard Very Severe, 5b   Unknown
Climb the slab easily up to below the crack splitting the left-hand block. Climb out rightwards following the crack to pull hopefully onto the front face and an easy finish. Technically trying but excellent protection.

                        LED STEVE 4/2000
13. Splitting The Difference   Hard Severe   Unknown
A direct line up the slab to between the two large blocks.

14. Vegetable Crack   Difficult   Unknown
Start at the lowest part of the slab above two dead trees. Climb the grass filled crack, hard to start, first up leftwards then back right to finish up the right side of the block overhang.

*** 15. Schmutzig LEAD STEVE 4/2000 Severe   Unknown
Start at the two dead trees climbing straight up the slab, difficult to start, move right onto the main slab which leads to excellent holds. Finish slightly right across the slab above the perched blocks. A smart route taking the full challenge of the slab at reasonable standard.

16. Emerald Point   Very Difficult   Unknown
Contrived but with a good finish. Start at the very lowest right-hand side of the slab by a large block and ash tree. Pull over blocks onto a slab then over a bulge to gain the main upper slab. Traverse left along the lip of the slab and up into the obvious corner, follow this to the top.

Stuart Cathcart on Bawls like a Bull, Pandy Outcrop

** 17. Banana Boat LEO STEVE 4/2000 Severe, 4a   Unknown
Although short it is well worthwhile. A grassy terrace leads in across the slabby area from halfway down the descent gully. At the end of the terrace is an obvious slabby groove which leads to an exit via a small overhang usually taken on the left.

*** 18. Duck Flight   Hard Severe   Unknown
A really enjoyable and escapable girdle across the main slab. Start at the base of the descent gully as for Villeta (11).

1) Move up to follow the obvious traverse crack rightwards to the grassy crack and further following excellent jugs to belay on the obvious block ledge 15ft below the top.
2) Step up onto the slab above the belay to reach a horizontal finger crack moving right along this to the arête. A steep swing down right into the groove will prove easier than it looks after finding the hidden hold! Continue right across the slab at the same height to the next arête which is rounded to finish up a roof crack.

PINNACLE WALLS

** 19. Floodtide   Very Severe, 4c   Unknown
After a scramble down to the base of the crag an enjoyable struggle pursues up the steep excellent rock via an offwidth crack splitting the block right of the oak tree.

20. Floodgate   Very Severe, 4b   Unknown
Not as good as Floodtide, climbing the other steep crack on the right of that route.

* 21. Floods Of Fear   E1 5b   Unknown
Good delicate climbing with a slightly serious finish. Start 3m right of Floodtide at a thin crack up a steep slabby wall. Climb the crack to step right to the base of the steep arête which is followed on improving holds to the top.

Two other routes can be found just right of Floods of Fear, one up the vegetated groove and the other on the slabby walls on its right, neither is very continuous although on very good rock.

THE OLD QUARRY

*   22. Dimpled Slab   Hard Very Severe, 5b   Unknown
Not high in its grade but an entertaining route. Start at the lowest part of
the quarry face on the left-hand side at a rounded arête. Climb steeply up
a thin crack in the arête, good wire on the right, to pull over onto a grass
ledge. Step up into a very smooth scoop below the golden wall which
flanks the left side of the large fin shape block, and gingerly move up
leftwards conquering the smooth wave like slab.

23. Rhydycroesau Cowboy   Very Severe, 5a   Unknown
Up right of the start of Dimpled Slab is the largest of the young ash trees.
Start on a grass terrace up and right of the ash tree. Climb a groove to gain
the upper slab just left of the prominent protruding rock. Follow the right
side of the smooth slab to an old PR and either continue straight up or,
much better, pull over onto the slab on the right level with the PR and climb
this to the top.

*** 24. Lethal Flattery   E2 5c   Unknown
If climbed properly without resorting to easier ground this is one of the best
routes at Pandy with necky but basically excellent protection. Start directly
above the largest of the young ash trees at a grass and bracken covered
ledge. Climb the blocky groove above past a PR to gain a ledge at the base
of the very blank slab. Climb straight up the slab past a PR to a bulge and
runner on the right, move left to pull over the bulge finishing more easily.

HENDRE (PANDY) QUARRY

O.S. Map 125 GR 191345
by Stuart Cathcart and Dave Barker

Pandy Quarry currently has no access agreement and is only included in this guidebook for historical reasons. The present owners have made it very clear that climbing will not be permitted under any circumstances. This situation is unlikely to change in the immediate future. If access is successfully negotiated, a statement will be made in the climbing press.

The approach is from Chirk, on the A5, following the B4500 and the pleasant Glyn Ceiriog Valley for some ten miles until just south of the village of Pandy. An enormous gash in the hillside is conspicuously evident on the opposite side of the valley.

From the public footpath adjacent to the quarry entrance, a compact diamond shaped buttress can be seen flanked on the right by a scree cone. The route descriptions start here and continue eastward along the north wall.

25. Elucid   Hard Very Severe   1970
Start on a broken terrace up and left of the toe of the buttress.

    30m 4c Climb up leftwards across the wall to a ledge. Step left from the end of the steep wall before moving right into a groove and up to a loose traverse line. Move right on shattered rock around a spiky prow to a tree belay.

* 26. Anne Boleyn   E2   1970
The obvious left to right diagonal line slanting across the face from a grassy recess near the base of the buttress.

    30m 5b Climb the left side of the recess to where a traverse right across a steep slab (spike runner) enables a pull to be made into a corner. Move up the slab on the right to a small overhang. Step left towards a small tree (spike runner) and make a few difficult moves up the wall above to a PR. Swing right onto a block and up to easier ground. Traverse right to round the arête into the niche on Cats Eye which is followed to the top. Abseil descent.

* 27. Winning Streak   E2   1986
Start 6m right of Anne Boleyn below a steep rib.

    25m 5c Gain the grassy ledge and climb the steep black wall on the left of the rib to a BR. Swing onto the rib to clip a second BR and lunge for a good hold and easier climbing to below an undercut flake roof. Move right until all the footholds disappear and a hard move over the bulge can be made into a niche. Traverse right passing a dubious block and into the niche on Cats Eye which is followed to the top. Abseil descent.

28. Cats Eye   Hard Very Severe   1970
Good climbing starting halfway up the scree cone right of Winning Streak.

    25m 4c Climb the arête and wall until a step left to a ledge can be made at the foot of a groove. Make a move up the groove and step left onto the wall, PR. Climb up into the prominent niche and follow this leftwards to a steep finish up a short corner. Abseil descent.

*   29. Une Hombre   E2   1986
A hard route that provides fierce but well protected climbing on good rock. Start as for Cats Eye.

    25m 6a Climb into the obvious v-groove with a white left wall. Without the aid of holds, climb the groove past a BR to a good finishing hold. Step left out of the groove and move up the bulging wall above to a large hold and BR on the right. Avoid easy but loose ground on the left by climbing direct up to the bolt chain belay. Abseil descent.

30. Angel Way   Very Severe   1970
Start at the top of the scree cone and right of the small trees below a shallow v-groove.

    30m 4b Gain the v-groove via a short wall, BR. Exit right from the groove onto the rib to gain a slab which leads to a ledge and a bolt chain belay. Abseil descent.

31. Quaver   Hard Very Severe   1970
Following an obvious diagonal line across the crag starting just right of Angel Way. The route crosses some very dangerous ground!

1) 30m 5a Climb the gangway up rightwards below a white quartz covered wall. Move right round some blocks to the base of the steep slab on Landing Circle, PR and BR above. Move right around the rib to an old PR and into the deep niche using a detached block. Nut belay.

2) 40m 4b Climb the crack behind the stance past blocks to the shattered band (dangerous) and traverse right passing two trees to a large block belay.

3) 20m 5a The steep slab and groove above lead to the base of the obvious right angled corner and PB.

4) 15m 5a Climb the corner and hand traverse left in an exposed position to a ledge below the last wall which is climbed with difficulty past a PR. Belay well back. Descend by a path leftwards along the cliff top and down through trees.

*   32. Landing Circle   E2   1986
Steep well protected climbing on good rock 6m right of Quaver at a slim
rightward slanting groove.

1)   40m 5c Climb the slim groove past a PR and two BRs to a ledge. Step
left to climb a short steep wall to easier ground and a PR on the left in a
large block. Step right and up to the base of the steep black slab. Climb
past three BRs to an airy finish on the right. Easier ground leads to a bolt
chain belay. Abseil descent.

33. Soul On Ice   E2   1971
Another route with a dangerous section on the first pitch. The route starts
at the foot of the scree slope just right of Landing Circle and ascends the
wall known as Khumbu Wall.

1)   25m 5c Climb the vague groove up rightwards for 6m to make a move
left and back right to below a quartz streaked wall. Using a dubious block
move left past a reasonable runner, past another block to gain a niche.
Surmount the overhang above to gain a groove and up this, PR, to a
delicate step left and over a bulge to a good PB.
2)   18m 5a Step right to a gorse bush and climb the steep groove until a
move right is possible to gain the left side of a pillar leading to another
groove and PB.
3)   20m 5b Continue above the groove above the groove above until
below the groove. Finish left to a tree on the shattered band as for Quaver.
(This is not a typing error.)
4)   20m 5a As for Pitch 3 of Quaver.
5)   15m 5a As for Pitch 4 of Quaver.

34. Sour Grapes   E2   1971
Part of the first pitch has fallen away and large portions of the upper section
appear poised to follow suit. Start (if you dare) below a large overhang left
of a prow of rock rounded by a path just as the main Fin wall comes into
view. This area is known as KHUMBU CORNER, an ice fall on Everest
was named after it!

1)   25m 5c Up easy rock and groove to climb a small overhang onto a slab
below the large roof. Traverse left over dubious rock to below a short steep
groove which breaks through the roof. Climb the groove (hard) to exit left.
Up the grass terrace to belay below a short groove.
2)   30m 6a Climb the short groove with difficulty to move left and layback
a flake which leads to easier ground and the base of a large, blank groove.
Climb the groove past three old PRs to a careful exit right of a large
levitating block - very precarious. Up to the shattered band and block belay
on the right.

3) 20m 5a As for Pitch 3 of Quaver.
4) 15m 5a As for Pitch 4 of Quaver.

35. Suspended Sentence   Hard Very Severe   1970

Most of the first pitch has fallen down and the top pitch looks likely to follow suit. An apt route name! Start at the rock prow just right of Sour Grapes where Fin wall comes into view.

1) 27m 5a Climb the prow below the massive blocks - an alpine start and a good frost might just keep them in place. Move right to a ledge at the top of the prow and continue up a slab and loose arête to the grass terrace at the left end of Fin wall.
2) 38m 5a Gain the groove at the left edge of Fin wall and climb to a small tree and ledge on the right. Continue up the crack behind the tree to easier climbing and up right to the arête finishing at a large loose block. Scamper diagonally left to a good ledge and belay.
3) 30m Bags of death potential here! Grovel carefully to the top.

*** 36. The Laughing Christ   E5   1988

This imposing route takes the only real line of weakness up the Fin wall. BRs provide some of the security on an excellent sustained climb. Start by gaining the wide grassy ledge via an easy scramble in from the right. BB.

1) 35m 6a Move left and climb the easy slab to gain the base of the obvious groove. Follow this and a faint line above, 2 BRs, to a good rest below the bulges at half height. BR. Step right and climb the short hanging groove (crux) to a ledge on the right. Power up the brilliant crack to a good jug and then climb the more leisurely headwall direct to the belay. Abseil descent.

The next routes start on the terrace to the right of and level with the base of Fin wall. This is reached via an easy scramble of 25m from the quarry floor.

37. Triethnos   E2   1970

Start at the left end of the terrace below a groove that curves up leftwards and bounds the right flank of Fin wall.

1) 15m 5c Climb the thin overhanging groove until the angle eases and a difficult move right to a ledge. Move right to a belay.
2) 35m 5b Left of the belay a crack leads back into the main groove which is followed to its end. Move left across the steep wall until it is possible to climb up to a stance of sorts below the final broken section.
3) 35m 4a Traverse right to climb the broken arête and wall which leads into a loose gully and the top.

38. Acis   Hard Very Severe   1971

A good route if only for the first pitch. Start just right of Triethnos at a clean rib.

1) 27m 5a Climb the right side of the rib to gain a groove exiting right with care from below some overhung blocks. Continue up pleasant slabby rock and a rib to a ledge and belay. If the ground ahead looks too horrible for words a short traverse right gains a rocky bay thoughtfully equipped with an iron stake and bolt for abseil. If you feel like cracking on, then...

2) 23m 4c Climb the short corner to loose blocks and traverse right for 5m then up leftwards to the shattered band and a belay.

3) 20m Ascend the loose scoop above to a tree belay well back.

The next four routes all share the iron stake and bolt in the rocky bay.

*   **39. Ripple**   E3   1986

Technical and fingery moves to start lead to an unusual finish. At the right end of the terrace is a tree stump below a left trending groove.

1) 25m 6a Climb the left wall of the black groove to clip a PR before stepping down to climb the groove direct by some hard bridging past a BR to a difficult landing on a sloping ledge at the base of the v-groove. A block in the groove allows it to be ascended by a series of contortions. Mantle up rightwards at the top to gain the rocky bay. Abseil off or pitch 2 of the Wobblies.

***   **40. The Wobblies**   E1   1986

A very fine route on impeccable rock - a Pandy classic.

1) 25m 5b Move rightwards around the arête onto the slabby wall and ascend to the base of a beautiful groove with a quartz coated left wall. Pause to admire the texture of the rock before climbing the groove past a PR to a steepening and BR on the right. Finish direct into the rocky bay.

2) 25m 5b Move up left to a ledge then up and traverse right with difficulty past a hidden PR to a narrow ledge and BR above. Climb the steep groove above past a PR to a sloping ledge. Abseil descent.

*   **41. Milky Way**   Hard Very Severe   1970

The pleasant first pitch is usually climbed as a route in itself followed by an abseil descent. Those devotees of loose mixed ground may continue to the top of the crag.

1) 25m 5a Move right as for the Wobblies onto the slabby wall but move across and up to a prominent and slightly dubious looking block. Swing up right below the block onto a grass ledge. Climb the corner above to step left onto the arête which is climbed past a quartz flake (care!) and BR.

Move up leftwards at the top into the rocky bay and belay. Abseil descent or...

2)   45m 4c Traverse right to climb a wall and arête to a small tree. Broken ledges and easy ground lead to a belay below the final wall.

3)   15m Move right and up over easy ledges to the top. Belay well back.

Round Khumbu Corner is an area of huge blocks (below Fin Wall) and just beyond these at the foot of the crag is a small triangular wall split by a thin crack ("Fags in Space" marked on the rock...tut-tut!)

*   42. Image Road   E1   1986
A poor first pitch leads to an increasingly technical second pitch on perfect rock.

1)   17m 4b Climb the crack in the wall and scramble up rightwards to a birch bush at the base of the obvious leftward curving black groove.

2)   18m 5b From the bush climb up and slightly leftwards across the black slabby wall on good holds to a small ledge below a quartz covered fin, BR. Either move up and make a difficult couple of moves left onto a sloping rock ledge (balancey) or move slightly down and left from the BR and use a sharp edge to swing up onto the sloping ledge, BR. Balance delicately left along the ledge and make a difficult step up into the groove. Climb the groove and move left to the rocky bay on Milky Way. Abseil descent.

** 43. Outer Darkness   E2   1970
One of the best of the original routes with good climbing on pitches two and three. Start as for Image Road.

1)   17m 4b As for Image Road to the bush belay.

2)   25m 5b Up left to the first BR on Image Road. Move back down and traverse right across the steep wall to gain a good ledge above the bush and overhang, BR in the slim groove above. Climb the right arête and wall of the slim groove past a PR and sling on a borehole to a good flat ledge. Easily up rightwards to a good bolt and chain belay.

3)   43m 5b Move out left to the arête and climb this more or less directly avoiding easier ground left or right until the foot of a short groove is reached. Climb the groove to the base of a short smooth slabby wall and climb the extreme left edge of this before stepping right into a grassy bay. Traverse out right onto the exposed but easy wall and up to a bolt chain belay. Either scramble carefully to the top and the long walk back to your gear or make two abseils back to the quarry floor.

*** 44. Fags In Space   E4   1986

A scrappy start does nothing to detract from this really fine route, the last pitch in particular being very much out there. Good belays, good rock and good protection. Start at the base of the crag as for Image Road by the top most of the massive boulders at the foot of a triangular wall split by a thin crack.

1) 30m 4c Climb the crack in the wall on good holds but with poor protection, stepping left before the very top to continue by scrambling up rightwards to a birch bush. Belay at the base of the obvious leftwards black curving groove.

2) 25m 5c A bold pitch. Step up right onto the steep slabby wall and climb up to a BR. Move left on underclings just above the BR to make a hard move up to gain the sloping ledge at the foot of the main groove, PR. Continue up the groove more easily, but this requires a certain amount of steadiness as the gear is limited, to clip a BR high on the right. Finish straight up the groove avoiding easier ground to the left. Belay chain and bolts above on the right.

3) 15m 5b Climb up into the steep narrow groove above the belay past a poor PR. Climb the groove, hard to start past a BR and finishing on the right, moving a few feet along the ledge to a PB at the foot of a steep crack.

4) 33m 6c A long hard pitch. Blast up the steep crack above the belay past a BR, wire and PR on the right. At the top of the crack a unique ledge leads rightwards! It is possible to continue straight up from the top of the crack to join Andromeda but this defeats the whole object. After traversing rightwards along the ledge past two BRs to its end climb out onto the very steep wall. Climb the wall past a PR and BR to gain a desperately poor crack which leads straight up with the aid of one PR and a BR to gain a very exposed ledge on the left. Phew! Climb the wall above past a BR to finish on a flat slab. Bolt and tree belay 15ft back. An abseil descent can be made from the chain belay just below this belay.

5) 70 ft 4b As for pitch 4 of Outer Darkness. Descent path to left.

** 45. Andromeda   Hard Very Severe   1970

Described as a magnificent route in the old guide and justifiably so, although there is some loose rock at the start of pitch 2 the effort is rewarded. 15m up from the massive boulders at the foot of the crag one can scramble up rightwards into a vegetated corner, climb this to step onto a grass ledge. Move left to below a small tree growing out of the obvious large leftward narrowing slab, belay using the tree.

1) 30m 5a Climb the crack, dubious rock to start, just left of the tree up the slab to the bulge move up the layback crack for a few feet until a swing right over the bulge leads to a grass ledge with a steep wall on the left. Move out left with difficulty across the wall to ledges and a chain and bolt

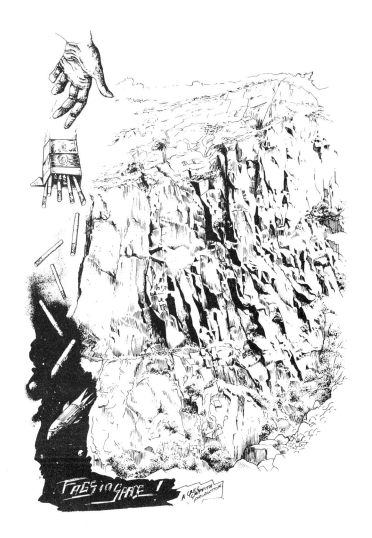

belay also used for the descent if needed.

2) 40m 5a Traverse right for 7m around some dubious blocks to a short slightly vegetated ramp and groove back up leftwards. This gains the belay ledge at the top of pitch 3 on Fags In Space. Move left and up onto a grass ledge, at the foot of an obvious corner. Climb the corner, PRs, to swing right at the top in a superb position. Continue up more easily on excellent holds moving slightly left to a bolt and chain belay. Abseil descent from here to the top of pitch 1 or...

3) 23m 4b as for pitch 4 of Outer Darkness

*** 46. Sky Trap   E2   1986
An immaculate line one of the best routes at Pandy with good gear and perfect rock once over the first few feet of the first pitch. Start as for Andromeda at the tree belay.

1) 35m 5c Start up the crack in the slab as for Andromeda left of the tree for a few feet to a point where a diagonal line out left can be taken to a small ledge by a bush on the left arête of the slab. Climb a thin crack up the slab to where it meets the layback crack and bulge, follow this almost to the overhang on the left. Using a flat hole in the centre of the slab on the left, can be wet after prolonged rainfall, drop down left with feet below a small roof and then make a difficult move up to the left end of the roof and a PR. Continue up left following the narrowing slab to its end beneath a roof, BR on the slab. Above the lip of the roof is another BR to protect a final move directly over the overhang into a small niche and a bolt chain belay above.

2) 40m 5c Climb directly up the steep wall behind the chain to a BR and sling above the bulging section. Make a set of hard moves up past the BR and up the green wall above avoiding a traverse left after clipping the BR to easier ground which also would miss out on the best part of the climb. On reaching a horizontal break climb straight up the juggy slab to a good crack on the right. Move right below the crack and up into a bay. Climb the prominent v-groove above the bay which has an obvious thin crack splitting the wall above. Step left from the crack at the top of the groove to climb easily upright across a slab to a bolt and chain belay. This pitch can be split in the bay below the v-groove. Abseil descent or..

3) 20m 4b as for pitch 4 of Outer Darkness.

47. Magnetic Pull   E1   1986
A slightly contrived route which takes in some interesting climbing. Start as for Andromeda.

1) 40m 5a Move out right across a broken slabby rock below a small roof to climb up shallow grove directly below the large roof. Traverse right below the roof to a grass ledge move left following the small white quartz slab to an arête. Climb the slab above to the groove with an old PR. At the

top of the groove swing left avoiding loose ground to the right. On good holds continue leftwards finally to be in a position to pull up onto the large sloping ledge, move back right to a PB below a short overhanging wall which sports a bore hole in the very lip at the top of the wall.

2) 40m 5c Move up the wall to a semi horizontal crack splitting the wall and follow this until in a position to make a phenomenal move to stuff ones fingers up the hole! Then if possible throw a long sling over the top and down the hole to form a runner suitable for holding the QE2, once accomplished stuff ones fingers down the top end of the hole after making a weird move up and 'King Kong' up over the lip to duff easy ground. Climb up and right into a corner at the right side of the main Fags In Space wall. Move right onto the arête and climb a crack past a PR to within 2m of the large roof, BR. Traverse right across the superb yellow on good holds to pull onto a ledge. From the ledge climb straight up past a PR steep to start onto ledge and a bolt and chain belay on the right. Abseil descent to Meadow Terrace and another abseil to the quarry floor from the middle of the three trees on the terrace.

** 48. Shadow Shift   Hard Very Severe   1986
The first pitch was probably part of an old line known as Batacomb but due to the poor description and mass of vegetation most of it has grown over. The present line is far cleaner and safer. Start left of Orion at a small slab and corner with a tree growing out of the corner at 3m. Two good pitches marred slightly by a scrappy start to the second pitch.

1) 40m 4c Climb up past the tree to the start of the obvious finger crack which veers up leftwards over two or three stepped sections to finish at the extreme left-hand end of the Meadow Terrace. Belay on the tree at one the end of the terrace.

2) 30m 5a Traverse left from the terrace at the same height onto the rib moving up this and into the crack on the left of the immaculate yellow slab, PR. Move up to just below the large roof, BR, and traverse on good holds below the roof right to a ledge, from the ledge climb straight up past a PR which is steep to start onto ledges and a bolt and chain belay on the right. Abseil descent as for Magnetic Pull.

*** 49. Orion   Hard Very Severe
A good route on perfect rock with two contrasting pitches. Start jus
of Shadow Shift at a grey slabby wall.

1) 38m 5a Climb the slab to a small ash tree at 6m, on its left is an excellent bore hole TR. Move up left from the tree to the base of a black wall with a bore hole scar through it and a PR high on the right. Climb the wall to an excellent hold and easier climbing leads into the base of the narrowing v-groove. Continue up the groove, small wire runners, to finish

direct with a belay on Meadow Terrace on the left hand tree.

2) 30m 5a This pitch climbs the prominent crack rising from the left end of the terrace. Enter it from the same height as the terrace avoiding climbing up over the large block flake. Move up the crack to where it steepens and layback strenuously up onto a small ledge continue up a second less   difficult section to a small cave roof. Pull straight over the roof to finish on a good ledge at the bolt and chain belay. Abseil descent as for Magnetic Pull.

*** 50. Power Dance   E2   1986
A bold first pitch leads to a second pitch rated as one of the best at Pandy, all on excellent rock. Right of Orion, a large prominent corner with a white quartz flake right wall and immaculate left wall split by a finger crack can be found. This route starts in the recess formed by this corner.

1)   40m 5b Follow the leftward slanting slab easily 3m left of the base of the main corner. Move up the steeper wall to a small roof split by a shallow crack. Move left below the roof onto a steep black wall and a good foothold just right of the PR of Orion. The PR is semi hidden down to the left but it is wise to reach down and clip it! With difficulty move up to where a step right onto an easy angled slab can be made, up this to a block. Step up left onto a slabby wall which leads to the Meadow Terrace. Belay on the tree at the left-hand end.

2)   25m 5c Directly behind the tree a thin flake crack veers up to the right for 3m. Climb the crack and another quartz filled finger much more strenuously up to the left into a short groove, a real finger mincer! Move up right out of the groove onto a small pillar which is climbed to its top, BR on left. Gain a good hold by a long reach up the ever steepening wall above the BR and start a series of excellent cranks up for more good holds in diagonal cracks either to finish direct or swing left to a large block. From the ledge at the top of the wall climb easily up and left to a large block. From the ledge at the top of the wall climb easily up and left to another ledge and a bolt and chain belay. Abseil descent as for Magnetic Pull.

51. A Carrion With Jane   E2   1970
This route is not recommended. It is a combination of two routes climbed in 1970 by K Coyne, B Cardus, M Reeves and J Gosling called Carrion and Jane respectively and takes in the best of both routes. The last pitch climbs very dubious ground. Start as for Power Dance.

1)   35m 5b Follow the leftward slanting slab easily to a steep wall below an overhang. Swing up right and place a PR, continue straight up over a roof into a small recess, exit right and climb a slab to a small tree. Continue up the poor crack and corner behind the tree to the Meadow Terrace and a belay on the middle of the three trees.

2) 40m 5a Behind and a few feet to the right of the tree is a short rib. Climb the rib to where a traverse right can be made to a ledge, PR. Move up and left to gain an obvious rightward sloping gangway. Climb the gangway and continue more easily in the same line to a poor belay on broken ledges.

3) 21m 3a Continue over ledges poor rock and short walls trending left to finish. Descent path to the left.

*** 52. Phantom Of The Wall   E3   1985

A climb which provides excellent technical moves, impeccable rock, especially on the first pitch and good protection. Start just left of the main corner of White Sister at a thin crack.

1) 35m 5c Climb the crack to a PR and make a difficult few moves out and up left to a good layaway and a BR. Move up and left onto an easy angled slab, BR, left slightly to below a small roof and hanging groove above it. Climb the overhang into the square cut groove past a BR, moving right below a small bush onto an easy slab. Move right around the arête to another slab and a short corner which leads to the Meadow Terrace. Belay on the middle of the three trees.

2) 30m 5b Climb a crack midway between the two left-hand trees on the terrace which leads to a short steep crack and groove and finishes by a step right onto a ledge. Above twin parallel cracks veer up rightwards with an overhanging left wall. Climb steeply up the twin crack past a PR to a point near the top where a PR can be clipped out left on the cracked wall. Swing strenuously out left past the PR to cross the wall onto the long ledge. Move to its left end and climb up to a bolt and chain belay. Abseil descent as for Magnetic Pull.

*** 53. Smear Or Fly   E4   1986

An impressive crack splitting the left wall of the White Sister corner. Start as for Phantom Of The Wall at a thin crack.

36m 6a Climb the crack to a PR and make a desperate move up to the right to gain a small foothold. Move back left and up the crack past the V slot, very hard to start, past a PR to a ledge below the final short steep wall. Climb the continuation crack up the wall, PR, using a good hold to finish on the left. Finish easily up a groove onto the Meadow Terrace. Abseil descent from the middle of the three trees or walk to the end of the terrace, right, and scrabble up over loose rock and a groove to drop down a loose descent gully.

* 54. White Sister   E1   1985

Thought to have been climbed by a team from Wrexham many years ago but after lots of heavy cleaning it is doubtful. A good classic line with the hardest moves at the start. Good protection. Start at the foot of the obvious large corner.

1) 30m 5b Climb the initial bulge to a good hold and PR. Continue up past another PR to a resting ledge and a PR. A good runner above protects a swing above to the right to a large flake runner. Step back left and move up to a large quartz flake with good holds above. Move up and step left across the top of the corner to finish more easily up a groove and onto the terrace. Abseil or scramble descent as for Smear Or Fly.

55. Serpico   Hard Very Severe   1980

A poor line but an interesting start. Start on the left-hand side of the massive dubious quartz flake which forms part of the right wall of the White Sister corner.

1) 38m 5a Climb the left edge of the quartz flake to stand on its top! Make a difficult move up to stand in a square recess and then step onto the arête on the right, PR. Move up the ramp which the PRs are in and swing right onto the slab and traverse right along the obvious line just above the trees. Continue rightwards up a flake crack to finish up a smooth groove and onto the very extreme right-hand end of the Meadow Terrace. Descent by abseil or scrambling as for Smear Or Fly.

56. Randy Pandy   E1   1984

Around the corner right of Serpico is a large slabby wall, start on the right-hand side at the foot of a vegetated corner.

1) 30m 5b Climb up leftwards above the green lichen to a poor BR good small wires above. With difficulty climb straight up over the slight bulge avoiding moving left. Once over the bulge traverse left easily to the arête. Two important PRs can be clipped around to the left of the arête. Step back right and pull directly over the bulge onto the slab move right and climb straight up the slab to finish just left of a small roof. Easier climbing leads to the Meadow Terrace.

57. Pandymonium   Very Severe   1970

A bold route for its grade on generally very good rock. Start right of the Randy Pandy slab at the foot of a slaty arête.

1) 35m 4c Traverse out onto the arête from the right into a groove and up to a small overhang. Make a difficult move over the overhang and follow a fine groove to move right at the top across a slab past an old PR and iron spike. Continue further up rightwards to a ledge and tree belay.

2) 10m 5a Climb onto the large block on the left and make a very, very trying move, usually a belly flop, onto an easy angled groove. Descent by scrambling up the easy groove on the right to gain the shoulder and down an easy gully on the other side.

Phantom of the wall.

Two short and not very worthwhile routes have been done on the wall immediately right and up from the start of Pandymonium. The routes are Hard Very Severe, and E1 respectively in order of left and right looking at the cracks up the wall and 5a and 5b.

The approach path along the base of the crag after the Randy Pandy slab climbs steeply up a scree covered slope to a small wooded area. The path hugs the base of a grey wall with the wood in front of it. This grey wall contains two routes, one reasonable, the other poor.

58. Deadline   Hard Very Severe   1986
Start below the obvious crack on the left of the wall.
1) 20m 5a Climb the crack direct mainly on the right wall to start and making a long reach at half height to a good hold on the left. Well protected. Belay on a tree well back, descent to right.

59. Who Cares, Who Wins?   E1   1986
Start 3m right of Dead Line in the centre of the horrible wall.
1) 20m 5a Climb up to the centre of the wall to a very poor PR, preferably climb back down, or continue straight up on even more desperate rock quality than the PR, using pull off flakes etc. Belay if you make it, on a tree well back. Descent to the right.

Continuing up the path past Dead Line the slope steepens considerably and is covered with grass. At the top of the slope a superb hanging slab comes into view on the left, known as Barkers Slab.

*   60. The Long Crawl   Hard Very Severe   1986
A much better route than would appear and a lot harder. 10m left of the start to Barkers Slab is a large tree at the start of an obvious rightward slanting ramp line which eventually meets the initial slab on that route. Start on the right of the tree.
1) 40m 5a Climb the short wall to gain the base of the ramp and follow the ramp rightwards past a good wire placement in the overhanging wall, and make a difficult move up onto a ledge halfway along, PR. Continue up right to join Barkers Slab. Move straight up and then leftwards up a superb finger crack through some dubious looking blocks, so far proved to be safe, finally to pull onto the skyline arête. Swing right and traverse across the top of the main slab belay on the bolt chain. Abseil descent from here.

*** 61. Barkers Slab   E2   1984
The easiest of the three slab routes. Excellent technical climbing on good rock. A must if visiting the quarry, with a really testing start. Start at the

214

ridiculously blank short leftward sloping slab below the main slab itself.

1) 30m 5c Climb leftwards across the short hanging slab past a BR, hard and getting harder, to the left arête. Move up a few feet and swing right onto the main slab and up to a flake runner. A thin crack containing a PR veers up right from the flake, this is climbed until after a short way good holds lead to a sloping ledge and the chain and bolt belay above. Abseil descent.

*** 62. Under Pressure   E3   1984

A perfect little route on 100% rock. Start in the centre of the main slab.

1) 28m 6a Traverse left across a small slab into a short corner and pull up left onto the main slab. Move straight up to a BR and with difficulty move up past it and right to gain a finger crack which trends rightwards to join an easier crack with a PR veering back up to the left. The crack is followed to step left at the top onto the sloping ledge and a chain and bolt belay. Abseil descent.

*** 63. El Lobo   E4   1986

This is a modern masterpiece whose creator flew especially from Spain to dedicate his energies to it for a whole day. It's bold, thin, strenuous, inspiring, catastrophically technical and in keeping with the modern idiom SHORT. Start as for Under Pressure.

1) 22m Technically Ungradable (according to Mr Waters)! Pull straight over the bulge onto the main slab and move up to a BR. With steel fingers and a steady head climb straight up the slab to the PR at the base of the final crack on Under Pressure. The route actually finished here as the master was exhausted but a finish has been added by moving left from the PR onto the steepening slab, climbing direct to the chain and bolt belay. Abseil descent.

From Barkers Slab the quarry walls curve around into a huge bay with a small wood and level ground. Approximately 17m onto the bay from the slope up from Barkers Slab an obvious slabby ramp line can be seen high up on the right ending at a tree. This ramp line is taken by:

** 64. Peregrine   Hard Severe   1986

A good route on generally sound rock. Start at a short broken wall down and left of a deep crack.

1) 43m 4b Climb the short wall and move up to the base of the deep crack. Avoiding the crack move right onto a shallow hanging slab, crouching to avoid the roof above. From the slab swing out right on good holds and traverse right to the base of the slabby ramp. Climb the ramp, enjoyable, to exit left at an iron stake runner. Move up a flake rack and right across a slab to finish on a large boulder ledge. Tree belay above. Descent

by abseil from trees on the opposite side of the quarry.

| 65. Pariha | Hard Severe | Unknown |

1) 28m Directly opposite Barkers Slab on the other side of the quarry is a smooth wavy slab. Climb this past a BR at 8m.

FIRST ASCENTS

Pre 1970	PARIHA	
1970	ELUCID	K Bell & V King
1970	ANNE BOLEYN	J A Gosling & M Reeves
1970	CATS EYE	V King & K Bell
1970	ANGEL WAY	K Coyne & D A Cowans
1970	QUAVER	K Coyne & D A Cowans
1970	SUSPENDED SENTENCE	C Jackson & R D Conway
1970	TRIETHNOS	V King, K Bell & P Seramur
1970	MILKY WAY	J A Gosling & M Reeves
1970	ANDROMEDA	J A Gosling & M Reeves
1970	PANDYMONIUM	W Cheverst & S Beresford
1970	ORION	B A Cardus, K Coyne & T Norton

FFA 1975 S M Cathcart & T Curtis

| 1970 | OUTER DARKNESS | J A Gosling, M Reeves & B A Cardus |
| 1970 | SHADOW SHIFT | C Jackson & R D Conway |

FFA 1986 S M Cathcart & D Barker

| 1970 | A CARRION WITH JANE | J A Gosling & party |

The route was originally two separate routes called Jane and Carrion until some wag took the best of both routes and changed the name to suit!

1971	SOUL ON ICE	R D Conway, B A Cardus & J A Gosling
1971	SOUR GRAPES	R D Conway, B A Cardus & J A Gosling
1971	ACIS	J A Gosling & B A Cardus
1975	ORION	S M Cathcart & T Curtis

First climbed in 1970 by B A Cardus & party.

1980	SERPICO	S M Cathcart & P Waters
1984	RANDY PANDY	S M Cathcart, D Barker & B Phillips
1984	BARKERS SLAB	S M Cathcart, D Barker & M Cameron

Named in honour of a great Oswestry climber (Dave Slab).

| 1984 | UNDER PRESSURE | S M Cathcart & D Barker |

1985	PHANTOM OF THE WALL	S M Cathcart, D Barker & B Phillips
1985	WHITE SISTER	S M Cathcart & D Barker
1986	WINNING STREAK	S M Cathcart, D Barker & B Phillips
1986	UNE HOMBRE	S M Cathcart & D Barker
1986	LANDING CIRCLE	S M Cathcart & D Barker
1986	RIPPLE	S M Cathcart & D Barker
1986	THE WOBBLIES	S M Cathcart & D Barker
1986	IMAGE ROAD	S M Cathcart & B Phillips
1986	FAGS IN SPACE	S M Cathcart, D Barker & B Phillips

"Whilst attempting desperately to remain in contact with the headwall on pitch 4, I lost my fags - they just floated right on out there man!"

1986	SKY TRAP	S M Cathcart & D Barker
1986	MAGNETIC PULL	S M Cathcart & D Barker
1986	SHADOW SHIFT	S M Cathcart & D Barker

First climbed in 1970 by C Jackson & R D Conway

1986	POWER DANCE	S M Cathcart & C Leventon
1986	SMEAR OR FLY	S M Cathcart & D Barker
1986	DEADLINE	D Barker & B Phillips
1986	WHO CARES, WHO WINS?	A Brown & T Heminsley
1986	THE LONG CRAWL	S M Cathcart & B Phillips
1986	EL LOBO	P Waters, Unseconded
1986	PEREGRINE	S M Cathcart & B Phillips
1988	THE LAUGHING CHRIST	J Moulding

A fine effort this. On an earlier "look" at this wall, Cathcart's pioneering abseil ended up in the arms of an extremely irate landowner accompanied by the local "Plod".

MISCELLANEOUS

SMALLER QUARRIES

Some of these quarries are in serious need of work to bring them up to good working order, others have already been worked but are too small to warrant a complete description.

CEFN MAWR   O.S.116 GR 282427
> Good climbing on sandstone walls with several lines already claimed. Situated behind the large chemical plants at Acrefair above a playing field.

PWLLGLAS QUARRY   O.S 116 GR 126554
> A small limestone quarry, half a mile from Ruthin escarpment, that has had some routes put up on it although none of them merit a full description.

PRESTATYN QUARRY   O.S.116 GR 072818
> A large but loose quarry situated in the hillside above the town of Prestatyn on the Clwyd coast. In need of development.

WHITE QUARRY   O.S.116 GR 167759
> A chossy quarry with climbing on broken walls and slabs up to 25 metres high.

BOULDERING

What finer way is there to finish a day off than to spend a half an hour bouldering with some friends to make sure them arms are fully worked or to get rid of the frustrations of the day.

CRAIG Y CYTHRAUL   O.S.117 GR 237476
> A delightful limestone wall that reaches up to 12m at its highest point. Walk up the path as for Worlds End upper tier and on into the woods and the wall can be found on the right hand side.

WAUN Y LLYN   O.S.117 GR 283584/284580
> Two small sandstone quarries a short distance from the car park at the top of the mountain at Horeb and close to the lake. Good quality rock with some interesting problems.

HOPE MOUNTAIN BOULDERS   O.S.117 GR 298574
   A series of boulders set in a dip in the hillside just down from the small lane
   that follows Hope mountain on its east side from Cymau (GR 294560).

MONUMENT BOULDERS   O.S.117 GR 245430
   A lovely set of boulders and walls sitting on the left skyline as you drive
   from Trevor to Garth. Park 100 metres past the monument on the left and
   walk up to, and past, the monument, following the path diagonally up the
   hillside.

GRAFFITI WALLS   O.S.117 GR 247427
   The graffiti covered walls on the bend in the road between Trevor Rocks
   and Garth Village. Park as not to obstruct other vehicles.

CLIMBING WALLS

THE WALLS, CHESTER
Superb, Foundry style indoor wall with routes ranging from 4a through to 6c.
Two vertical walls, one slab wall and one overhanging, arm-wrenching wall.
Open Tuesday to Sunday. Tel: 0244 682626

CHESTER RACECOURSE WALLS   GR 402656
Finger tearing, vertical sandstone walls that make up the base of the
Grosvenor bridge that spans the River Dee. The Chester side of the bridge is
the best.

ELLESMERE PORT INDOOR CENTRE
Mediocre indoor climbing wall made up of pieces of natural rock imbedded into
the breeze block wall. Tel. 051 355 6432

CHESTER NORTHGATE ARENA
Not a training wall as such! Access is limited and the wall is a grim shade of
concrete. The addition of a series of bolt-on holds is its one saving grace. Tel.
0244 380444